YAMAHA 500 TWIN Owners Workshop Manual

by Jeff Clew
Member of the Guild of Motoring Writers

Models covered:

TX500	first introduced USA only 1972
TX500A	first introduced USA and UK 1973
XS500B	first introduced USA late 1974, UK March 1975
XS500C	first introduced USA late 1975, UK May 1976

All the above models have the eight valve, 498cc double overhead camshaft engine

ISBN 0 85696 308 9

 J H Haynes and Company Limited 1976

All rights reserved. No part of this book may be reproduced or transmitted in any form or by any means, electronic or mechanical, including photocopying, recording or by any information storage or retrieval system, without permission in writing from the copyright holder.

Printed in England

J H Haynes and Company Limited
Sparkford Yeovil Somerset England

distributed in the USA by
Haynes Publications Inc
9421 Winnetka Avenue
Chatsworth
California 91311 USA

Acknowledgements

Our grateful thanks are due to Jim Patch, of Yeovil Motor Cycle Services, Abbey Hill Trading Estate, Preston Road, Yeovil, Somerset who supplied the machine on which this title is based and the parts used in the rebuild. Brian Horsfall provided the necessary assistance with the overhaul and devised the ingenious methods for overcoming the lack of service tools. Les Brazier took the photographs and Tim Parker edited the text.

We would also like to acknowledge the help of the Avon Rubber Company, who kindly supplied illustrations and advice about tyre fitting, the Champion Sparking Plug Company Limited, for the use of their illustrations relating to spark plug maintenance and electrode conditions and Renold Limited for their advice about equivalent chains of British manufacture.

About this manual

The author of this manual has the conviction that the only way in which a meaningful and easy to follow text can be written is first to do the work himself, under conditions similar to those found in the average household. As a result, the hands seen in the photographs are those of the author. Unless specially mentioned, and therefore considered essential, Yamaha special service tools have not been used. There is invariably some alternative means of loosening or removing a vital component when service tools are not available but risk of damage should always be avoided.

Each of the six Chapters is divided into numbered Sections. Within these Sections are numbered paragraphs. Cross reference throughout the manual is quite straightforward and logical. When reference is made "See Section 6.10" it means Section 6, paragraph 10 in the same Chapter. If another Chapter were meant, the reference would read "See Chapter 2, Section 6.10". All the photographs are captioned with a Section/paragraph number to which they refer, and are relevant to the Chapter text adjacent.

Figures (usually line illustrations) appear in a logical but numerical order, within a given Chapter. Fig. 1.1 therefore refers to the first figure in Chapter 1.

Left-hand and right-hand descriptions of the machines and their components refer to the left and right of a given machine when the rider is seated normally.

Whilst every care is taken to ensure that the information in this manual is correct no liability can be accepted by the authors or publishers for loss, damage or injury caused by any errors in or omissions from the information given.

Introduction to the Yamaha 500 Twin

Although the history of Yamaha can be traced back to the year 1887, when a then very small company commenced manufacture of reed organs, it was not until 1954 that the company became interested in motor cycles. As can be imagined, the problems of marketing a motor cycle against a background of musical instruments manufacture were considerable. Some local racing successes and the use of hitherto unknown bright colour schemes helped achieve the desired results and in July 1955 the Yamaha Motor Company was established as a separate entity, employing a work force of less than 100 and turning out some 300 machines a month.

Competition successes continued and with the advent of tasteful styling that followed Italian trends, Yamaha became established as one of the world's leading motor cycle manufacturers. Part of this success story is the impressive list of Yamaha 'firsts' - a whole string of innovations that include electric starting, pressed steel frame, torque induction and 6 and 8 port engines. There is also the "Autolube" system of lubrication, in which the engine-driven oil pump is linked to the twist grip throttle, so that lubrication requirements are always in step with engine demands.

It was during 1970 that Yamaha made their first serious breakthrough into the four-stroke field, when their 650 cc XS1 was introduced into the US market. Basically, it represented a new approach to the design of the classic vertical twin, employing an overhead camshaft arrangement in place of the generally accepted push rod layout, without increasing the complexity of the working parts of the engine. Although the new model was well received by the motorcycling fraternity, it still possessed the characteristic inherent with all engines of this design - engine vibration that was difficult to damp out. When later additions were made to the four-stroke range, in the form of 500 cc and 750 cc twins, each embodied another new Yamaha innovation - a chain-driven contra-rotating crankshaft balancer which eliminated the effects of engine vibration at the expense of added mechanical complexity. The 500 cc model proved to be the more popular of the two new additions. The 500 cc model was known initially as the TX500, but from the end of 1974 onwards it was redesignated the XS500, when the Yamaha coding system was changed to give more positive identification of models fitted with a four-stroke engine. Design changes have been made as the XS500 model has continued in production, the latest version being the XS500C, which has many cosmetic changes, disc brakes front and rear, and die-cast aluminium alloy wheels as an optional extra. Unique in having a double overhead camshaft cylinder head configuration and four valves per cylinder, the XS500 model represents the very latest in the development of the four-stroke parallel twin - and has a degree of performance that is in keeping.

The first model to reach the UK market was the XS500B, which was imported during March 1975. The re-styled XS500C version made its debut towards the end of that year and is well-established as being the modern answer to an old, traditional design that first saw the light of day some 40 years ago.

Contents

Chapter	Section	Page
Introductory Sections	Acknowledgements	2
	About this manual	2
	Introduction to the Yamaha 500 Twins	2
	Ordering spare parts	5
	Working conditions and tools	6
	Routine maintenance	6
Chapter 1/Engine, clutch and gearbox	Specifications	13
	Dismantling	20
	Examination and renovation	39
	Reassembly	47
	Fault diagnosis - Engine, clutch, gearbox	74
Chapter 2/Fuel system and lubrication	Specifications	76
	Carburettors	77
	Exhaust system	82
	Fault diagnosis	86
Chapter 3/Ignition system	Specifications	87
	Contact breakers	88
	Ignition timing	90
	Automatic advance unit	91
	Spark plug	93
	Fault diagnosis	93
Chapter 4/Frame and forks	Specifications	94
	Front forks	94
	Steering head bearings	99
	Frame	101
	Swinging arm	101
	Rear suspension unit	106
	Cleaning	107
	Fault diagnosis	108
Chapter 5/Wheels, brakes and tyres	Specifications	109
	Front wheel	109
	Rear wheel	116
	Adjusting brake pedal	119
	Cush drive assembly	119
	Final drive chain	120
	Tyres	121
	Fault diagnosis	123
Chapter 6/Electrical system	Specifications	124
	Alternator	125
	Battery	125
	Starter motor	126
	Headlamp	127
	Fault diagnosis	132
	Wiring diagrams	134
Metric conversion tables		136
Index		138

1976 Yamaha 500 cc XS500C model

Modifications made to the Yamaha 500 Twin

This title is based on the XS500C model, an example of which was completely stripped and rebuilt in our workshop. Although the basic design concept has not changed, certain minor differences occur when the XS500C model is compared to earlier versions. Wherever possible, these changes have been mentioned in the text, even though they will have no significant effect on the way in which the machine is dismantled and reassembled. It should, however, be appreciated that sometimes an Allen screw is substituted for a bolt, or the shape and/or composition of a gasket changed, where field service experience has shown any such change to be beneficial. The electrical system has benefitted most in this respect, by separating the individual circuits so that each has its own fuse. Except under exceptional circumstances, a short circuit will no longer 'black out' the entire electrical system and providing the source of the trouble is not within the ignition circuit itself, the machine can be ridden in an emergency capacity until the source of the trouble is found and remedied.

The most noticeable difference between late and early models is the type of rear brake fitted - disc or drum. A full description is given of each system and the way in which either can be overhauled and examined for wear.

Ordering spare parts

When ordering spare parts for the Yamaha 500 twin, it is advisable to deal direct with an official Yamaha agent, who will be able to supply many of the items required ex-stock. Although parts can be ordered from Yamaha direct, it is preferable to route the order via a local agent even if the parts are not available from stock. He is in a better position to specify exactly the parts required and to identify the relevant spare part numbers so that there is less chance of the wrong part being supplied by the manufacturer due to a vague or incomplete description.

When ordering spares, always quote the frame and engine numbers in full, together with any prefixes or suffixes in the form of letters. The frame number is found stamped on the right-hand side of the steering head, in line with the forks. The engine number is stamped on the right-hand side of the upper crankcase, close to the starter motor cover.

Use only parts of genuine Yamaha manufacture. A few pattern parts are available, sometimes at cheaper prices, but there is no guarantee that they will give such good service as the originals they replace. Retain any worn or broken parts until the replacements have been obtained; they are sometimes needed as a pattern to help identify the correct replacement when design changes have been made during a production run.

Some of the more expendable parts such as spark plugs, bulbs, tyres, oils and greases etc., can be obtained from accessory shops and motor factors, who have convenient opening hours, charge lower prices and can often be found not far from home. It is also possible to obtain parts on a mail order basis from a number of specialists who advertise regularly in the motor cycle magazines.

Engine number location (right-hand side of engine unit)

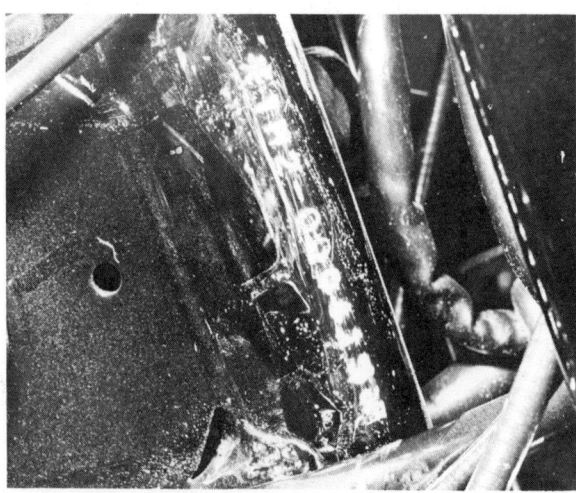

Frame number location (steering head)

Working conditions and tools

When a major overhaul is contemplated, it is important that a clean, well-lit working space is available, equipped with a workbench and vice, and with space for laying out or storing the dismantled assemblies in an orderly manner where they are unlikely to be disturbed. The use of a good workshop will give the satisfaction of work done in comfort and without haste, where there is little chance of the machine being dismantled and reassembled in anything other than clean surroundings. Unfortunately, these ideal working conditions are not always practicable and under these latter circumstances when improvisation is called for, extra care and time will be needed.

The other essential requirement is a comprehensive set of good quality tools. Quality is of prime importance, since cheap tools will prove expensive in the long run if they slip or break and damage the components to which they are applied. A good quality tool will last a long time, and more than justify the cost. The basis of any tool kit is a set of open-ended spanners, which can be used on almost any part of the machine to which there is reasonable access. A set of ring spanners makes a useful addition, since they can be used on nuts that are very tight or where access is restricted. Where the cost has to be kept within reasonable bounds, a compromise can be effected with a set of combination spanners - open-ended at one end and having a ring of the same size on the other end. Socket spanners may also be considered a good investment, a basic ½ inch drive kit comprising a ratchet handle and a small number of socket heads, if money is limited. Additional sockets can be purchased, as and when they are required. Provided they are slim in profile, sockets will reach nuts or bolts that are deeply recessed. When purchasing spanners of any kind, make sure the correct size standard is purchased. Almost all machines manufactured outside the UK and the USA have metric nuts and bolts, whilst those produced in Britain have BSF or BSW sizes. The standard used in the USA is AF, which is also found on some of the later British machines. Other tools that should be included in the kit are a range of crosshead screwdrivers, a pair of pliers and a hammer.

When considering the purchase of tools, it should be remembered that by carrying out the work oneself, a large proportion of the normal repair cost, made up by labour charges, will be saved. The economy made on even a minor overhaul will go a long way towards the improvement of a tool kit.

In addition to the basic tool kit, certain additional tools can prove invaluable when they are close to hand, to help speed up a multitude of repetitive jobs. For example, an impact screwdriver will ease the removal of screws that have been tightened by a similar tool, during assembly, without risk of damaging the screw heads. And, of course, it can be used again to retighten the screws, to ensure an oil or airtight seal results. Circlip pliers have their uses too, since gear pinions, shafts and similar components are frequently retained by circlips that are not too easily displaced by a screwdriver. There are two types of circlip plier, one for internal and one for external circlips. They may also have straight or right-angled jaws.

One of the most useful of all tools is the torque wrench, a form of spanner that can be adjusted to slip when a measured amount of force is applied to any bolt or nut. Torque wrench settings are given in almost every modern workshop or service manual, where the extent to which a complex component, such as a cylinder head, can be tightened without fear of distortion or leakage. The tightening of bearing caps is yet another example. Overtightening will stretch or even break bolts, necessitating extra work to extract the broken portions.

As may be expected, the more sophisticated the machine, the greater is the number of tools likely to be required if it is to be kept in first class condition by the home mechanic. Unfortunately, there are certain jobs which cannot be accomplished successfully without the correct equipment and although there is invariably a specialist who will undertake the work for a fee, the home mechanic will have to dig more deeply in his pocket for the purchase of similar equipment if he does not wish to employ the services of others. Here a word of caution is necessary, since some of these jobs are best left to the expert. Although an electrical multimeter of the Avo type will prove helpful in tracing electrical faults, in inexperienced hands it may irrevocably damage some of the electrical components if a test current is passed through them in the wrong direction. This can apply to the synchronisation of twin or multiple carburettors too, where a certain amount of expertise is needed when setting them up with vacuum gauges. These are, however, exceptions. Some instruments, such as a strobe lamp, are virtually essential when checking the timing of a machine powered by a CDI ignition system. In short, do not purchase any of these special items unless you have the experience to use them correctly.

Although this manual shows how components can be removed and replaced without the use of special service tools (unless absolutely essential), it is worthwhile giving consideration to the purchase of the more commonly used tools if the machine is regarded as a long term purchase. Whilst the alternative methods suggested will remove and replace parts without risk of damage, the use of the special tools recommended and sold by the manufacturer will invariably save time.

Routine Maintenance

Periodic routine maintenance is a continuous process that commences immediately the machine is used. It must be carried out at specified mileage recordings, or on a calendar basis if the machine is not used frequently, whichever is the sooner. Maintenance should be regarded as an insurance policy, to help keep the machine in the peak of condition and to ensure long,

Routine maintenance

trouble-free service. It has the additional benefit of giving early warning of any faults that may develop and will act as a regular safety check, to the obvious advantage of both rider and machine alike.

The various maintenance tasks are described under their respective mileage and calendar headings. Accompanying diagrams are provided, where necessary. It should be remembered that the interval between the various maintenance tasks serves only as a guide. As the machine gets older or is used under particularly adverse conditions, it would be advisable to reduce the period between each check. Some of the tasks are described in detail, where they are not mentioned fully as a routine maintenance item in the text. If a specific item is mentioned but not described in detail, it will be covered fully in the appropriate Chapter. No special tools are required for the normal routine maintenance tasks. The tools supplied with every new machine will prove adequate, in most cases, but if additional tools are needed, it is advisable to purchase only those of good quality, which will not damage any parts of the machine on which they are used.

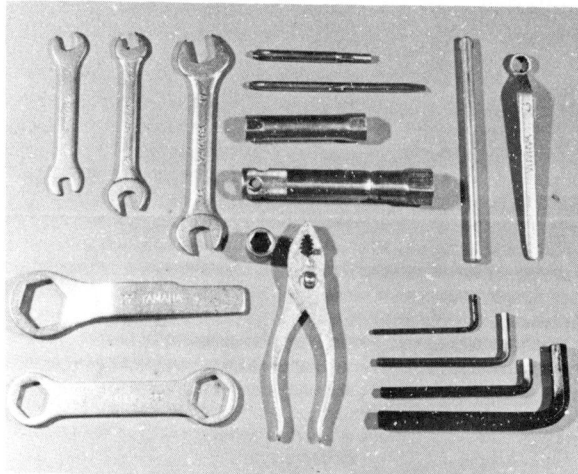
The complete tool kit supplied with the XS500C model

Weekly, or every 250 miles

Tyre pressures
1 Check the tyre pressures with a pressure gauge that is known to be accurate. Always check the pressures when the tyres are cold. If the tyres are checked after the machine has travelled a number of miles, the tyres will have become hotter and consequently the pressure will have increased, possibly as much as 8 psi. A false reading will therefore always result.

The recommended tyre pressures are:

Front tyre	23 psi (1.6 kg/cm^2)	normal riding
Rear tyre	28 psi (2.0 kg/cm^2)	normal riding
Front tyre	28 psi (2.0 kg/cm^2)	high speed riding
Rear tyre	33 psi (2.3 kg/cm^2)	high speed riding

When a pillion passenger is carried, it is advantageous to increase the rear tyre pressure by at least 4 psi (0.3 kg/cm^2).

Engine oil level
2 Check the engine oil level when the engine is cold, after making sure that the machine is standing on level ground. There is a dipstick mounted in the forward left-hand side of the crankcase, immediately to the rear of the alternator housing. Check the level with the dipstick resting on the edge of the hole into which it threads, and replenish, if necessary, with oil of the recommended viscosity (SAE 20W/40). Do not overfill or let the oil drop below the minimum level mark. Because the big-end and main bearings are of the shell type, they will fail very rapidly if the oil pressure decreases or oil starvation occurs.

The oil filler cap is found immediately to the rear of the left-hand cylinder. The total oil capacity is 3 litres.

Hydraulic fluid level
3 Check the level of the hydraulic fluid in the master cylinder reservoir mounted on the handlebars. The level can be seen through the transparent reservoir and should be between the upper and lower level marks. Ensure that the handlebars are in the central position when a level reading is taken and also when the cap and diaphragm are removed. Replenish the reservoir with an hydraulic fluid of the recommended specification.

In the case of the XS500C model, this will also apply to the rear brake master cylinder reservoir, which is found under the right-hand side cover, immediately above the rear brake pedal. It is imperative that the correct grade of fluid is used.

Safety check
4 Give the machine a close, visual inspection, checking for loose nuts and fittings, frayed control cables, etc.

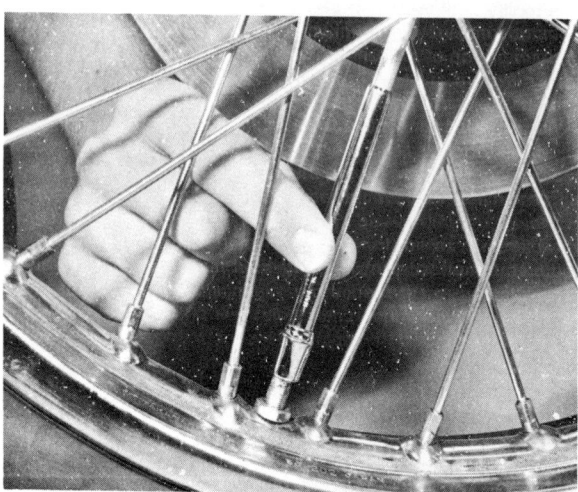
Check tyre pressures with a gauge known to be accurate

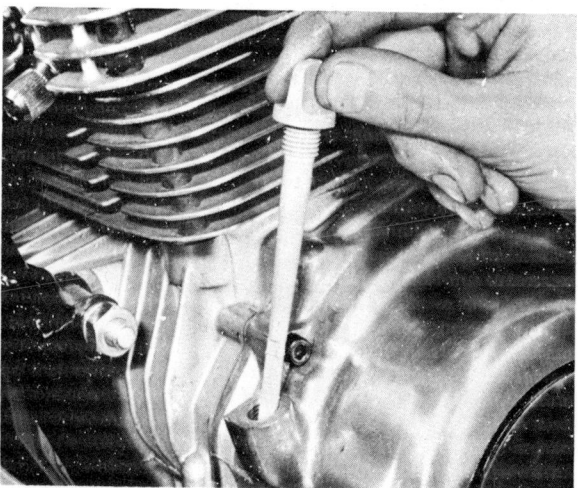
Use a dipstick to check oil level

Routine maintenance

Legal check
5 Ensure that the lights, horn and traffic indicators function correctly, also the speedometer. If any bulbs have to be renewed, make sure they have the same rating as the original. Remember that if different wattage bulbs are used in the traffic indicators, the flashing rate will be altered.

Monthly, or every 500 miles

Complete the tasks listed under the weekly/200 mile heading and then carry out the following checks.

Tyre damage
1 Rotate each wheel and check for damage to the tyres, especially splitting on the sidewalls. Remove any stones or other objects caught between the treads. This is particularly important on the front tyre, where rapid tyre deflation due to penetration of the inner tube will almost certainly cause total loss of control of the machine.

Spoke tension
2 Check the spokes for tension, by gently tapping each one with a metal object. A loose spoke is identifiable by the low pitch noise emitted when struck. If any one spoke needs considerable tightening, it will be necessary to remove the tyre and inner tube in order to file down the protruding spoke end. This will prevent it from chafing through the rim band and piercing the inner tube.

In the case of cast aluminium alloy wheels, as fitted as an optional extra to the XS500C model, they should be examined very carefully for any signs of cracking or other damage. Cracking or splitting is most likely to occur at the point where the spokes join either the rim or the hub.

Rear brake adjustment
3 When the rear brake is in correct adjustment the total brake pedal travel measured at the toe tread should be within the range 20 - 30 mm (0.8 - 1.2 in.). If the travel is greater or less than this carry out the necessary adjustment by means of the shouldered nut at the brake arm end of the cable.

Final drive chain lubrication
4 In order that final drive chain life can be extended as much as possible, regular lubrication and adjustment is essential. This is particularly so when the chain is not enclosed or is fitted to a machine transmitting high power to the rear wheel. The chain may be lubricated whilst it is in situ on the machine by the application of one of the proprietary chain greases contained in an aerosol can. Ordinary engine oil can be used, though owing to the speed with which it is flung off the rotating chain, its effective life is limited.

The most satisfactory method of chain lubrication can be made when the chain has been removed from the machine. Clean the chain in paraffin and wipe it dry. The chain can now be immersed in one of the special chain graphited greases. The grease must be heated as per the instructions on the can so that the lubricant penetrates into the areas between the link pins and the rollers.

Final drive chain adjustment
5 Check the slack in the final drive chain. The correct up and down movement, as measured at the mid-point of the chain lower run, should be 15 - 20 mm (0.6 - 0.8 in). Adjustment should be carried out as follows: Place the machine on the centre stand so that the rear wheel is clear of the ground and free to rotate. Remove the split pin from the wheel spindle and slacken the wheel nut a few turns. Loosen the locknuts on the two chain adjuster bolts. Rotation of the adjuster bolts in a clockwise direction will tighten the chian. Tighten each bolt a similar number of turns so that wheel alignment is maintained. This can be verified by checking that the mark on the outer face of each chain adjuster is aligned with the same aligning mark on each fork end. With the adjustment correct, tighten the wheel nut and fit a new split pin. Finally, retighten the adjuster bolt locknuts.

Battery electrolyte level
6 Release the seat catch and hinge the dualseat up so that access to the battery may be gained. Detach the battery retaining strap and the breather pipe and lift the battery sufficiently that the level may be checked. The electrolyte solution should be between the upper and lower level lines. If the electrolyte solution is low it should be replenished, using distilled water. This is best done when the battery is removed from the machine. Disconnect the positive lead and the negative lead, and lift the battery away.

Two-monthly, or every 1,000 miles

Complete each of the checks listed under the weekly/200 mile and monthly/500 mile headings, then carry out the following additional checks:

Braking system
1 Check the complete braking system, front and rear, paying special attention to the condition of the brake pads and the angle of the rear brake operating arm in the case of machines fitted with a rear drum brake. The brake pads can be examined by lifting a small plastic flap in the top of the caliper unit. This will show the extent of the wear that has taken place in relation to the red line inscribed round the periphery of each pad. If either pad has worn down to the red line or is very close to it, BOTH pads must be renewed immediately. It is dangerous to exceed this wear limit.

In the case of the drum rear brake fitted to the earlier models, the brake operating arm gives the best guide to the extent of wear of the brake shoes. For maximum braking efficiency, the angle of this arm in relation to the brake rod should not be greater than 90° when the brake is applied. When this point is reached, the rear wheel should be removed as described in Chapter 4 of this manual and the brake shoes examined for wear, renewing them if necessary.

Spark plugs
2 Remove both spark plugs and readjust the points gaps so that they are within the range 0.6 - 0.7 mm (0.024 - 0.028 in). Always bend the outer electrode to adjust the gap and never the central electrode, otherwise the ceramic insulation will be destroyed, with consequent plug failure and the possibility of particles of insulator dropping into the engine.

If the electrodes are badly eroded or have worn away to any noticeable extent, it is preferable to renew both plugs and restore full performance. Make sure the replacements are of the same grade and check their gaps prior to insertion into the engine.

Reference to the end of Chapter 3 will show how spark plug electrode conditions can be interpreted, with some experience, to act as a guide to engine operating conditions.

Wheels and tyres
3 In addition to checking the wheels for loose or broken spokes, run out etc, and the tyres for wear, damage and correct pressures, it is also advisable to check wheel balance, especially with regard to the front wheel. If the front wheel is allowed to go out of balance, as may occur through uneven tyre wear, a most unpleasant hammering effect will be noticed as road speeds increase. The wheel should be balanced by placing weights opposite the valve so that when the wheel is spun, it will come to rest in any random position. Balance weights of differing ratings are available from Yamaha repair specialists, designed to fit around the spokes and spoke nipples with absolute security. The alternative is to wrap lead wire or solder around the appropriate spokes until the correct counter-balance is obtained.

Although the rear wheel can be balanced in similar fashion, it is doubtful whether there is any real advantage to be gained

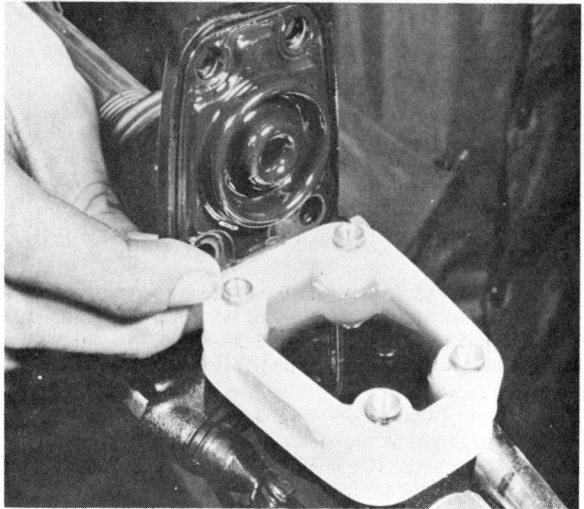
Check hydraulic brake fluid level in handlebar mounted reservoir

XS500C model has separate rear brake reservoir, above brake pedal

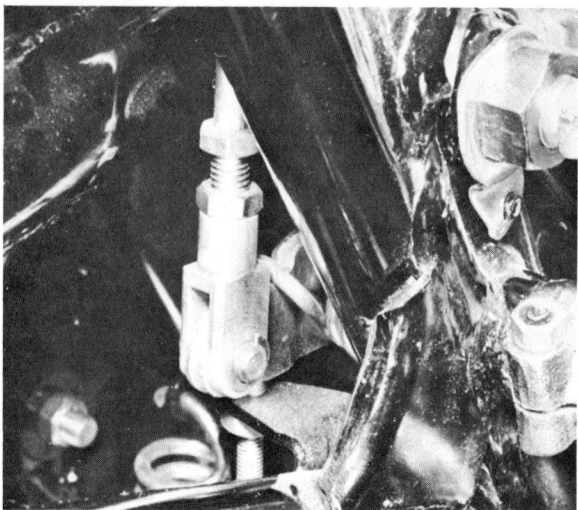
Adjuster for rear brake pedal travel (XS500C model)

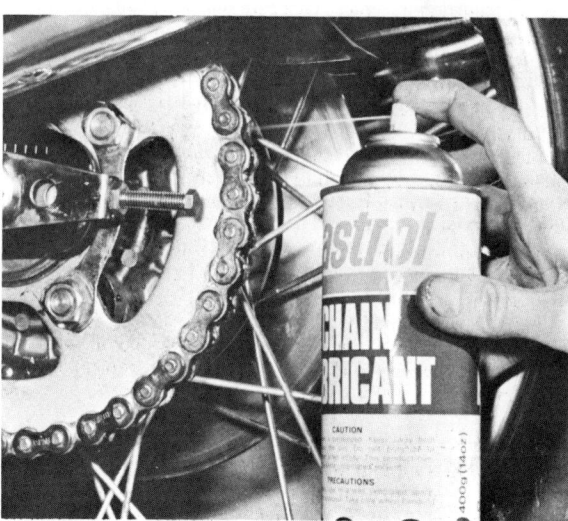
Aerosol-type lubricants permit chain to be lubricated in-situ

Electrolyte must be between these two levels (battery shown is unfilled)

Brake pad wear can be checked by raising flap

since an out of balance rear wheel will have only minimal effect on the handling of the machine.

Do not omit to check the wheels for alignment, since if they are out of line, the handling characteristics of the machine will be impaired. Checking by laying a straight wooden plank alongside the wheels, each side in turn, and make whatever adjustments are necessary by means of the final drive chain adjusters. If adjustments are called for, do not omit to check the chain tension after correct wheel alignment has been verified. Make sure both adjusters are turned an equal amount, when adjusting the chain, to preserve wheel alignment.

Final drive chain
4 When correctly adjusted, the final drive chain should have from 15 - 20 mm (0.6 - 0.8 in) of slack in the middle of the upper run, without the rider seated, but with both wheels touching the ground. If the chain is too tight, an excessive load will be placed on the sprockets and the gearbox bearings, causing premature wear. If the chain is too slack, there is danger of it jumping the sprockets and causing transmission snatch.

When adjusting the chain, take care that wheel alignment is preserved by turning both adjusters an equal amount.

If the chain is dirty, or shows signs of running dry, it should be removed from the machine and washed in a petrol/paraffin mix so that all the road filth and other matter is cleaned off. After drying, it should then be immersed in one of the proprietary chain lubricants that has been heated until it is molten, removed and hung up to drain of excess lubricant, prior to replacement on the machine. This will ensure the lubricant really penetrates the chain and is more effective than lubricating with engine oil, which is rapidly flung off. The alternative is to apply chain lubricant from an aerosol pack, whilst the chain is still in position on the machine.

Check the security of the spring clip, if the chain is not of the endless type. The closed end must face the direction of travel of the chain, to prevent it from being displaced whilst the chain is in motion.

Quarterly, or every 2,000 miles

Complete each of the tasks listed under the weekly/200 mile, monthly/500 mile and two-monthly/1,000 mile headings, then complete the following additional tasks:

Clutch
1 The clutch adjustment should be checked, to ensure there is from 2 - 3 mm (0.08 - 0.12 in) free play at the handlebar lever. There are two adjustment points, the adjuster on the end of the clutch lever itself and a screw and locknut in the centre of the clutch operating mechanism, blanked off by a removable plug in the left-hand crankcase cover. Under normal circumstances, adjustment at the handlebar lever should suffice.

It is important that the correct amount of free play is maintained, otherwise a continual, heavy load is placed on the clutch operating mechanism that may ultimately lead to clutch slip.

Air cleaner
2 The air cleaner element should be removed by raising the dualseat and taking off the top of the air cleaner box, which is retained by two wing nuts. The air cleaner element can then be pulled out, together with the wire clip or spring that retains it in position. Provided the element is not wet, oily, or torn, it can be blown clean with an air line, applying the pressure from the INSIDE. If very dirty, it is preferable to renew the element, rather than attempt to clean it.

The air cleaner element should be renewed, irrespective of condition, every SECOND service. Before replacing the element, check that there are no leaks in the system, which would reduce the effectiveness of the system and cause carburation changes.

Petrol tap filters
3 It is advisable to remove and clean the detachable filter screen within each petrol tap by turning off the tap and removing the three slotted bolts that retain the rear of the petrol tap body. This will give access to the screen. If desired, the tap can be drained of fuel first, by removing the small screw and fibre washer in the front of the tap body, which acts as a drain plug.

There should be no necessity to remove either tap from the underside of the fuel tank, in order to gain access to the main filter, which is an integral part of the tap. When such action is necessary, the tank must be completely drained of fuel first.

Contact breaker points
4 The condition of the contact breaker points should be examined by removing the circular cover in the right-hand crankcase main cover. It is retained by three screws and has a gasket to seal the joint. Check the condition of the faces of each of the two sets of contact breaker points. Slight burning or pitting can be removed while the contact breaker unit is in situ on the machine, using emery paper (No. 400) backed by a thin strip of tin. If pitting or burning is excessive the contact breaker unit should be removed for points dressing or renewal. (See Chapter 3, Section 4). After the points have been cleaned, they should be adjusted to restore the correct gap as follows:

Rotate the crankshaft in a forward direction (ie; clockwise) until one set of points is in the fully open position. Check the gap with a 0.35 mm (0.014 in) feeler gauge. If the gap is incorrect, loosen the fixed point retaining screw and by placing a screwdriver in the points adjuster slot, rotate the fixed point until the gap is correct. The feeler gauge should be a light slide fit between the points faces. Tighten the fixed point retaining screw and recheck the gap. The remaining set of contact breaker points should now be checked and adjusted, following the same procedure. After contact breaker adjustment has been carried out, clean the points faces with methylated spirits or carbon tetrachloride applied with a clean piece of rag. Do not use petrol or paraffin as both these fluids will leave an oily deposit.

After cleaning or renewing the contact breaker points, it is advisable to check the accuracy of the ignition timing, by following the procedure described in Section 8 of Chapter 3. Alignment of the timing marks will show whether the setting is approximately correct, but for real accuracy, a strobe lamp check is recommended, which in most cases will necessitate a visit to a Yamaha service agent. Engine performance and fuel consumption are related to the accuracy with which the ignition timing is set, and in consequence the setting should be verified from time to time.

Carburettors
5 It is important that the carburettors are synchronised with each other, so that both have identical settings throughout the entire throttle opening range. A vacuum gauge set is necessary in this instance and in consequence it will be necessary to enlist the help of a Yamaha service agent who will have the necessary equipment and the setting-up experience. For those who have access to a vacuum gauge set, the relevant details are given in Section 8 of Chapter 2.

Remove the float chamber from the underside of each carburettor by unscrewing the four screws that retain it in position. A short, stubby screwdriver will be necessary, in view of the limited amount of clearance when the float chamber is removed with the carburettor in position. Clean the float chamber interior so that no sediment remains and make sure that none of the jets is blocked. Use compressed air only to clear a blocked jet, never wire or a pointed instrument of any kind which would enlarge the jet orifice and create carburation problems. When replacing the float chamber, make sure the sealing gasket is in good order and that the float assembly has not been disturbed. Tighten the four retaining screws.

Compression test
6 In order to check whether the valves and cylinder head are

seating correctly, each spark plug should be removed in turn and the engine rotated whilst a compression test gauge is inserted into the plug hole. The standard reading should be 10 kg/cm^2 (142 psi). A reading higher than 11 kg/cm^2 (154 psi) indicates a build-up of carbon in the combustion chamber and on the piston crown of the cylinder concerned, outlining the need for a decoke. A reading below 9 kg/cm^2 (127 psi) indicates a valve or cylinder head joint leakage, or a worn cylinder bore and/or piston. To check, introduce a small amount of oil into the spark plug hole and check the reading again. If the reading increases, cylinder bore and/or piston wear is the more likely.

Lubrication

7 Drain the engine oil by removing BOTH drain plugs from the underside of the crankcase and the oil filler cap. It is preferable to complete this task when the engine is warm, so that the old oil will drain off more readily. A large receptacle will be needed to collect the oil that drains off; approximately 3 litres (5.28 pints) will be released. When all the oil has drained off, refit and tighten the drain plugs, after checking that their sealing washers are in good condition. Refill the crankcase sump with 3 litres (5.28 pints) of a good quality SAE 20W/40 engine oil and check with the dipstick that the oil level is correct. Replace the filler cap.

Lubricate the control cables, using either a proprietary lubricator made for this purpose, or a simple plasticine funnel. It will be necessary to detach one end of each cable in this latter case.

Lubricate the speedometer and tachometer drive cables by detaching the cable at the driving end and withdrawing the inner cable. High melting point or graphited grease should be used, taking care not to grease the last six inches of the cable at the instrument head end. If this precaution is overlooked, grease will work into the instrument head and immobilise the movement.

Grease the twist grip throttle by separating the split housing that also contains the switchgear. Disconnect the battery first and make sure no lubricant finds its way on to the switch contacts or parts. Do not reconnect the battery until the twist grip is reassembled.

Use light oil to lubricate the brake pedal shaft, the gearchange pedal shaft and the centre and prop stand pivots. Apply high melting point grease to the swinging arm pivot.

Dismantle the wheel bearings, as described in Chapter 5, Sections 7 and 9, and repack them with fresh high melting point grease. Special care is necessary when removing and replacing the bearings, as they are easily damaged if they are driven in or out incorrectly.

Steering head bearings

8 Check the steering head bearings for play by applying the front brake hard and seeing whether there is any movement as the machine is rocked backwards and forwards. If adjustment is necessary, slacken the pinch bolt through the upper fork yoke and turn the centre nut of the steering head column in the desired direction. Retighten the pinch bolt, and re-check. Do not overtighten, or the machine will show a tendency to roll at low speeds. Do not confuse movement at the steering head with worn fork sliders.

Half-yearly or every 4,000 miles

When this point is reached, all the foregoing checks should be carried out first, working from the weekly/200 mile service right through to the quarterly/2,000 mile list. Two further checks are then necessary:

Carburettors

1 Both carburettors should be removed from the machine, dismantled and cleaned and examined very carefully, prior to reassembly. The relevant information is given in Chapter 2, Section 6. It is also advisable to check the tickover setting and

Also applies to rear brake of XS500C model

Check contact breaker gaps with feeler gauge

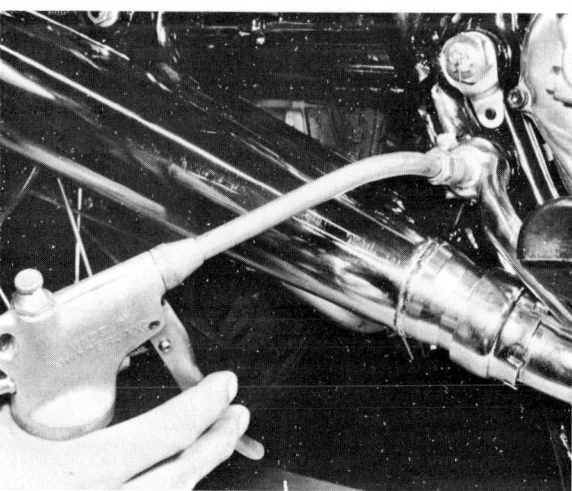
Do not omit to grease swinging arm pivot

synchronisation after reinstallation on the machine, as detailed in Sections 7 and 8 of the same Chapter.

Oil filter element
2 The oil filter element is of the disposable type. It is located almost immediately below the final drive gearbox sprocket, on the left-hand side of the machine. Only the rearmost portion of the left-hand crankcase cover need be removed to gain access; the cover is retained by five Allen screws. The oil filter element will unscrew from position by placing a spanner over the hexagon shape formed on the end. It has a normal, right-hand thread.

The element can be changed without having to drain the sump first. Use only a replacement filter element of Yamaha manufacture and make sure the inner 'O' ring at the mounting point is in good condition. It should be greased before installation. Tighten the element fully, to preclude the leakage of oil or loss of oil pressure.

Speedometer drive gearbox
3 Grease the speedometer drive gearbox via the grease nipple provided, using high melting point grease.

Front forks
4 Place the machine on its centre stand and remove the drain plugs from the front fork lower legs, so that the damping oil will drain off. Approximately 147 cc will drain from each leg, which will be aided by removal of the filler cap at the top of each fork leg. To release the cap, pull out the rubber plug, press downwards on the cap, and release the internal circlip that retains it in place.

When all the old oil has drained, replace the drain plugs, making sure their sealing washers are in good condition, and refill each fork leg with 147 cc of SAE 10W/30 oil. Replace the filler caps, their retaining circlips and the rubber blanking plugs.

Repack the steering head races with fresh high melting point grease. This will involve a considerable amount of dismantling, as described in detail in Section 2 of Chapter 4, and subsequent readjustment of the bearings, after greasing and reassembly. If necessary, the individual ball bearings should be renewed during this operation, whilst access is easy.

Contact breaker
5 Lubricate very sparingly, with light machine oil, the felt wick of the contact breaker assembly. The wick bears on the contact breaker cam and the oil will help reduce the amount of wear on the fibre heels of the two moving contact points.

Do not over-oil. If oil finds its way on to the contact breaker points, it will act as an insulator and immobilise the ignition system.

Yearly, or every 8,000 miles

Hydraulic brake fluid
1 Drain and refill the complete hydraulic brake system(s), using new fluid of the recommended specification. Note that it will be necessary to bleed the system(s) of air after each refill, using the technique described fully in Section 3 of Chapter 5, paragraphs 8 to 11.

Use only fluid of the recommended specification and not fluid that has been stored in an open container or used on a previous occasion. Brake fluid absorbs water, which is why it is necessary to change it at regular intervals.

Note: The manufacturer recommends that many of the foregoing tasks should be carried out by a Yamaha service agent, especially those from the quarterly/2,000 mile service onwards, where more detailed attention is needed.

During the initial running-in period, service to many of the items listed will be required at more regular intervals. During this period, the recommended intervals listed in the owner's manual, supplied with every new machine, should be rigidly adhered to, otherwise there is risk of damage to the machine and subsequent invalidation of the manufacturer's guarantee.

Above all else, if you wish to carry out your own routine maintenance on a new machine, check first that it will not invalidate the guarantee. In a great many cases the initial service, and perhaps those immediately following, are the responsibility of the dealer who supplied the machine new.

Chapter 1 Engine, clutch and gearbox

Contents

General description ... 1	Cylinder block: examination and renovation ... 25
Operations with engine in frame ... 2	Pistons and piston rings: examination and renovation ... 26
Operations with engine removed ... 3	Cylinder head: dismantling, examination and renovation ... 27
Method of engine removal ... 4	Checking and resetting the valve clearances ... 28
Removing the engine unit ... 5	Camshafts, rocker arms and rocker spindles: examination and renovation ... 29
Dismantling the engine unit: general ... 6	
Dismantling the engine unit: removing the cylinder head cover, crankcase covers and cylinder head ... 7	Camshaft drive chain, tensioners and sprockets: examination and replacement ... 30
Dismantling the engine unit: removing the cylinder block, pistons and starter motor ... 8	Primary drive pinion, clutch assembly, camshaft drive and tachometer drive pinion: examination and replacement ... 31
Dismantling the engine unit: removing the alternator rotor ... 9	Gearbox components: examination and replacement ... 32
Dismantling the engine unit: removing the crankshaft balancer drive and final drive sprocket ... 10	Crankshaft balancer, drive chain and sprockets: examination and replacement ... 33
Dismantling the engine unit: removing the contact breaker, camshaft drive sprocket and camshaft drive chain ... 11	Gearbox bearings: examination and replacement ... 34
	Engine and gearbox reassembly: general ... 35
Dismantling the engine unit: removing the primary drive pinion, clutch and kickstart assemblies ... 12	Engine and gearbox reassembly: replacing the gearbox components and crankshaft assembly ... 36
Dismantling the engine unit: removing the gearchange mechanism ... 13	Engine and gearbox reassembly: fitting the crankcase strainer and sump ... 37
Dismantling the engine unit: removing the sump, oil pressure release valve and strainer ... 14	Engine and gearbox reassembly: replacing the gearchange mechanism, crankshaft balancer and kickstart assembly ... 38
Separating the crankcase halves ... 15	
Dismantling the engine unit: removing the crankshaft assembly and gear cluster ... 16	Engine and gearbox reassembly: replacing the clutch assembly, primary drive and camshaft chain drive ... 39
Dismantling the engine unit: removing the oil pump ... 17	Engine and gearbox reassembly: replacing and timing the crankshaft balancer and the starter drive chain ... 40
Dismantling the engine unit: removing the gear selector mechanism ... 18	Engine and gearbox reassembly: replacing the cylinder block 41
Dismantling the engine unit: removing the crankshaft balancer and the tachometer and oil pump drive ... 19	Engine and gearbox reassembly: replacing the cylinder head and timing the valves ... 42
Examination and renovation: general ... 20	Replacing the engine unit ... 43
Big ends and main bearings: examination and renovation ... 21	Starting and running the rebuilt engine ... 44
Crankshaft assembly: examination and renovation ... 22	Taking the rebuilt engine on the road ... 45
Connecting rods: examination and renovation ... 23	Fault diagnosis: engine ... 46
Oil seals: examination and replacement ... 24	Fault diagnosis: clutch ... 47
	Fault diagnosis: gearbox ... 48

Specifications

Engine:

Type ...	Inclined four-stroke parallel twin, with double overhead camshaft valve operation and four valves per cylinder. All alloy construction
Bore and stroke ...	73.0 x 59.6 mm (2.874 x 2.346 in)
Capacity ...	498 cc (30.39 cu in)
Compression ratio ...	8.5:1
Valve clearances (engine cold):	
Inlet ...	0.15 - 0.20 mm (0.006 - 0.008 in)
Exhaust ...	0.20 - 0.25 mm (0.008 - 0.010 in)
Valve seat angle ...	45° inlet and exhaust valves
Valve seat width ...	1.0 ± 0.1 mm (0.040 ± 0.004 in) inlet and exhaust valves
Wear limit ...	1.5 mm (0.060 in)
Valve springs:	
Outer free length ...	39 mm (1.53 in)
Wear limit ...	37.50 mm (1.48 in)
Inner free length ...	38.2 mm (1.51 in)
	36.70 mm (1.45 in)
Cam height:	
Inlet cams ...	34.07 mm (1.342 in)

Exhaust cams	34.11 mm (1.344 in)
Base circle (inlet)	28.24 mm (1.1096 in)
Base circle (exhaust)	28.29 mm (1.1098 in)
Cylinder bore	73 mm (2.874 in) standard dimension
Wear limit	0.1 mm (0.004 in) see text for measurement procedure
Piston/cylinder clearance	0.050 - 0.055 mm (0.0021 in)
Piston ring gaps:	
Top and 2nd ring	0.2 - 0.4 mm (0.008 - 0.016 in)
Oil control ring	0.2 - 0.9 mm (0.008 - 0.035 in)
Top and 2nd ring wear limit	0.7 mm (0.027 in)
Oil control ring wear limit	0.9 mm (0.035 in)
Side float maximum	0.15 mm (0.007 in)
Piston oversizes available	+ 0.25 mm, + 0.50 mm, + 0.75 mm and + 1.0 mm
Crankshaft runout (maximum permissible)	0.05 mm (0.002 in) measured at any point
Cylinder head warpage	0.03 mm (0.0012 in) or less
Maximum permissible	0.05 mm (0.002 in) measured at any point
Connecting rod side play	0.15 mm (0.006 in)
Big end play	0.15 mm (0.006 in) or less *
Maximum permissible	0.40 mm (0.016 in) *
Small end play (maximum permissible)	2.0 mm (0.080 in)

measured at small end bearing

Clutch:

Clutch springs:	
Number	6
Free length	42.8 mm (1.691 in)
Wear limit	41.8 mm (1.651 in)
Clutch plates:	
Number	15 (8 friction, 7 plain)
Thickness (friction plates only)	3.0 mm (0.12 in)
Wear limit	2.7 mm (0.108 in)
Warpage (maximum permissible)	0.05 mm (0.002 in)

Gear ratios:

1st	35/15	2.333
2nd	31/20	1.550
3rd	31/26	1.192
4th	28/29	0.965
5th	25/31	0.806
Primary reduction ratio	79/26	3.038
Secondary reduction ratio	42/17	2.470

Torque wrench settings:

Parts to be tightened	Part size	Q'ty	Tightening torque
Valve clearance adjustment nuts	6 mm	8	1.2 – 1.5 m.kg
Camshaft cap nuts and studs	6 mm	12	0.8 – 1.0 m.kg
Camshaft cap nuts and studs	6 mm	12 (a)	0.8 – 1.0 m.kg
Cylinder head nuts and screws	10 mm	8	3.0 – 3.5 m.kg
Cylinder head nuts and screws	6 mm	9	1.0 – 1.2 m.kg
Cylinder head nuts and screws	8 mm	3	2.1 – 2.5 m.kg
Cylinder head nuts and screws	10 mm	8 (a)	1.5 – 2.0 m.kg
Connecting rod nuts	8 mm	4 (b)	3.5 – 4.0 m.kg
Crankshaft oil hole plug	1/8 in	2	3.7 – 4.0 m.kg
Oil pressure warning switch	1/8 in	1 (a)	2.0 – 2.3 m.kg
Oil filter element	22 mm	1	2.0 – 2.3 m.kg
Strainer housing screw	6 mm	4	0.8 – 1.0 m.kg
Delivery pipe (external)	10 mm	2	2.0 – 2.2 m.kg
Drain plug	30 mm	1	3.5 – 4.0 m.kg
Drain plug	14 mm	1	3.5 – 4.0 m.kg
Pump cover screws	6 mm	3	0.7 – 0.9 m.kg
Strainer cover screws	6 mm	11	0.7 – 0.9 m.kg
Kickstart bolt	8 mm	1	1.5 – 2.5 m.kg
AC generator rotor bolt	10 mm	1	4.0 – 4.5 m.kg
AC generator armature coil	6 mm	3	0.7 – 0.9 m.kg
AC generator field coil screws	6 mm	3	0.8 – 1.0 m.kg
Clutch springs	6 mm	6	0.8 – 1.0 m.kg
Clutch centre nut	18 mm	1	7.5 – 8.0 m.kg
Change stopper screw	8 mm	1 (a)	1.2 – 2.0 m.kg
Change adjusting screw	6 mm	1 (a)	0.8 – 1.0 m.kg
Neutral switch screws	5 mm	3	0.25 – 0.45 m.kg

Chapter 1: Engine, clutch and gearbox

Change pedal bolt	6 mm	1	0.8 – 1.2 m.kg
Drive sprocket locknut	18 mm	1	7.5 – 8.0 m.kg
Crankcase bolts	10 mm	6	1st 1.0 2nd 2.0 Final 3.5 m.kg
Crankcase bolts	6 mm	14	1st 0.5 Final 1.0 m.kg
Primary drive gear bolt	10 mm	1	4.0 – 5.0 m.kg
Spark plugs	18 mm	2 (b)	1.5 – 2.0 m.kg
Primary gear nut	6 mm	1 (a)	0.8 – 1.2 m.kg

a: Use Locktite
b: Use molybdenum oil

1 General description

The engine fitted to the Yamaha 500 cc vertical twin four stroke is of the combined engine and gearbox type in which the gearbox forms part of the main crankcase assembly. All the main castings are in aluminium alloy, to help reduce the overall weight of the machine, the engine itself being of advanced design, having four valves per cylinder and a chain-driven double overhead camshaft arrangement to operate them. The big-end and main bearings are of the shell type, necessitating a very thorough lubrication system that relies upon two trochoid-type oil pumps. A two-throw crankshaft arrangement is employed, in an attempt to help reduce the vibration factor inherent in parallel twin engines. An added refinement is Yamaha's patented Omni-phase Balancer, a chain-driven contra-rotating system of balance weights that cancel out any vibrations that remain.

The gearbox is of the five-speed constant mesh type, operated by a short gearchange lever on the left-hand side of the machine. Although a folding kickstart is fitted, the overall specification of the machine includes an electric starter. Power to the gearbox is transmitted by a gear primary drive, through a multiplate clutch immersed in oil. Final drive is by chain and sprockets.

The engine unit is heavy, despite the extensive use of aluminium alloy for the various castings. In consequence, it is a two person job to lift out and replace the engine unit during any major overhaul. Apart from the need for a good set of metric spanners, an impact screwdriver, with a selection of crosshead bits, is also an essential requirement if the machine has not been dismantled since it left the factory. A thread sealant is used on many of the internal engine screws and they will otherwise prove very difficult to remove without mutilating their heads, if the correct tool for the job is not used.

2 Operations with engine in frame

It is not necessary to remove the engine unit from the frame, unless attention is required to some major assembly, such as the crankshaft, main bearings or gearbox components. Many operations can be achieved with the engine in frame, such as:

1. *Removal and replacement of alternator*
2. *Removal and replacement of primary drive components*
3. *Replacement of the kickstart spring*
4. *Removal and replacement of the gear selector mechanism*
5. *Removal and replacement of the clutch*

When several operations have to be undertaken simultaneously, for example, during a major overhaul, it will probably be more advantageous to remove the complete engine unit from the frame; an operation that will take approximately 2-2½ hours. As mentioned earlier, this is a two person job, as the engine unit is quite heavy.

An added advantage of having the engine unit on the work bench is that better access is available. If a simple engine stand is made up so that the engine unit can be bolted rigidly to the bench, both hands can then be used during any dismantling routine, as the engine will not need to be steadied.

3 Operations with engine removed

1. *Removal and replacement of the main bearings*
2. *Removal and replacement of the crankshaft assembly*
3. *Removal of the cylinder head and cylinder block*
4. *Removal and replacement of the overhead camshafts and valve gear*

Note that when the cylinder head is removed, it is necessary to separate the overhead camshaft drive chain by pressing the pins of a special link through their side plates. A spring connecting link is NOT fitted. It also follows that when the chain is separated, the valves will have to be re-timed, before the chain is rejoined in the recommended manner.

Research has shown that it is just possible to renew the big-end bearings alone by following car practice, after dropping the sump and working from the underside of the machine. Whilst this technique may be employed whilst the engine is still in the frame, it is doubtful whether there are any real advantages to be gained. If the big-end bearings have failed, it is highly probable that other bearings may require attention at the same time.

4 Method of engine removal

As mentioned previously, the engine and gearbox are built in unit. The engine unit cannot be dismantled completely until the unit has been lifted from the frame and refitting cannot take place until it has been reassembled. A certain amount of dismantling is necessary before the engine unit can be lifted out of the frame, including removal of the exhaust system, carburettors and side covers and the disconnection of the final drive chain, the electrical connections and the tachometer drive cable.

Access to the gearbox is not available until the engine has been dismantled and the crankcases separated at their horizontal joint. It will also be necessary to separate the crankcases and expose the gearbox components, when working on the lower half of the engine.

5 Removing the engine unit

1 Place the machine on its centre stand, so that it is standing firmly, on level ground. Place a container that will hold at least 1 gallon (4.5 litres) under the crankcase sump and remove both drain plugs, so that the oil can drain off. This task will be made much easier if the engine is run prior to the commencement of these dismantling operations, so that the oil is warm and will drain off more readily. Allow the oil to drain completely, then replace and tighten both drain plugs after making sure their sealing washers are in good condition.

2 Disconnect both fuel pipes from the petrol taps, after making sure the latter are in the 'off' position. The pipes are retained by wire clips and may be freed by pulling whilst the ears of the clips are pressed together. To release the fuel tank, remove the two bolts and washers that pass through rubber grommets

5.3 Remove battery connections to isolate electrics

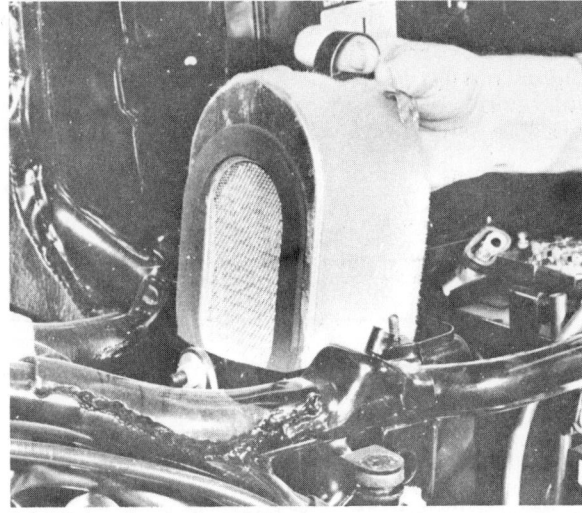
5.4 Lift out the air cleaner element

5.5 Disconnect throttle cable from operating lever

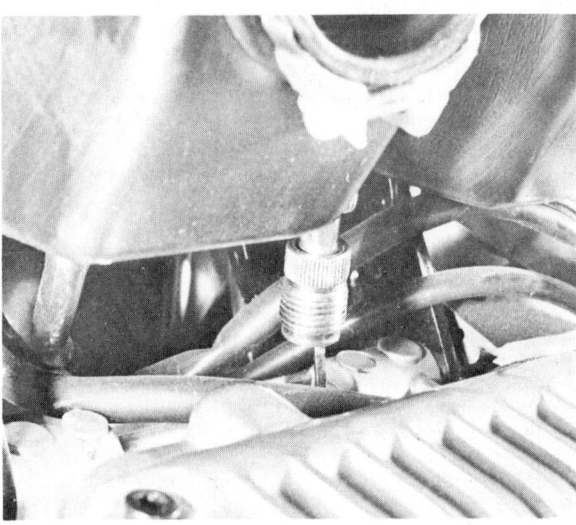
5.6a Unscrew tacho drive cable, now readily accessible

5.6b Milled Allen screws retain exhaust pipe flange

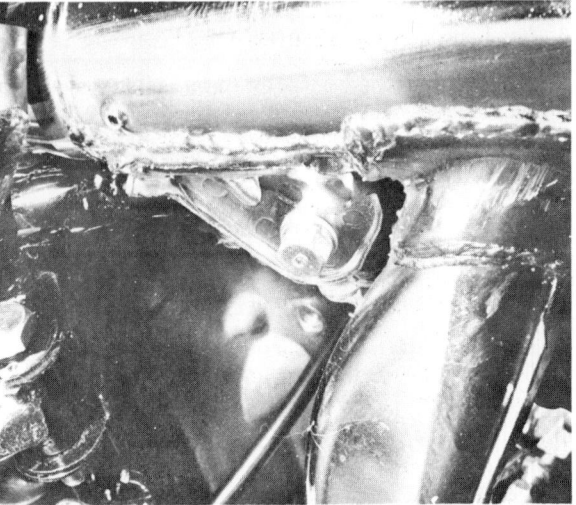
5.6c Note how silencers bolt to underside of frame

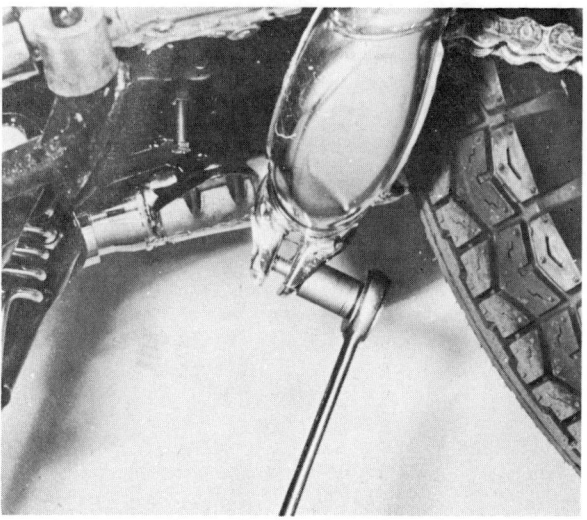
5.6d Clamp bolt of cross-pipe is under engine unit

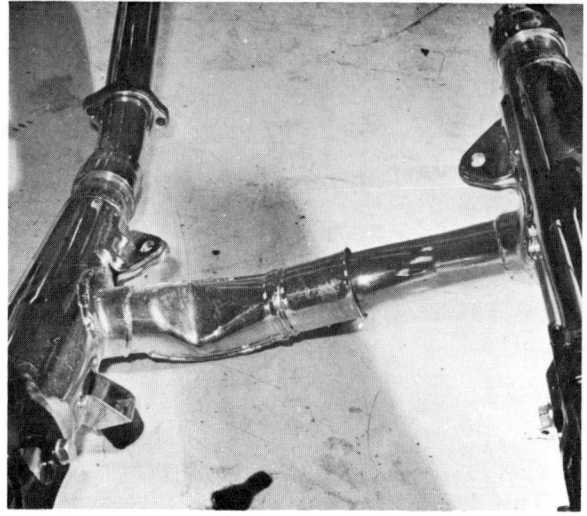
5.6e How the cross-pipe joins the separate exhaust systems

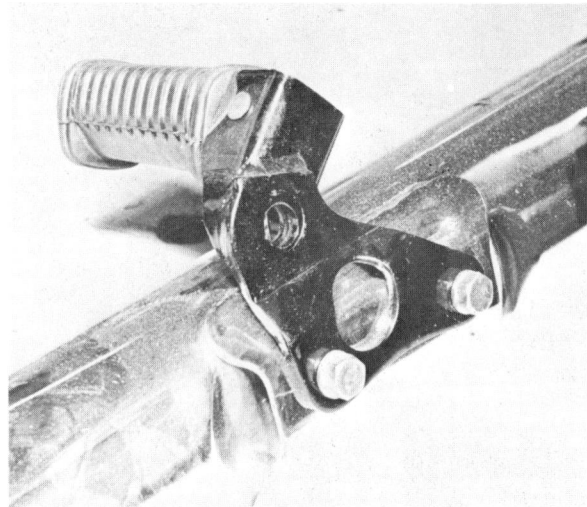
5.6f Pillion footrests bolt direct to silencer bracket

5.7 Remove long bolt that holds rider's footrests

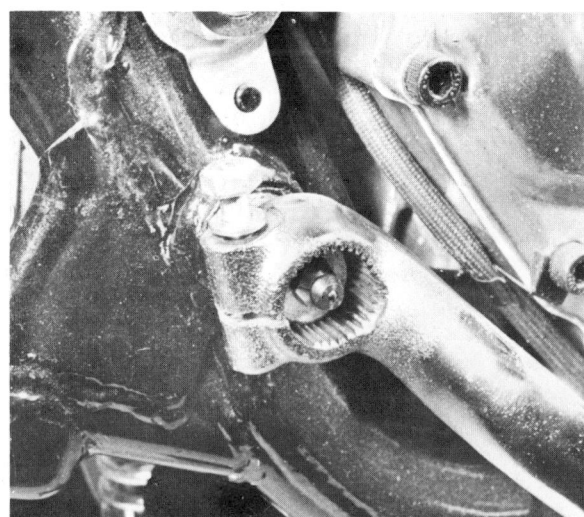
5.8 Relocate brake lever to give clearance when lifting out engine

5.9 Remove metal duct from cylinder head cover

5.10 Remove final drive cover for access to clutch cable

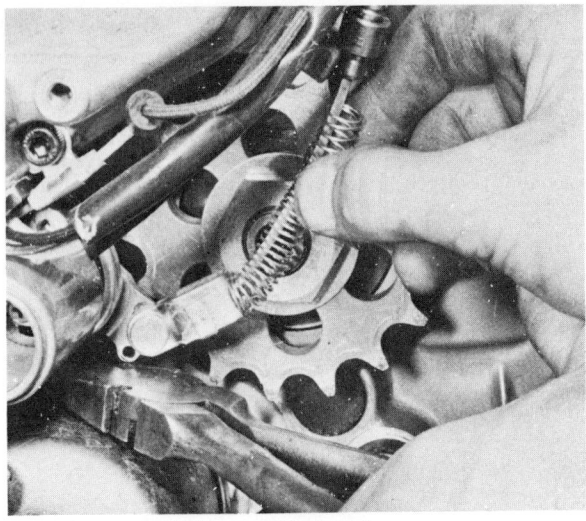

5.11a Stop will pull from crankcase anchorage

5.11b Clutch cable will disconnect from trunnion

5.12a Disconnect electrical leads on right-hand and ...

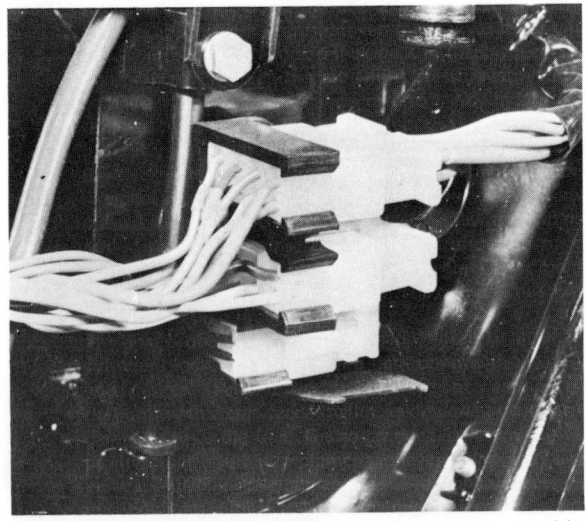

5.12b ... left-hand side of machine, at block connectors provided

15.13a Take off the starter motor cover

Chapter 1: Engine, clutch and gearbox

at the rear of the tank. It will be necessary to raise the dualseat first. When the bolts have been removed, lift the rear end of the tank and withdraw it backwards, so that the rubber buffers at the nose of the tank disengage from their mounting points on each side of the steering head. The tank should lift away quite easily. Store it in a safe place, away from any naked flames, as the petrol vapour within will constitute a fire/explosion hazard.

3 Disconnect the battery, which will be found under the forward part of the seat. Disconnect at the battery terminals, noting that the battery has a negative earth. Remove both spark plug leads. Slacken the hose clamps around the carburettor mouths and pull off the air cleaner connections.

4 Remove the top of the air cleaner box, which is retained by two wing nuts. Pull out the flap spring that holds the air cleaner element in place and then withdraw the plastic foam element itself. Remove the plastic side covers and loosen the air cleaner box by removing the two retaining bolts, one on each side. Note that an earthing strap is attached to one of them. Freeing the air cleaner box is necessary to give sufficient clearance for the carburettors to be removed as an inter-connected pair. It is advisable to remove the battery completely at this stage.

5 Slacken the clamp screws of the carburettor induction clamps. Pull off the breather pipe from the cylinder head cover and detach the throttle cable(s) from the throttle operating pulley or lever. With careful manipulation, the twin carburettor assembly can be slid out of position, towards the left-hand side of the machine. Move the air cleaner box as far back as it will go, to provide sufficient clearance. Place the carburettors in a safe place to prevent damage, until attention is given to them later.

6 Disconnect the tachometer drive cable from the rear of the engine, as it is now more accessible. Remove the two exhaust pipes by withdrawing the two allen screws that retain each flange to the cylinder head. At the rear end of the exhaust system, the silencers are retained to the underside of the frame by a single bolt on each side, which passes through a bracket welded to each silencer. Before these bolts are removed, withdraw the clamp bolt around the interconnecting pipe between the two silencers (not fitted to early models). This will make separation of the system easier. The exhaust pipes will pull out of the silencers and the whole system can thus be broken down and taken away from the machine. Unlike many other Japanese machines, the pillion rider's footrest bolts direct to each silencer bracket and does not perform the dual role of retaining the silencer to a convenient point of the frame assembly.

7 Remove the rider's footrests by slackening and withdrawing the retaining nut on the left-hand side of the machine. The long bolt that retains them in position should be withdrawn from the right of the machine; this bolt also acts as one of the engine mounting bolts. Take off the gearchange pedal and the kickstart lever, found on the left and right-hand sides of the machine respectively. Both are retained on splines by a single pinch bolt, which must be removed completely before the lever in question can be withdrawn. It is advisable to mark both lever and shaft with a centre punch mark prior to removal, so that the levers can be replaced in identical positions.

8 The engine unit has to be lifted out from the right-hand side of the machine and to facilitate this, the rear brake pedal should be removed or relocated on its splined shaft so that it is well out of the way. Here again, it is convenient to mark the original pedal position in some clear manner. Remember that the pedal may be needed later, to lock the rear wheel.

9 Take off the small metal cylinder head duct, found close to the steering head of the machine. It is retained by two allen screws.

10 Remove the final drive cover from the left-hand side of the machine. This forms part of the main cover and is retained by five allen screws. Separate the final drive chain at the spring

5.13b Remove earth strap from rear crankcase bolt

5.13c Disconnect the lead wire from the oil pressure switch

5.14a Remove the rear engine plates first ...

5.14b ... then the lower right-hand engine plate and finally ...

5.14c ... the upper front engine mounting bolt

7.3 Improvised but safe means of removing the special joining link

link, which is painted orange to aid location. Lay a clean sheet of newspaper on the floor so that the trailing chain does not get dirty or pick up grit.

11 Disconnect the clutch cable by pulling it from the stop at the rear of the crankcase. The nipple will then disengage from its anchorage quite easily. Do not lose the coil spring, which is very easily displaced.

12 Disconnect the various electrical leads at their block connectors. If there is any doubt about their identification, now is the time to mark them to aid reassembly. They will be found on the left-hand side of the machine.

13 Remove the battery earth strap from the rear left-hand side of the engine unit and take off the starter motor cover, which is retained by three allen screws. Pull back the protective cover and disconnect the main lead to the starter motor. Detach the lead to the oil pressure switch, which is retained by a single crosshead screw. The oil pressure switch will be found in the top of the crankcase, to the rear of the cylinder block.

14 Withdraw the upper rear engine mounting bolt and the rear mounting plates on each side of the engine unit. Pull through the electrical leads so that they cannot snag in the frame as the engine unit is lifted out. Withdraw the front engine mounting bolt, but do not withdraw it completely. Take out the lower right-hand engine mounting bolt and plate. This is only a short bolt. Take out the lower left-hand engine mounting bolt, noting that there is no plate on this side of the engine. Withdraw completely the upper front engine mounting bolt that is already partially removed. The complete engine unit is now free to be lifted out of the frame.

15 Before lifting the engine out of the frame, check to make sure there is nothing to retain the engine unit to the frame. Re-check that none of the electrical leads will snag or become trapped during the lifting operation. Lift the engine unit out towards the right-hand side, having an assistant to steady the frame throughout this operation. The engine unit is very heavy and there is very little clearance available. Whilst it can be lifted out single handed, the assistance of a third person will make this part of the task very much easier.

6 Dismantling the engine unit: general

1 Although it is anticipated that the whole of the machine will have been cleaned thoroughly prior to dismantling, to prevent the ingress of grit or dirt that may find its way into the internal working parts, the engine unit should receive special attention in this respect. A motor cycle engine has very little protection from road dirt which will sooner or later find its way into the dismantled engine if this simple precaution is not observed.

2 One of the proprietary engine cleaning compounds such as Gunk or Jizer can be used to good effect, especially if the compound is allowed to penetrate the film of oil and grease before it is washed away. When washing down, make sure that water cannot enter the carburettors or the electrical system, particularly if these parts are now more exposed.

3 Never use force to remove any stubborn part, unless mention is made of this requirement in the text. There is invariably good reason why a part is difficult to remove, often because the dismantling operation has been tackled in the wrong sequence.

4 Dismantling will be made easier if a simple engine stand is constructed that will correspond with the engine mounting points. This arrangement will permit the complete unit to be clamped rigidly to the work bench, leaving both hands free for the dismantling operation.

7 Dismantling the engine unit: removing the cylinder head cover, crankcase side covers and cylinder head

1 Unscrew the eighteen allen screws that retain the cylinder head cover and lift the cover from the cylinder head. This will expose the valve gear and the timing chain that drives the overhead camshafts.

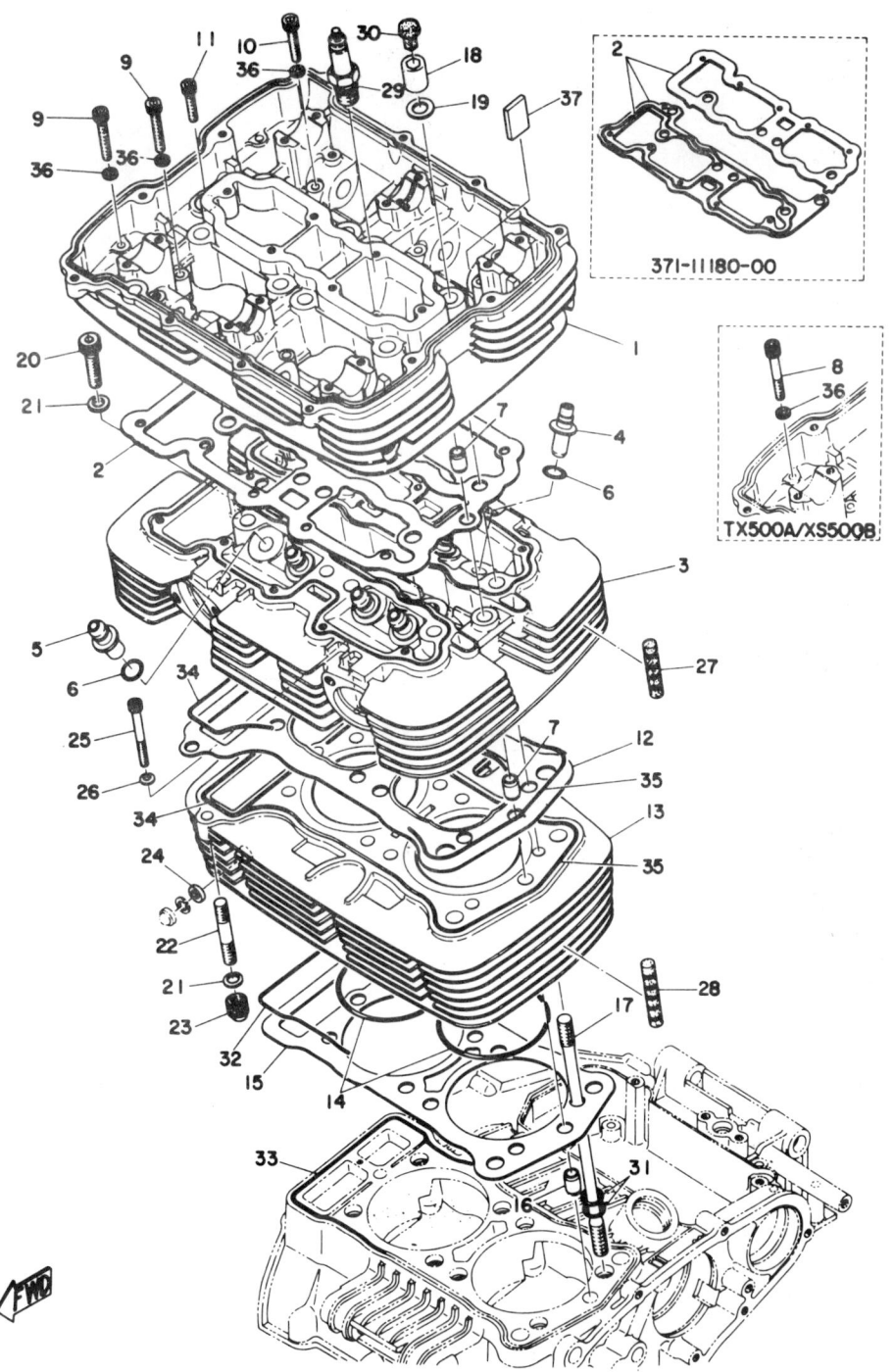

Fig. 1.1. Cylinder head, cambox and cylinder head cover

1 Cambox
2 Cylinder head/cambox gasket
3 Cylinder head
4 Inlet valve guide - 4 off
5 Exhaust valve guide - 4 off
6 'O' ring seal - 8 off
7 Dowel pin - 4 off
8 Allen screw - 2 off
9 Allen screw - 4 off
10 Allen screw - 4 off
11 Allen screw
12 Cylinder head gasket
13 Cylinder block
14 'O' ring - 2 off
15 Cylinder base gasket
16 Dowel pin - 2 off
17 Stud - 8 off
18 Nut - 8 off
19 Washer - 8 off
20 Allen screw
21 Plain washer - 3 off
22 Stud - 2 off
23 Nut - 2 off
24 Oil seal
25 Allen screw
26 Plain washer
27 Damper rubbers - 10 off
28 Damper rubbers - 2 off
29 Spark plug - 2 off
30 Blind plug - 8 off
31 'O' ring - 16 off
32 Cylinder base seal 1
33 Cylinder base seal 2
34 Cylinder head seal 1
35 Cylinder head seal 2
36 Washer - 10 off
37 Breather plate

Note: the design and number of some of the above components may vary as the result of design changes incorporated in XS500C model

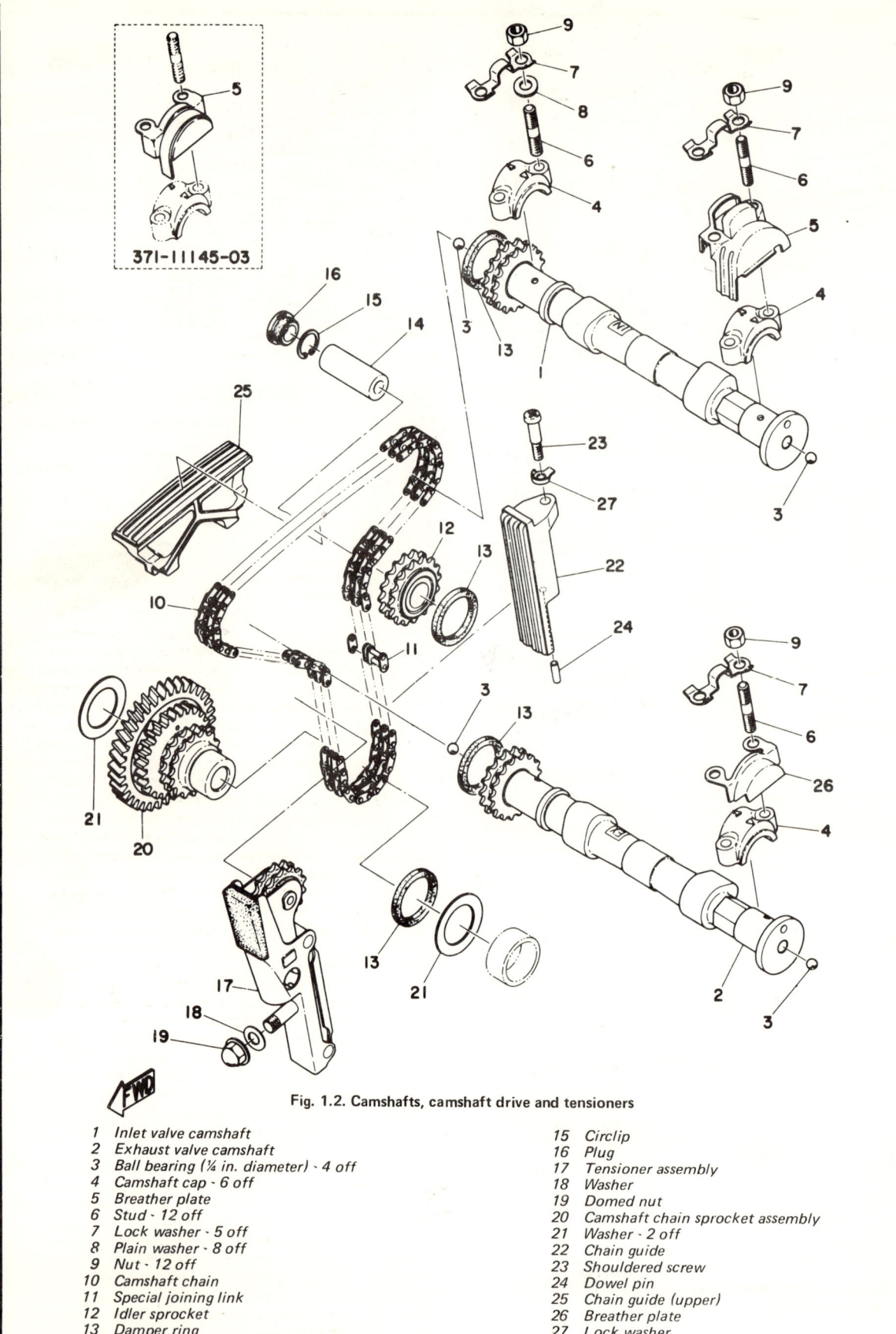

Fig. 1.2. Camshafts, camshaft drive and tensioners

1 Inlet valve camshaft
2 Exhaust valve camshaft
3 Ball bearing (¼ in. diameter) - 4 off
4 Camshaft cap - 6 off
5 Breather plate
6 Stud - 12 off
7 Lock washer - 5 off
8 Plain washer - 8 off
9 Nut - 12 off
10 Camshaft chain
11 Special joining link
12 Idler sprocket
13 Damper ring
14 Shaft 1
15 Circlip
16 Plug
17 Tensioner assembly
18 Washer
19 Domed nut
20 Camshaft chain sprocket assembly
21 Washer - 2 off
22 Chain guide
23 Shouldered screw
24 Dowel pin
25 Chain guide (upper)
26 Breather plate
27 Lock washer

Chapter 1: Engine, clutch and gearbox

7.5 Detach the rear external oil feed to cylinder head

7.6a There are two milled Allen screws on underside of cylinder head

7.6b Don't forget single Allen screw near right-hand spark plug

7.7 Raise cylinder head up holding down studs

2 Take off the contact breaker cover on the right-hand side of the engine unit, which is retained by three allen screws. Take off the alternator cover on the left-hand side of the machine, which is retained by nine allen screws and two dowels. Remove the dowels to prevent them from falling out during the subsequent dismantling processes.

3 Before the cylinder head can be lifted, it is necessary to separate the camshaft chain, which is of the endless type. Rotate the engine by placing a spanner on the alternator bolt until the special chain link for separation is positioned mid-way between the two camshaft chain sprockets. It is readily identified because the pins have clenched over ends and are not rivetted in the normal manner, to make separation easier. A special Yamaha service tool is recommended for this somewhat delicate task, but the problem can be overcome by the use of an improvised rig, as shown in the accompanying photograph. All that is required is a carpenter's G clamp, a small diameter hardened roller from an old bearing and a bolt in which the shank is drilled to accept the roller. Apply even pressure and push each pin slowly through the end plate, until the chain is separated. Take care that the chain does not fall through the tensioner tunnels and become jammed.

4 Chain separation is made easier if the chain tensioner is slackened off prior to this operation. This is achieved by slackening off the dome nut at the base of the right hand cylinder, pushing the camshaft tensioner sprocket as far downwards as it will go and locking it in this position by tightening the dome nut again whilst pressure is still applied.

5 Detach the rear external oil feed to the cylinder head. It is retained by two banjo unions, both bolts of which should be unscrewed and removed, complete with washers.

6 Slacken the eight cylinder head bolts in an even and diagonal sequence, then remove them. Slacken off the domed camshaft tensioner locknut. Unscrew the two milled nuts with a hexagon insert, found on the underside of the cylinder. Do not omit to remove the single allen screw found close to the right-hand spark plug. The cylinder head is now free to be removed.

7 Most probably the cylinder head will remain attached to the cylinder block as the result of a tight bond with the cylinder head gasket. It should be displaced by gently tapping around the joint with a soft-faced mallet, taking great care not to damage any of the fins. On no account use a screwdriver or any other pointed implement to lever the joint apart. This will cause irrepairable damage to the jointing surfaces, resulting in subsequent oil leaks. When the head is free, lift it from the engine unit, guiding the camshaft chain through the tunnels. The chain guide to the rear of the right-hand cylinder can be lifted out after bending back the tab washer and removing

8.1a Remove recessed Allen screw in camshaft chain tunnel

8.1b Cylinder block will now slide up holding down studs

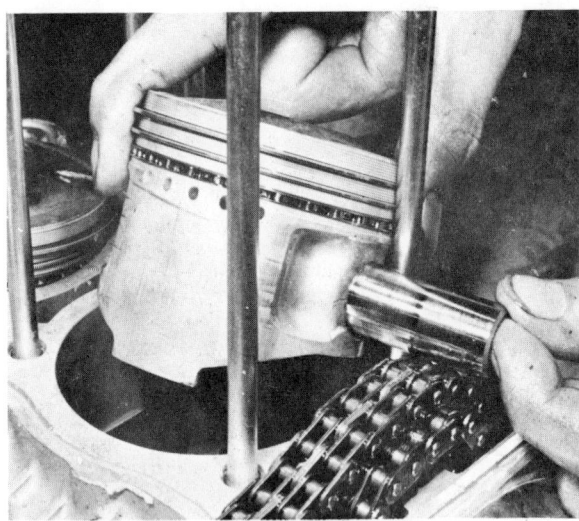
8.1c Withdraw gudgeon pins to free pistons

8.4 Remove starter motor after pushing sprocket forward, to increase clearance

9.1 Rotor retaining bolt is tight

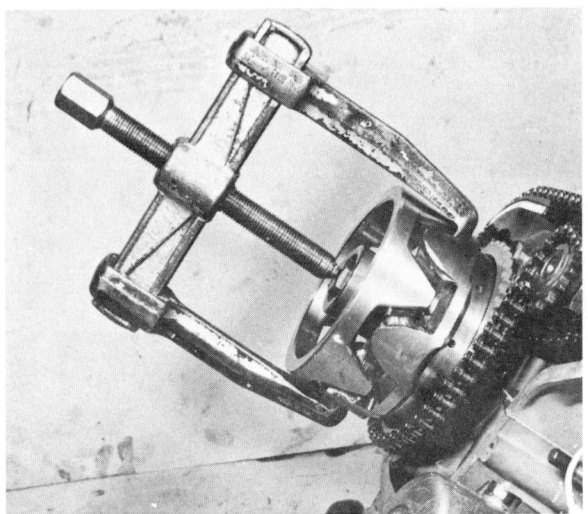
9.2 Two-leg sprocket puller can be used to withdraw rotor

Chapter 1: Engine, clutch and gearbox

the single retaining bolt.
8 There is no point in dismantling the cylinder head further at this stage unless this is the only component requiring attention. Place it aside in a safe place, until further dismantling is required, as described in Section 27 of this Chapter.

8 Dismantling the engine unit: removing the cylinder block, pistons and starter motor

1 Remove the allen screw located in the camshaft chain tunnel and lift out the camshaft chain tensioner by pressing it inwards, then pulling it upwards out of its housing, after removing the retaining dome nut and washer. Raise the cylinder block up along the holding down studs, tapping the joint with the crankcase first, if necessary, to break the joint. Make provision to catch the pistons as they emerge from each cylinder bore, to obviate risk of damage caused by striking the crankcase mouth. If only a minor overhaul is contemplated, it is advisable to pad the crankcase mouths with clean rag as soon as the block is raised a trifle, so that there is no risk of anything falling into the crankcase and necessitating more extensive work to retrieve it. This is a wise precaution if any of the piston rings are likely to have broken.
2 To remove the pistons, use a small screwdriver to remove the wire circlips fitted to each gudgeon pin boss. Discard these circlips as they must not be reused. The gudgeon pin should now press out, allowing each piston to be removed from its connecting rod. Mark the pistons inside the skirt, to ensure they are subsequently replaced in their original cylinder bores.
3 If a gudgeon pin is a tight fit, immerse a clean rag in very hot water, wring it out and place it on the piston crown. This should transfer sufficient heat to expand the piston and release its grip on the gudgeon pin. Do not attempt to drive the gudgeon pin out, especially if the connecting rod is unsupported. There is grave risk of bending the rod or causing premature failure of the big-end bearing.
4 To remove the starter motor, first unscrew the oil pressure switch, which may otherwise be damaged during the following operations. It should unscrew quite easily from the upper rear of the crankcase assembly. The starter motor is retained by four allen screws and a clamp, through which two of them pass. When these are withdrawn, the starter motor can be lifted from position by raising the rear end, after pushing it forward to push the starter sprocket shaft through the ball journal bearing to give added end clearance. There is a minimum clearance, but sufficient to lift the starter motor away if these instructions are observed.

9 Dismantling the engine unit: removing the alternator rotor

1 There is a special Yamaha service tool for extracting the alternator rotor, which screws into the centre of the crankshaft, after the alternator retaining bolt has been removed. This should be used, if it is available.
2 As an alternative, a two leg sprocket puller can be used to equally good effect, provided care is taken to ensure neither of the legs are likely to cause damage to the welded joints. Tighten the sprocket puller as far as it will go without using undue force, then give the end of the puller a sharp blow with a hammer, which should be sufficient to break the taper joint. A short bolt should be fitted inside the crankshaft during this operation, so that the threaded centre portion of the puller will bear on the head of this bolt and not cause damage to the internal thread of the crankshaft. Alternatively, the alternator retaining bolt can be left in position, after it has been slackened off.
3 After the alternator rotor has been lifted off, the thrust washer behind should be placed in a safe place until reassembly commences. This also applies to the rotor key in the crankshaft taper.
4 The large sprocket of the free-running clutch assembly

9.3 Note thrust washer between rotor and free-running clutch

9.4 Starter chain is of endless type. Pull off sprockets simultaneously

behind the rotor can now be pulled off the crankshaft, together with the endless drive chain and the starter idler sprocket. The starter sprocket shaft will pull quite easily through the ball journal bearing in which it centres.

10 Dismantling the engine unit: removing the crankshaft balancer drive, oil filter and final drive sprocket

1 Remove the balancer drive chain tensioner bracket by withdrawing the three bolts that retain the casting to the crankcase. Take careful note of how the balancer is timed before proceeding further, as its correct assembly during replacement is vitally important. Dots on the sprockets should align with lines on the casting projections. Note the oil deflector plate behind the bracket.
2 Remove the tension from the chain by turning the eccentric cam of the lower sprocket shaft. The endless chain can then be detached. Pull out the lower eccentric shaft and sprocket.
3 The circular oil filter found immediately below the final drive sprocket will unscrew. It has a normal, right-hand thread. Take care to collect the oil that will be released, to avoid a messy work bench.
4 Bend back the tab washer of the final drive sprocket and hold the sprocket very firmly whilst the centre nut is unscrewed.

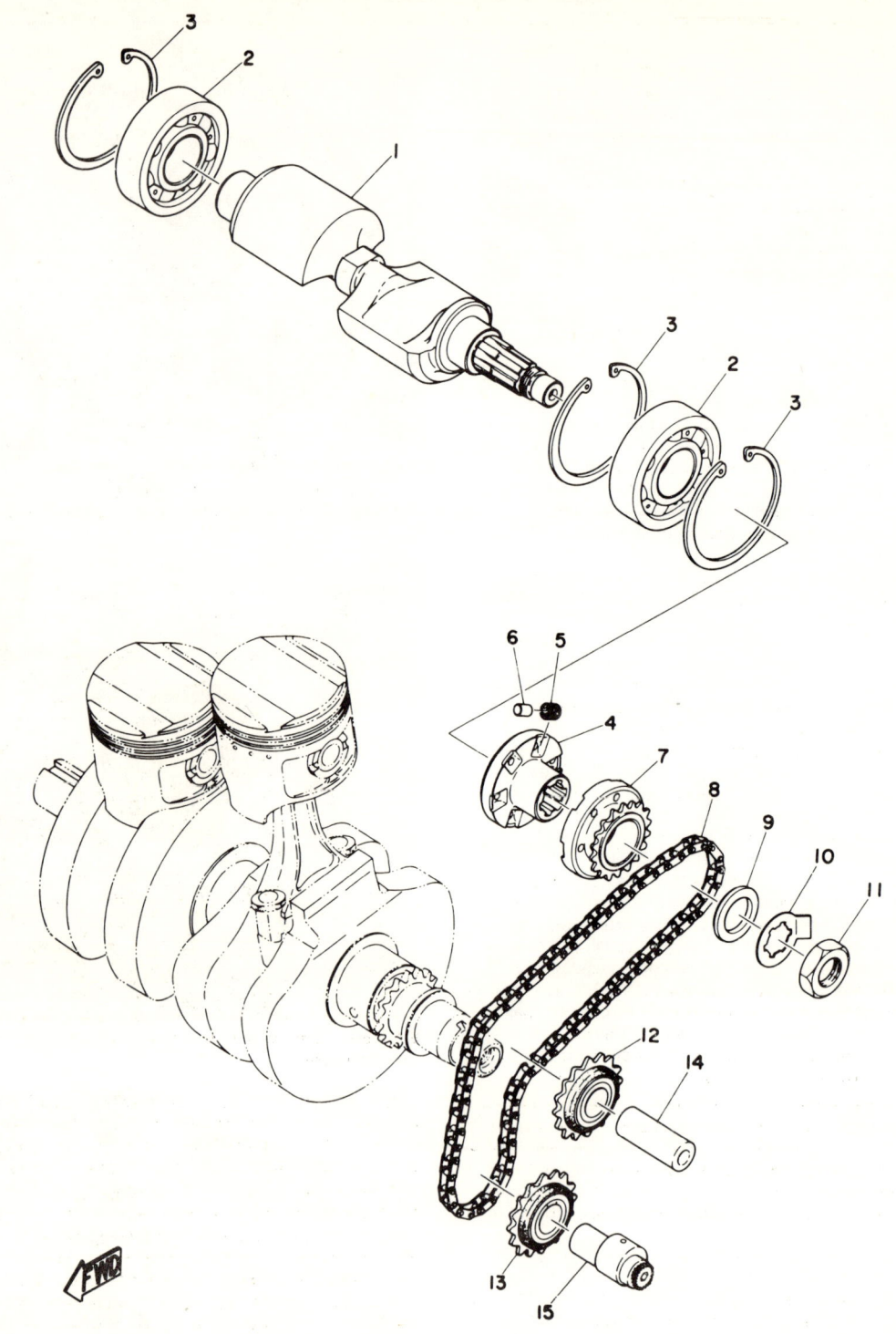

Fig. 1.3. Crankshaft balancer

1 Contra-rotating weight
2 Bearing · 2 off
3 Circlip
4 Shock absorber boss
5 Compression spring · 3 off
6 Dowel pin · 3 off
7 Sprocket
8 Drive chain
9 Spacer
10 Tab washer
11 Nut
12 Idler sprocket
13 Idler sprocket
14 Shaft
15 Eccentric shaft

10.1 Remove the balancer drive chain tensioner bracket, held by three bolts

10.2a Note how endless chain layout is arranged

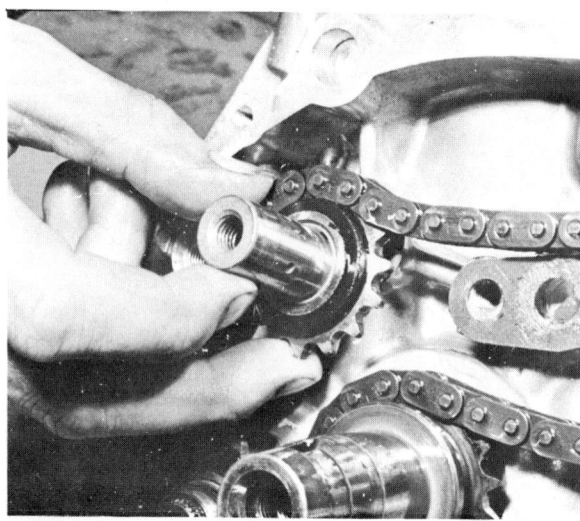
10.2b Upper sprocket will pull out with shaft

10.2c Lower sprocket fits over eccentric shaft, which provides tensioning

10.4a Note how neutral indicator lead wire is routed before ...

10.4b .. removing final drive sprocket. Note bunched chain to lock sprocket

Since the nut is very tight, it will be necessary to lock the sprocket solid, a convenient method being the replacement of the final drive chain so that both ends can be gripped in a vice or by allowing the chain to 'bunch' so that the sprocket cannot move. Once the nut has been removed, the sprocket will pull off the end of the output shaft.

11 Dismantling the engine unit: removing the contact breaker, camshaft drive sprocket and camshaft drive chain

1 Working on the right-hand side of the engine unit remove the contact breaker assembly complete by withdrawing the two screws that retain the base plate to the right-hand crankcase cover. It is advisable to mark the exact position of the baseplate in relation to the crankcase cover with scribe lines, since this will save having to retime the ignition on reassembly. Lift the assembly away, complete with lead wire and connector, after sliding the moulded grommet from the base of the contact breaker housing.
2 Unscrew the centre nut and remove it, together with the spring and plain washers found underneath. The contact breaker cam can now be pulled off the shaft, together with the automatic ignition advance assembly. Note how the contact breaker cam is dowelled, so that it is always replaced in an identical position.
3 Remove the right-hand crankcase cover, which is retained by twelve allen screws. One of them is recessed within the contact breaker housing. This will expose the primary transmission.
4 Take off the contact breaker shaft outrigger bracket, which is retained by three bolts. Take off the thrust washer in front of the small and large pinions, to prevent them from being misplaced. Note how the pinions are timed. Lift out the large pinion, after disengaging the camshaft drive chain from the rearward facing sprocket. Note that there is also another thrust washer on the inside of this assembly. The camshaft chain can now be removed from the engine.

12 Dismantling the engine unit: removing the primary drive pinion, clutch and kickstart assemblies

1 Bend back the tab washer of the forward mounted pinion on the end of the crankshaft and lock the engine by placing a stout metal bar through one of the connecting rod eyes, or by placing

11.3a Note how one Allen screw is recessed into contact breaker housing

11.3b Removal of outrigger bracket will expose primary and camshaft drives

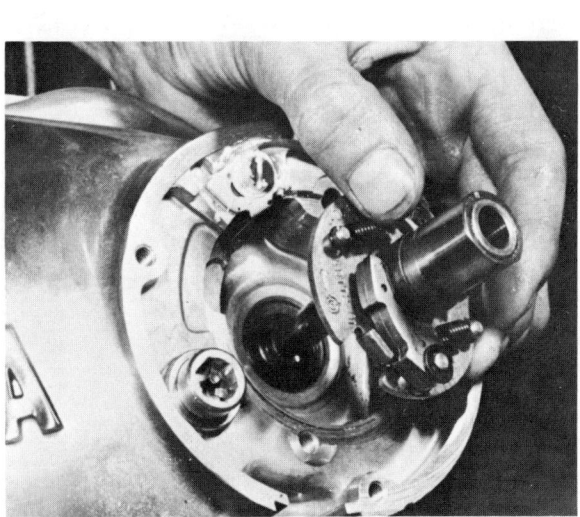
11.2 Auto-advance unit will pull off, with contact breaker cam

11.4 Take out large combined pinion and sprocket assembly first. Note rear thrust washer

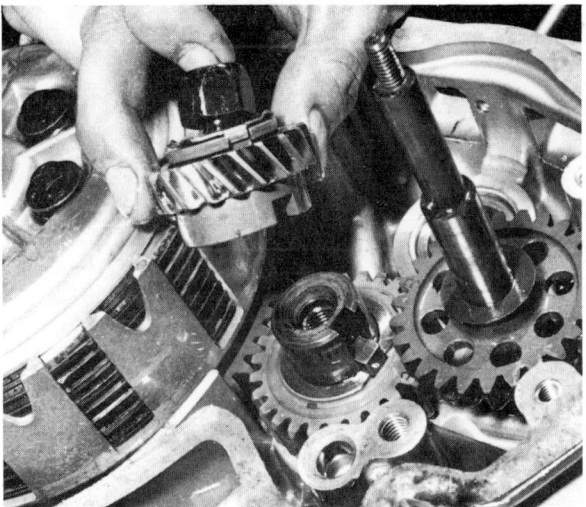
12.1a Remove the contact breaker drive pinion next ...

12.1b ... then pull out contact breaker drive assembly

12.2 Lever off primary drive pinion. Note key in shaft

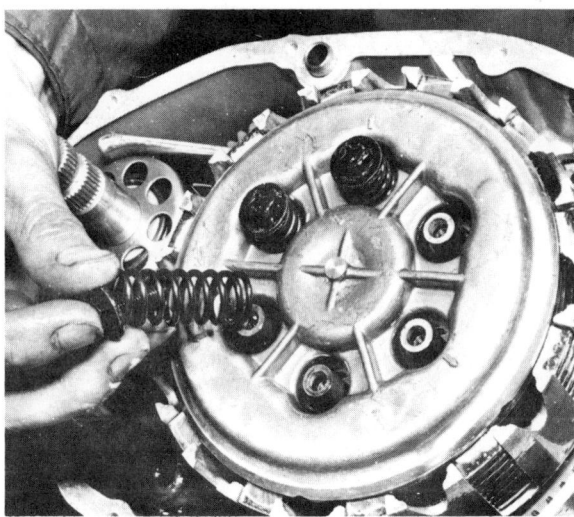
12.3a Remove the six crosshead screws to release clutch springs and pressure plate

12.3b Plates can be removed separately, or as a complete pack, whichever is easiest

12.3c Lift out clutch operating 'mushroom'

12.4a Clutch centre and outer drum must be 'spragged' before nut can be unscrewed

12.4b Use two screwdrivers to lever off clutch centre

12.4c Note large thrust washer under clutch centre

12.5a Clutch outer drum and pinion will now lift off

12.5b Note centre bearing bush and thrust washer

12.5c If not removed, square key in end of adjoining crankshaft is easily lost

Chapter 1: Engine, clutch and gearbox   31

12.6a Circlip retains idler pinion in position

12.6b Belville washer fits below pinion

12.7a Take off the kickstart spring cover

12.7b Unhook spring, to relieve tension

a rolled up rag between the primary drive pinion and clutch. Unscrew the pinion retaining nut, which is very tight, and withdraw the pinion from the crankshaft. The contact breaker shaft and pinion are now free to be withdrawn from the crankcase. Note the thrust washer behind this pinion, which must be put in a safe place until reassembly commences.

2 Pull, or lever off carefully with two screwdrivers, the inboard primary drive pinion still on the end of the crankshaft. It is keyed into position - do not misplace the key. Note how many shims are fitted behind this pinion, if any.

3 To dismantle the clutch assembly, remove the six bolts and washers from the clutch pressure plate in a diagonal sequence and lift out the clutch springs. The clutch plates can then be drawn out separately or as a complete pack, whichever is easier, after the clutch pressure plate has been lifted away. Take out the clutch operating 'mushroom' from the hollow mainshaft, as this will otherwise drop out later and may get lost.

4 Before the clutch centre nut can be removed, the tab washer must be bent back and the engine locked, this time by placing a stout metal rod through one of the connecting rod eyes. Slacken and remove the nut, which is tight, and draw the clutch centre off the splined end of the gearbox input shaft. It is a good fit on these splines and two screwdrivers may be needed to ease it off, using great care. There is a large thrust washer behind the clutch centre, which should be stored in a safe place until reassembly commences.

5 The clutch outer drum and its integral drive pinion can now be pulled off the shaft, together with its centre spacer and the large thrust washer that fits behind the back of the outer drum. It is advisable to tilt the crankcase forward at this stage, to displace the loose ball bearing that is normally interposed between the clutch operating 'mushroom' and the end of the clutch push rod.

6 Remove the circlip that retains the gearbox output shaft idler pinion in place and the washer under the circlip. The pinion is now free to be removed. Note that a Belville washer fits behind the pinion.

7 Take off the cover from the kickstart spring, and lever the end of the spring from its crankcase stop, using a screwdriver. The whole kickstart assembly can now be lifted out. Take great care that the thick washer on the underside of the assembly does not fall off. It can quite easily drop into the crankcase assembly, necessitating a complete stripdown to retrieve it.

8 Remove the nut and washers from the oil pump drive pinion and pull the pinion off its shaft. It is keyed into position, hence care should be taken to ensure the small Woodruff key is not lost.

12.7c Whole kickstart assembly will now lift out as a unit

12.7d Take great care, or this thrust washer will disappear inside crankcase

12.8 Remove the oil pump/tachometer drive pinion from its shaft

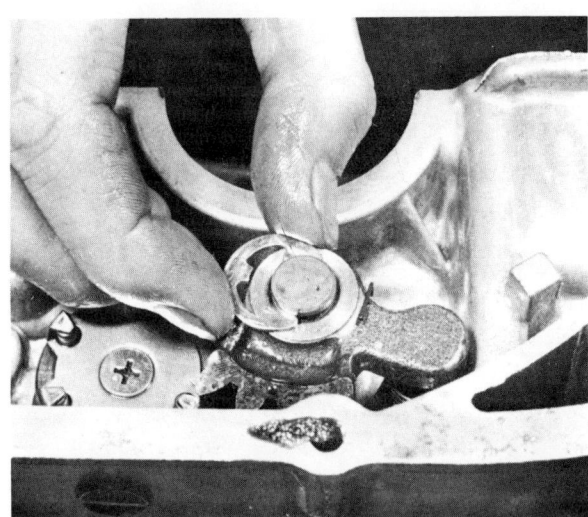
13.1a 'E' clip retains small internal lever

13.1b Note how stopper arm is attached to lever. No need to separate

13.2 The gearchange shaft will pull through from the right-hand side

Chapter 1: Engine, clutch and gearbox

13 Dismantling the engine unit: removing the gearchange mechanism

1 Prise off the E-clip that retains the internal gearchange lever in position on the end of one of the gear selector forks. It may be necessary to press down on the mating gearchange lever claw to achieve its satisfactory release, complete with stopper arm and spring attached.
2 Remove the E-clip and washer from the gearchange lever side (left-hand) of the main gearchange shaft, which is integral with the claw, and pull the entire assembly through from the right-hand side.

14 Dismantling the engine unit: removing the sump, oil pressure release valve and strainer

1 Invert the engine unit and unscrew the eleven allen screws that hold the finned base of the sump in position. Two of these screws have locking plates fitted, for the engine mounting bolts. Mark their positions, so that they are replaced correctly. Lift off the sump, noting the small magnet fitted in a recess, close to the strainer. This attracts any ferrous metal particles in the oil stream that would otherwise find their way into either of the oil pumps and cause damage.
2 Lift off the pressure release valve and strainer assembly, after removing the four retaining allen screws. Pull out the camplate plunger and spring. It is necessary to remove this assembly to free the main gasket, part of which is used to seal off the casting. The crankcase halves are now free to be separated.

15 Separating the crankcase halves

1 With the engine unit still inverted, remove the four large dome nuts that seat on copper washers and the two nuts inside the crankcase. Then unscrew the seven small bolts in the underside. Turn the engine up the correct way and take out the seven bolts in the upper side of the crankcase assembly, three of which are found within the starter motor housing.
2 Lightly tap around the crankcase joint, using a soft-faced mallet. Do not attempt to lever the joint apart. This is a somewhat delicate operation, the reluctance to part being caused by the very good bond of the joining gasket. As soon as a little movement is detected, the crankcase halves should part without much extra effort.

16 Dismantling the engine unit: removing the crankshaft assembly and gear cluster

1 The crankshaft assembly will lift out of the lower crankcase half without difficulty, by pulling on the connecting rods. Examine the assembly closely, noting how the connecting rods have matched, detachable end caps marked with identical identification numbers. This ensures that they are always correctly matched.
2 Note also that the end caps have an arrow mark, to denote the correct direction of fitting. The arrow must always point towards the primary drive (right-hand) side of the engine.
3 The main bearing shells can be lifted out at the same time, after marking the back of them to ensure they are returned to their original positions. Each has a small locating tab, to make sure it seats correctly.

14.1 Do not lose the circular magnet, retained in the sump

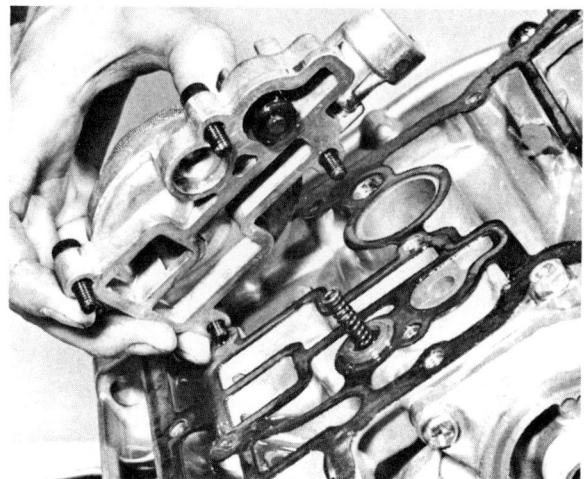
14.2a Lift off pressure release valve and strainer assembly

14.2b Cam plate plunger and spring are now released

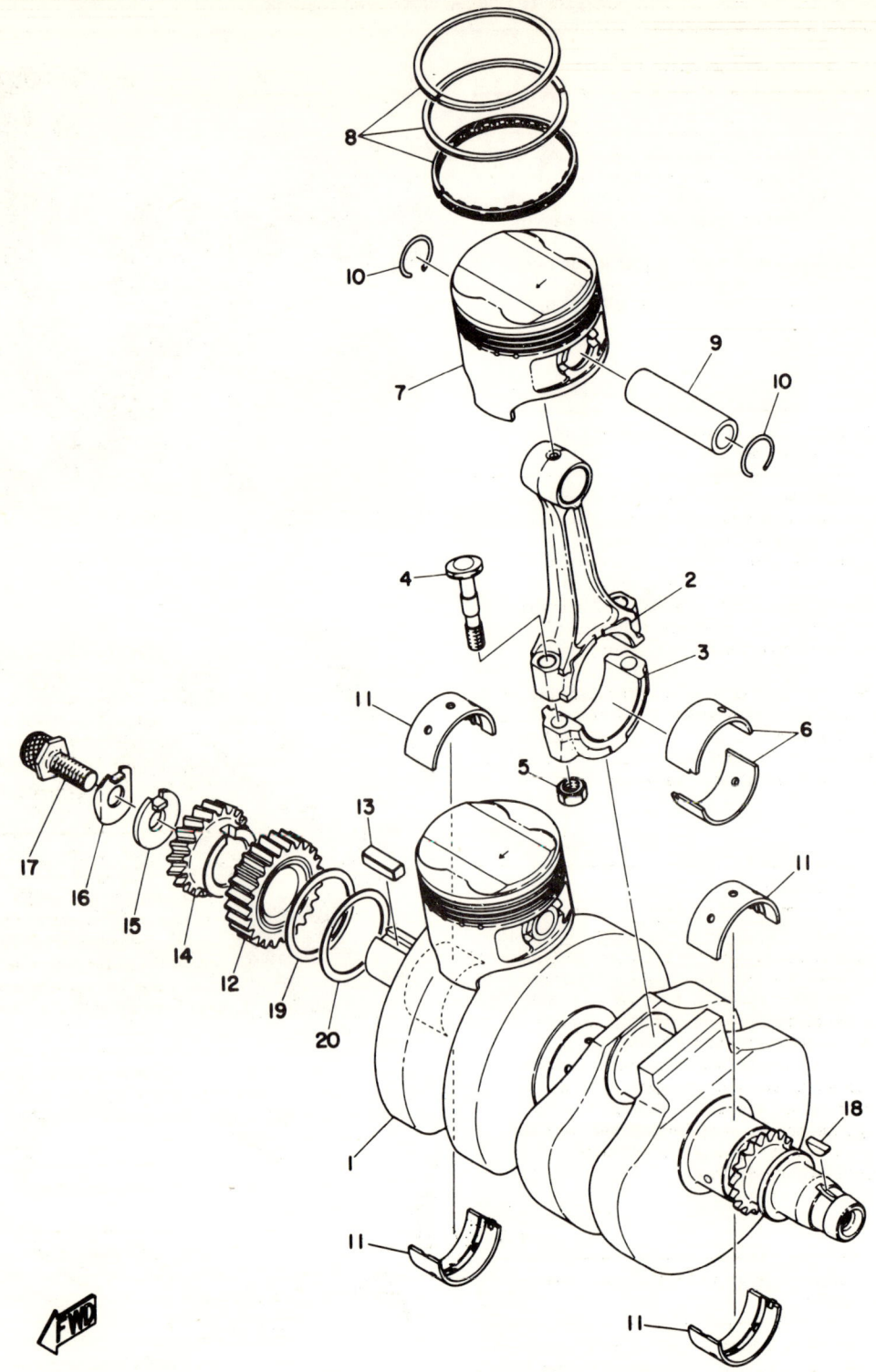

Fig. 1.4. Crankshaft assembly

1 Crankshaft assembly
2 Connecting rod assembly - 2 off
3 Connecting rod - 2 off
4 Connecting rod cap - 2 off
5 Big-end nut - 4 off
6 Connecting rod (big-end) bearing shell - 4 off
7 Piston - 2 off
8 Piston ring set - 2 off
9 Gudgeon pin - 2 off
10 Circlip - 4 off
11 Main bearing shell - 6 off
12 Primary drive gear pinion
13 Key
14 Drive pinion (19 teeth)
15 Claw washer
16 Lock washer
17 Bolt
18 Woodruff key
19 Crankshaft shim
20 Crankshaft shim

thickness as required

Chapter 1: Engine, clutch and gearbox

16.1 Crankshaft assembly will lift out of crankcase. Note arrow on big-end cap

16.4a Lift out gearbox input shaft as a complete unit

16.4b Gearbox output shaft will lift out in similar fashion

4   Lift out the gearbox input shaft as an assembled unit. There is no necessity to dismantle it unless gearbox troubles have been experienced and the individual components need to be examined very closely. This also applies to the output shaft, which will lift out in similar fashion. The clutch push rod may still be within the input shaft, in which case it can be slid out of position by tilting the shaft and allowing it to drop free.

17 Dismantling the engine unit: removing the oil pump

1   To remove the oil pump assembly, unscrew the three allen screws that hold the drive to the lower crankcase half. The pump assembly will pull away, leaving the lower half of the pump in situ, although it is possible that the lower rotor may remain attached to the drive spindle. Keep the rotors together for examination later, and do not lose either of the drive pins that pass through the oil pump drive shaft.
2   There is no possibility of inadvertently interchanging the component parts of either pump, as they are of differing depths. Great care should be taken of the oil pump components, so that they are not scratched or marked in any way.

18 Dismantling the engine unit: removing the gear selector mechanism

1   Tap out the forward facing selector rod from the right-hand side, so that it forces the rubber blind plug from position in the left-hand side of the crankcase. It will pass through the selector fork, freeing the latter.
2   Prise the E-clip from the groove of the second selector rod, which will be found inside the crankcase. The selector rod can then be tapped out of position towards the left-hand side of the crankcase, displacing another rubber blind plug. In this instance, two selector forks will be freed. Mark them all, to make sure they are replaced in their original locations.
3   To release the gear selector drum first unscrew the three screws that hold the oil filter adaptor in place, then remove the neutral switch cover, retained by three countersunk crosshead screws. These screws have been treated with thread sealant and will prove tight. An impact screwdriver will almost certainly be necessary. Note the tracking of the neutral switch wire, then remove the single crosshead screw that connects this wire to the switch cover. Pull the cover off, noting the small spring-loaded

17.1 Oil pump can be withdrawn after removing the three retaining screws

18.1a Tap out forward selector rod from right-hand side, to displace blind plug

18.1b Forward selector fork is now free

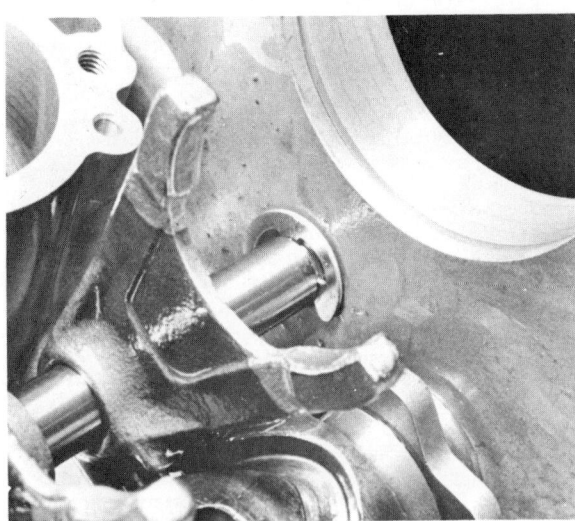
18.2a Remove internal 'E' clip to free rear selector rod

18.2b Rod can now be tapped from position to displace rear blind plug

18.3a Remove the oil filter adaptor first, then ...

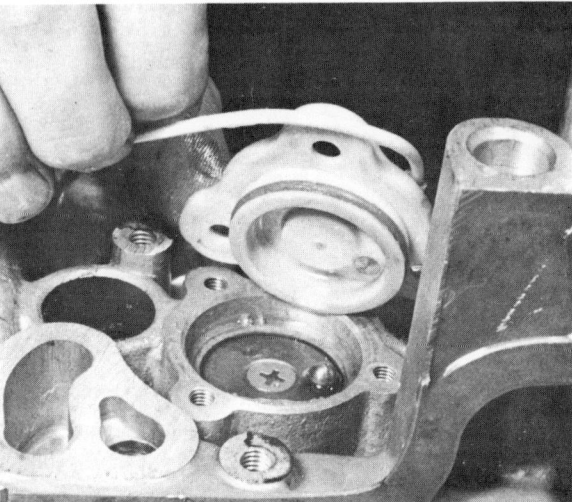
18.3b ... the neutral contact cover, after noting tracking of wire

Chapter 1: Engine, clutch and gearbox

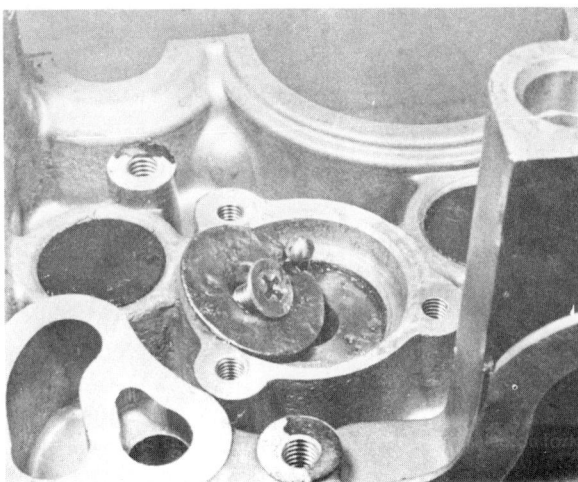

18.3c Contact is retained by large diameter washer and centre screw

18.3d Internal spring is easily lost

18.4 Large diameter external circlip retains cam on end of drum

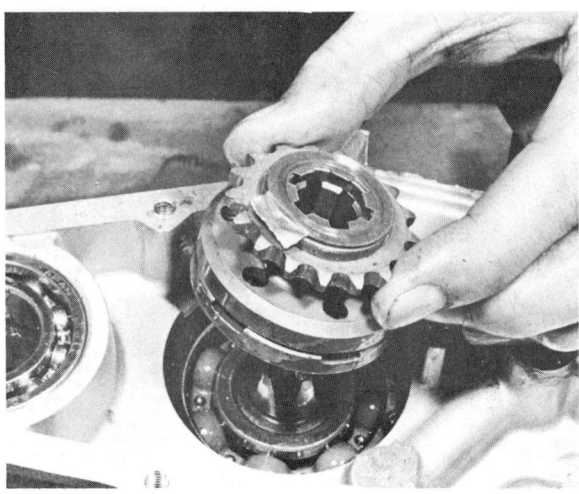

19.1 Take off chain sprocket splined on to balancer shaft

19.2 Drive balancer through bearing, from the left-hand side

contact within retained by the central washer and countersunk crosshead screw, which should be removed. Take out both the contact and the spring as both are small and very easily lost. The cover should have an 'O' ring seal around its periphery.

4 Remove the split pin from the underside of the crankcase, press down the detent plunger from the inside of the crankcase and pull the gear selector drum as far forward to the right-hand side as it will come. Then remove the large diameter circlip, to free the camplate end, which is dowelled into position. The lower crankcase half should now be completely free of all components.

19 Dismantling the engine unit: removing the crankshaft balancer and the tachometer and oil pump drive

1 Reverting to the upper crankcase half, remove the large diameter circlip that retains the crankshaft balancer in position. The chain drive sprocket is held by a nut and tab washer, and must be taken off first to give clearance for the circlip. Note that the sprocket assembly can be fitted only one way, due to the lead spline arrangement.

19.3 Starter motor drive will press outwards, through bearing

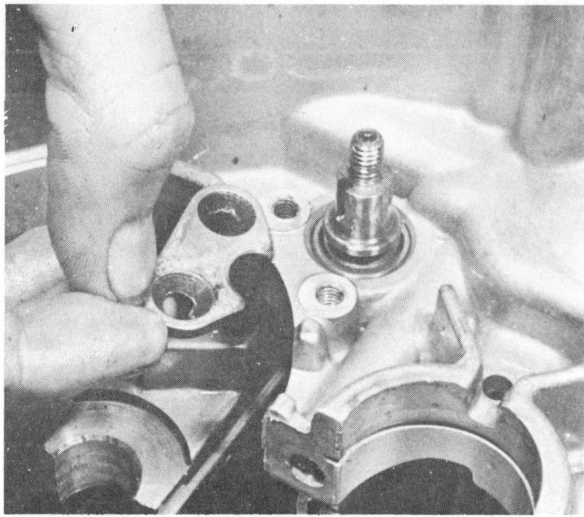
19.4 Locking plate retains the oil-pump/tachometer drive shaft

19.5 Skew pinion is retained on splined shaft by two 'E' clips

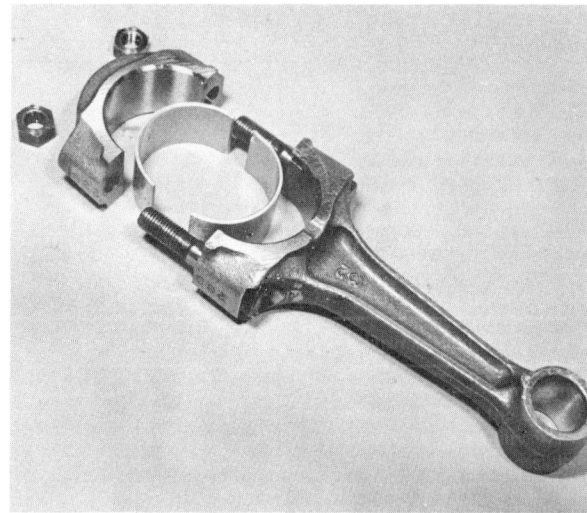
21.1a A dismantled connecting rod and big-end assembly

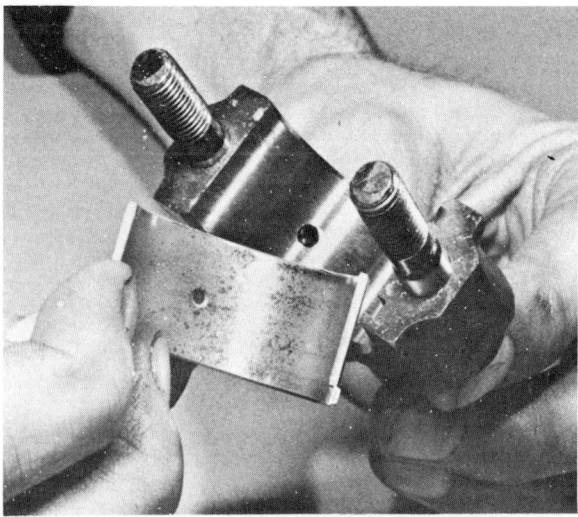
21.1b Check the surface of each shell for damage or wear

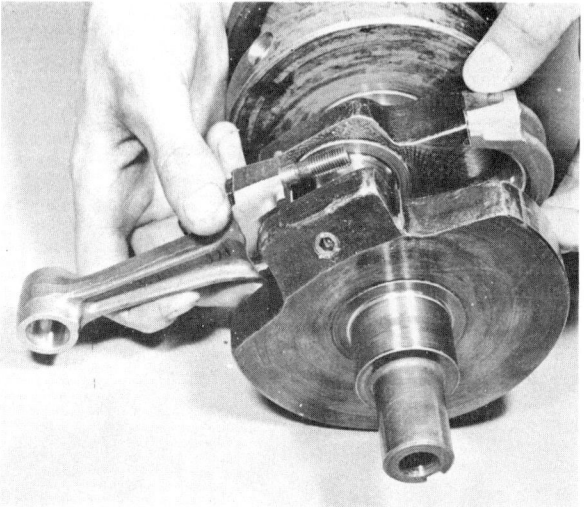
21.2 Big-end caps must be removed during each major overhaul

2 Drive the balancer out towards the right-hand side of the crankcase half, through the bearing. The left-hand bearing will not be displaced, as it is pegged in position.
3 Push out the starter motor drive through the ball journal bearing. It will press through, quite easily. If necessary, the bearing can be driven out of its housing from the right, taking care not to damage the oil seal that is located behind it.
4 The oil pump/tachometer drive shaft locking plate, is secured by two countersunk crosshead screws. These are tight, their threads having been treated with a sealing compound. It will be necessary to use an impact screwdriver. Do not lose the small Woodruff key that locates the pinion with the shaft.
5 Before attempting to withdraw the shaft, remove both the E-clips that retain the skew drive pinion in position. This pinion is a splined fit on the end of the shaft and will withdraw quite easily. The shaft can then be slid out of position, to the right-hand side. The upper crankcase half is now free of all components.

21.4a Arrows on end caps must face toward the primary drive side (right-hand)

20 Examination and renovation: general

1 Before examining the parts of the dismantled engine unit for wear, it is essential that they should be cleaned thoroughly. Use a paraffin/petrol mix to remove all traces of old oil and sludge that may have accumulated within the engine.
2 Examine the crankcase castings for cracks or other signs of damage. If a crack is discovered, it will require professional repair.
3 Carefully examine each part to determine the extent of wear, checking with the tolerance figures listed in the Specifications section of this Chapter. If there is any question of doubt, play safe and renew.
4 Use a clean, lint-free rag for cleaning and drying the various components. This will obviate the risk of small particles obstructing the internal oilways, causing the lubrication system to fail.

21.4b Connecting rods and end caps are numbered, to ensure correct reassembly

21 Big ends and main bearings: examination and renovation

1 The big-ends and main bearings are of the shell type and any wear will immediately be obvious. Even if the shells appear to be in good condition, check carefully for any score or scuff marks, or for any ridges or score marks in the bearing journals. If there is any doubt about the condition of the shells, they must be renewed without question. Specialist advice should be obtained from a Yamaha service agent, as the shells are made in a number of selective fits and will need to be matched up very accurately with the crankcase and/or crankshaft. If the bearing journals are damaged, it will almost certainly be preferable to renew the complete crankshaft assembly. Here again, the advice of a Yamaha service agent should be sought first.
2 It will, of course, be necessary to remove the end caps from both connecting rods, to examine the bearing shells. Before the caps are removed, the amount of bearing wear can be checked by moving the small end of the connecting rod sideways. When new, the amount of movement should be 0.15 mm (0.0059 in) or less, and after service, this must not be allowed to increase beyond 0.3 mm (0.012 in). Always check for wear after the oil has been washed out from the bearing. Worn big-end bearings will cause a pronounced knock or rattle whilst the engine is running and the engine should never be used when they are in this condition. Apart from the distinct possibility of seizure through reduced oil pressure, even more serious damage may result if a connecting rod breaks.

3 As mentioned earlier, renewal of either the main bearing or the big-end shells must be entrusted to a Yamaha service agent, on account of the system of selective fits used. It is imperative that the oil clearance between the big-end bearing and the crankshaft is within the range 0.041-0.064 mm (0.0016-0.0033 in). Bearing seizure will occur if the clearance does not correspond.
4 When replacing the connecting rods and big-end caps, make sure the connecting rod oil hole faces to the rear of the engine. Early models have a protuberance on the forward facing side of the connecting rod, which makes identification easier. It follows that the connecting rods must be replaced in their original positions, with their matching end caps, identified by the numbers stamped on them. The arrows on the caps must face towards the primary drive side of the machine and the securing nuts should have their ground shoulders used at the seating. Tighten to 3.5 - 4.0 m.kg after making sure the shells have located correctly, and check that the connecting rods will move quite freely on the crankshaft, without any play. The big-end bearings should be well lubricated with clean engine oil, prior to fitting - as should the main bearings.

22 Crankshaft assembly: examination and renovation

1   Examine the big-end and main bearing journals very carefully, to ensure they are not scuffed or scored and therefore likely to cause premature wear of any new bearing shells that are fitted. Slight damage can be rectified by a crankshaft repair specialist, but in view of the problem with selective fit bearings, it is preferable to entrust any work of this nature to a Yamaha service agent.
2   The crankshaft is a one-piece assembly and whilst the engine is stripped completely, it is advisable to check the run-out, using vee blocks and a dial gauge. If the run-out at any point is 0.05 mm (0.002 in) the assembly must be renewed. Excessive run-out will cause severe engine vibration and account for a noticeable drop in power.

23 Connecting rods - examination and renovation

1   It is unlikely that any of the connecting rods will bend during normal usage, unless an unusual occurrence such as a dropped valve has caused the engine to lock. Carelessness when removing a tight gudgeon pin can also give rise to a similar problem. It is not advisable to straighten a bent connecting rod; renewal is the only satisfactory solution.
2   The small end eye of the connecting rod is unbushed and it will be necessary to renew the connecting rod if the gudgeon pin becomes a slack fit. Always check that the oil hole in the small end eye is not blocked since if the oil supply is cut off, the bearing surfaces will wear very rapidly.
3   Balanced connecting rods are fitted and if renewal is necessary, the replacement(s) must have the same stamped marking. If both rods are renewed, the weight difference must not exceed 9 grams maximum (0.31 oz).

24 Oil seals: examination and replacement

1   Oil seals tend to lose their effectiveness as they harden with age and from the effects of heat. It is difficult to give any firm recommendations about frequency of replacement, other than to suggest that all oil seals are renewed without question, irrespective of their condition, when a complete overhaul is undertaken. This will obviate the need to strip the machine again, at a later date, should any of the original oil seals give cause for concern.
2   When fitting oil seals, special care is necessary to prevent damage to their feather edge seals. Always drive them into position very carefully, checking that they are fitted the correct way round, and if a shaft has to be inserted through the centre, grease both the shaft and the seal to prevent any drag or pick-up, which may destroy the seal.

25 Cylinder block: examination and renovation

1   The usual indication of badly worn cylinder bores and pistons is excessive smoking from the exhausts and piston slap, a metallic rattle that occurs when there is little or no load on the engine. If the top of the bore of the cylinder block is examined carefully, it will be found that there is a ridge on the thrust side, the depth of which will vary according to the rate of wear that has taken place. This marks the limit of travel of the uppermost piston ring.
2   Cylinder bore wear should be measured in three different positions. Two separate measurements should be taken in each position, at right angles to each other, using an internal micrometer. This makes a total of six measurements in all. For each bore the standard bore diameter is 73 mm (2.88 in), the actual dimensions of the cylinder in question being etched in ink at the base of the cylinder sleeve. The wear limit is 0.1 mm (0.004 in). The cylinder bores will also require attention if the amount of taper caused by wear exceeds 0.05 (0.002 in) at any of the measured points.
3   Attention will also be required if either cylinder bore is scored or indented in any way, as may have occurred if a gudgeon pin circlip has worked loose or if a piston has seized. Irregularities of this nature cause compression loss and a corresponding drop in performance.
4   If a rebore is necessary, four oversizes of piston are available, + 0.25 mm, + 0.50 mm, + 0.75 mm and + 1.00 mm. The piston crowns are stamped accordingly, with the exception of the largest (1.00 mm) oversize, which has the coding OO.
5   Make sure the external cooling fins of the cylinder block are not clogged with oil or road dirt, which will impede the free flow of air and cause the engine to overheat.

26 Pistons and piston rings: examination and renovation

1   Attention to the pistons and piston rings can be overlooked if a rebore is necessary, since new components will be fitted.
2   If a rebore is not considered necessary, examine each piston closely. Reject pistons that are scored or badly discoloured as the result of exhaust gases by-passing the rings.
3   Remove all carbon from the piston crowns, using a blunt scraper, which will not damage the surface of the piston. Clean away all carbon deposits from the valve cutaways and finish off with metal polish so that a clean, shining surface is achieved. Carbon will not adhere so readily to a polished surface.
4   Check that the gudgeon pin bosses are not worn or the circlip grooves damaged. Check that the piston ring grooves are not enlarged. Side float should not exceed 0.15 mm (0.007 in). It is not possible to measure side float in the case of the oil control ring, as it is made up of two rails and an expander, the upper and lower rails being forced against the ring groove by the action of the expander.
5   Piston ring wear can be measured by inserting each ring in turn in its respective cylinder bore, from the top, and pushing it down with the base of the piston, so that it locates squarely in the bore about 1½ inches down from the top. Measure the end gap with a feeler gauge. If the gap exceeds 0.7 mm (0.027 in) in the case of either compression ring, or 0.9 mm (0.035 in) in the case of the oil control ring, renewal is necessary. Always renew the rings as a complete set, never separately.
6   Check that there is no build up of carbon on the inside surface of the rings or in the grooves of the pistons. Any build-up should be removed by careful scraping.
7   The piston crowns will show whether the engine has been rebored on some previous occasion. All oversize pistons have the rebore size stamped on the crown as described in the preceding section. This information is essential when ordering replacement piston rings.

27 Cylinder head: dismantling, examination and renovation

1   Before giving attention to the cylinder head, it is advisable to remove the two overhead camshafts in order to gain access to the valve gear for later dismantling. Each camshaft is retained by two caps, which can be removed after their two holding down nuts are slackened and removed. Each has a tab washer, which must be bent back first. Mark the caps so that they are replaced in their original positions, during reassembly. The caps at the left-hand end of each camshaft have a special breather plate attached. The camshafts are clearly marked, so that they cannot be inadvertently interchanged. There is no necessity to detach the cambox from the cylinder head, to which it is bolted.

27.1a Camshaft end cap nuts are secured by twin tab washers

27.1b Mark caps prior to removal, so that they cannot be interchanged

27.1c Camshafts will lift out. Are pre-marked to avoid interchange

27.2a Remove end plugs to gain access to rocker spindles

27.2b Shouldered Allen screws retain spindles in position

27.2c Use long sump bolt to withdraw spindles. End of spindle is threaded internally

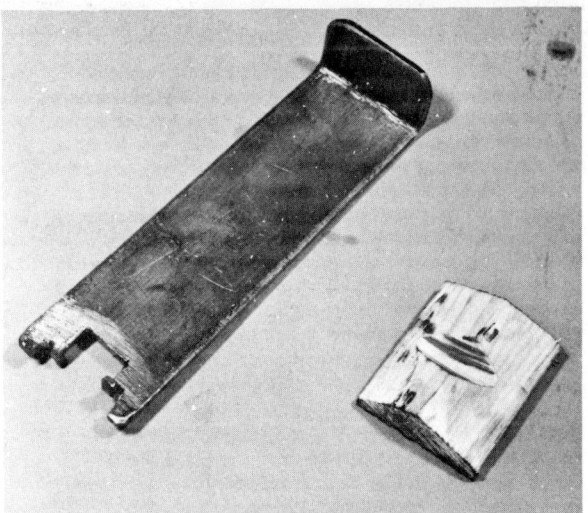

27.4 Home-made valve spring compressor and shaped wooden insert

27.5a Compress each valve spring set in turn, to release collets

27.5b When collets have been extracted, pressure can be released and springs removed

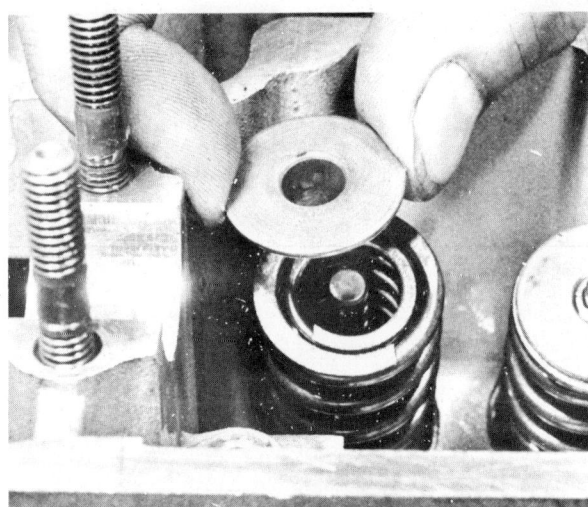

27.5c Note use of inner and outer spring with each assembly

27.5d Close coils of both springs must be next to cylinder head

27.5e There is a small oil seal around each valve stem

Chapter 1: Engine, clutch and gearbox

27.8 Valve seats will invariably need grinding-in to restore the seating

2 To remove the forked rocker arms - an ingenious method of operating each pair of valves simultaneously - it is necessary to extract the rocker spindles. This is achieved by unscrewing the end plugs found in the right-hand and left-hand sides of the cylinder head, and removing the shouldered bolts within the cylinder head, each of which engages with a slot in its respective rocker spindle. Each spindle can then be withdrawn from its housing by screwing one of the sump retaining bolts into the central threaded portion and pulling it from position. This will free the rocker arms. Mark the spindles and arms so that they are replaced in their original positions when reassembly takes place.

3 Before removing the valves, it is advisable to decarbonise the cylinder head, so that there is no risk of damaging the valve seats. Before commencing this operation, remove the spark plugs and replace them with a pair of old plugs that are no longer fit for service. This will prevent loose carbon from clogging the spark plug threads or the original plugs themselves. Use a blunt-ended scraper so that the surface of the combustion is not damaged and finish off with metal polish, to achieve a clean, shiny surface.

4 Before the valves can be removed, it will be necessary to obtain a special type of valve spring compressor or to make one up from a strip of mild steel, as shown in the accompanying photograph. A stock valve spring compressor will most probably prove useless for this particular task unless it has an extra wide shank to go round the outside of the cylinder head. If a home-made tool is used, it will be necessary to use it in conjunction with a shaped piece of wood, also shown in the same photograph. The piece of wood is shaped to conform to the cylinder head hemisphere, so that the valves cannot open when pressure is applied to the valve caps. A small cutaway in the centre of the block will accommodate the spark plug points. The alternative is to remove the cambox casting from the cylinder head, to give improved access.

5 Compress each pair of valve springs in turn, so that the split collets can be removed from within the valve spring cap and the pressure released. The valve, valve springs (two), end cap, collets and valve spring seating washer can then be removed. Note each valve has a small oil seal around the stem. Keep the valves and their associated components in separate containers, so that they cannot be interchanged with each other. They should eventually be reassembled in their original positions.

6 Before giving the valves and valve seats further attention, check the clearance between each valve stem and the guide in which it operates. If the clearance proves to be excessive, the valve guide will have to be renewed by -

warming the cylinder head and driving it out of position with a shouldered drift of the same internal diameter as the valve stem. Whilst the cylinder head is still warm, drive the replacement guide into position, using the same drift. If one guide is worn, it will almost certainly be necessary to renew the whole set, and to fit new valves.

7 Grinding in will be necessary, irrespective of whether new valve guides have been fitted. This action is necessary to remove the indentations in the valve seats caused under normal running conditions by the high temperatures within the combustion chambers. It is also necessary when new valve guides have been fitted in order to re-align the face of each valve with its seating.

8 Valve grinding is a simple task. Commence by smearing a trace of fine valve grinding compound (carborundum paste) on the valve seat and apply a suction tool to the head of the valve. Oil the valve stem and insert the valve in the guide so that the two surfaces to be ground in make contact with one another. With a semi-rotary motion, grind in the valve head to the seat, using a backward and forward action. Lift the valve occasionally so that the grinding compound is distributed evenly. Repeat the application until an unbroken ring of light grey matt finish is obtained on both valve and seat. This denotes the grinding operation is now complete. Before passing to the next valve, make sure that all traces of the valve grinding compound have been removed from both the valve and its seat and that none has entered the valve guide. If this precaution is not observed, rapid wear will take place due to the highly abrasive nature of the carborundum base of the grinding compound used.

9 When deep pits are encountered, it will be necessary to use a valve refacing machine and a valve seat cutter, set to an angle of 45°. This will also prove necessary after new valve guides are fitted. Never resort to excessive grinding because this will only pocket the valves in the head and lead to reduced engine efficiency. If there is any doubt about the condition of a valve, fit a new one.

10 Examine the condition of the valve collets and the groove on the valve stem in which they seat. If there is any sign of damage, new parts should be fitted. Check that the valve spring collar is not cracked. If the collets work loose or the collar splits whilst the engine is running, a valve could drop into the cylinder and cause extensive damage.

11 Check the free length of each of the valve springs. When new, the outer spring has a free length of 39 mm (1.53 in). It should not compress to more than 37.50 mm (1.48 in). The inner spring has a free length of 38..2 mm (1.51 in) and should be renewed when it compresses below 36.70 mm (1.45 in). Always renew both valve springs, even if only one appears below standard, and preferably the entire set. Poor engine performance can often be attributed to weak valve springs, which permit valve bounce.

12 Reassemble the valve and valve springs by reversing the dismantling procedure. Fit new oil seals to each valve guide and oil both the valve stem and the valve guide, prior to reassembly. Take special care to ensure the valve guide oil seal is not damaged when the valve is inserted. As a final check after assembly, give the end of each valve stem a light tap with a hammer, to make sure the split collets have located correctly.

13 Check the cylinder head for straightness, especially if it has shown a tendency to leak oil at the cylinder head joint. If the warpage exceeds 0.05 mm (0.002 in) at any point the cylinder head must be either machined flat or a new head fitted. Most cases of cylinder head warpage can be traced to unequal tensioning of the cylinder head nuts and bolts by tightening them in incorrect sequence.

28 Checking and resetting the valve clearances

1 Because the engine is of the overhead camshaft type, the valve clearances can be checked when the engine is complete and installed in the frame, or when the cylinder head itself is on the

28.3 Check gap with feeler gauge and adjust with spanner and screwdriver, if necessary

29.5 The pads must be free from score marks or other blemishes

30.5 Rubber ring helps quieten chain. Renew, if worn

work bench. In the former case, it will be necessary to remove the fuel tank and the cylinder head cover, in order to gain access to the rocker arms.
2 Rotate the engine until the valves of the cylinder to be checked are fully closed. This means the cylinder involved must be on the compression stroke. The best check is by removing the circular cover of the contact breaker housing and arranging the F mark of the cylinder involved with the pointer. The piston is now exactly at top dead centre on the compression stroke.
3 Measure the clearance between the adjustable tip of each rocker arm and the end of the valve stem. If the clearance is correct, the inlet valve clearance should be from 0.15 - 0.20 mm (0.006 - 0.008 in) and the exhaust valve 0.20 - 0.25 mm (0.008 - 0.010 in). Always check or set these clearances with the engine COLD and never check by inserting the feeler gauge between the tip of a cam and the pad of the rocker arm with which it makes contact.
4 If any adjustment is necessary, slacken the adjuster locknut and turn the adjuster either inwards or outwards to vary the setting - inwards to decrease the clearance and vice-versa to increase it. When the setting is correct, tighten the locknut fully, and recheck. Remember that badly adjusted valves will affect engine performance. If the clearance is too small, the valve will stick open, causing compression loss and the burning of the valve seat. If the clearance is too great there will be some loss of valve lift and the engine will become noisy.

29 Camshafts, rocker arms and rocker spindles: examination and renovation

1 The camshafts revolve in specially hardened seatings that form an integral part of the cylinder head assembly. Provided the lubrication system continues to function in a satisfactory manner, the camshafts and their seatings can be expected to give long service without need for attention.
2 Check the bearings and the camshaft journals for any score marks, scuffing or signs of uneven wear. Unless the machine has covered a very considerable mileage, most signs of damage to the bearings can be attributed to either lubrication failure or impurities in the oil. Renovation of the affected parts is virtually impossible and it will be necessary to purchase new replacements, including a new cylinder head casting.
3 Wear of the cams can be checked by measuring the height of the cam lobes at their point of maximum lift. The inlet valve cams have a standard height of 34.07 mm (1.342 in) and the exhaust cams 34.11 mm (1.344 in). Their respective base circles should measure 28.24 mm (1.1096 in) and 28.29 mm (1.1098 in). The camshafts cannot be interchanged. Each is quite clearly marked.
4 It is also necessary to check the camshafts for end float and any general wear in the bearing housing, which will tend to make the valve gear noisy. Here again, the worn parts will have to be renewed; they cannot be reclaimed easily.
5 Wear in the rocker arms and/or rocker spindles will be apparent on close examination. If an excessive amount of play is found, both components should be renewed. Special attention should be given to the rocker pad that bears directly on the camshaft. The specially hardened surface should not be chipped, scuffed or worn if the rocker arm is fit for further service. Note that if the pad is badly worn or damaged, it is highly probable that the camshaft will be worn in a similar manner, or vice-versa. The central oil hole must be clean and free from obstructions.
6 Check the condition of the valve adjusters that thread into the forked ends of the rocker arms, and their locknuts. The threads must be in good condition so that the adjuster can be tightened fully, without fear of it slackening off. Do not omit to check the hardened ends at the point of contact with

each pair of valves. The end must not be chipped, broken or indented, otherwise rapid wear will occur, necessitating frequent valve clearance adjustments. If any damage or wear is evident, the complete adjuster must be renewed.

30 Camshaft drive chain, tensioners and sprockets: examination and replacement

1 The camshaft drive chain is of the duplex type, running in near ideal conditions - fully enclosed, with positive lubrication and under spring loaded tension. Excessive wear is unlikely to take place unless the machine has covered a very extensive mileage or if the chain has been allowed to run slack by incorrect tensioning. It should be examined closely during a major overhaul, checking for broken or cracked side plates and missing rollers. If any damage is evident, the complete chain must be renewed.
2 The chain is of the endless type, a design feature that is quite intentional. Do not be tempted to fit a spring link when rejoining the chain after an overhaul, in the mistaken belief that it will make removal of the cylinder head easier on the next occasion. A spring link is less likely to withstand prolonged high rpm than the special clenched-over type of master link fitted by the manufacturer. It follows that when the chain is eventually rejoined, the new master link must be clenched over so that there is no chance of the detachable side plate working loose.
3 The chain tensioner is spring loaded and will provide the correct degree of chain tension, provided it is allowed to adjust itself in the approved manner, after engine reassembly. A check should be made to ensure the free-running sprocket is not damaged, or its bearing worn, and that the protective rubber strip has not worn through. This latter point applies to the fixed chain guides too.
4 If the chain is due for renewal, it is possible that the camshaft sprockets and those that form part of the drive chain will require renewal at the same time. It is always preferable to run new parts together, and not a mixture of old and new. The camshaft sprockets are integral with the camshafts. Note the rubber ring between the two sprockets, which quietens the camshaft drive chain. If the ring is worn or shows signs of general deterioration, it should be renewed.
5 Sprocket wear should not present a problem, as the chain and sprockets run in ideal conditions. After a very lengthy period of service, however, it is probable that the sprockets will show signs of wear that will call for renewal, in the form of shallow teeth or teeth which have become hooked or deformed. As mentioned previously, the sprockets are integral with the camshafts, which will necessitate renewal of the complete camshaft assembly. However, by the time the sprockets will require attention, it is highly probable that the cams will need attention too, making the renewal of the whole assembly a vital necessity.

31 Primary drive pinion, clutch assembly, camshaft drive and tachometer drive pinion: examination and replacement

1 Check the primary drive pinion for chipped, cracked or broken teeth - also the clutch pinion with which it meshes. If one pinion is damaged in any way, it is highly probable that the other will require attention, too. It is always best to renew components that run together as a pair, otherwise the resultant rate of wear from running old and new parts together will be much higher than normal.
2 The camshaft drive and tachometer drive pinions should be examined in similar fashion, not omitting the small skew gear that is splined onto the end of the tachometer/oil pump drive shaft.
3 The eight friction plates of the clutch have a bonded on lining, which gives each plate an overall thickness of 3.0 mm $\pm$ 0.1 mm (0.12 in). Measure each friction plate to check whether the thickness has reached, or is about to reach, the service limit of 2.7 mm (0.108 in) or whether the lining has worn unevenly. If there is any doubt about the condition of the lining, renew ALL the friction plates as a complete set.
4 It is also advisable to check the seven plain clutch plates for warpage, renewing any that have warped by more than 0.05 mm (0.002 in). Check also for signs of scuffing or pick-up and whether there has been any overheating, denoted by discolouration of the plates in certain areas. The clutch has to transmit a considerable load to the gearbox and it is important that it is maintained in first class condition, if clutch slip and other maladies are to be avoided.
5 After an extended period of service, the clutch springs will tend to compress and lose some of their effectiveness. Measure the length of each spring, which should be 42.8 mm (1.691 in) in the free state. If any have compressed more than 1.0 mm (0.040 in) the complete set must be renewed.
6 Examine the clutch assembly for burrs on the edges of the protruding tongues of the inserted plates and/or slots worn in the edges of the outer drum with which they engage. Similar wear can occur between the inner tongues of the plain clutch plates and the slots in the clutch inner drum. Wear of this nature will cause clutch drag and other troubles, since the plates will become trapped and will not free fully when the clutch is withdrawn. A small amount of wear can be treated by dressing with a file; more extensive wear will necessitate renewal of the worn parts.
7 Check the clutch push rod for straightness by rolling it on a flat surface. If any evidence of bending is detected, the rod should be renewed rather than straightened. A bent clutch push rod is often responsible for heavy clutch action. At the same time, check the clutch operating mechanism that is still attached to the inside of the left-hand crankcase cover. It is easily dismantled by removing the two retaining screws that retain the quick-start worm housing to the cover.
The worm must move inwards and outwards quite freely, without any undue play. It should not wear any appreciable amount, unless it has suffered from under lubrication. The hardened end of the adjuster and that of the clutch push rod, where it makes contact, must be free from chipping, cracking or pronounced wear. If frequent clutch adjustment has proved necessary, it is highly probable that the hardened ends have worn through, permitting the softer metal underneath to wear at a much more rapid rate. Running with insufficient clearance in the clutch cable is the usual cause, since the continual load on the thrust mechanism causes it to overheat and the hardened ends to soften as a result. Renew all worn parts.
8 There is an oil seal around the push rod, which prevents oil leaking into the left-hand crankcase cover. This too must be checked, and renewed, if necessary. A simple dust seal protects the quick-start worm.

32 Gearbox components: examination and replacement

1 Give the gearbox components a close visual examination for any signs of wear or damage, such as broken or chipped teeth, worn dogs, damaged or worn splines and bent selectors. Unless necessary, there should be no need to dismantle the individual gear trains unless gearbox troubles have been experienced. Under these circumstances, dismantle each assembly very carefully, making notes on the position of the various thrust washers and shims so that they are eventually replaced in their original positions. Their correct positioning is vital if the gearbox is to function correctly. Renew any worn parts and when two pinions run together, both pinions, if one of them is worn or damaged.
2 Check the condition of the various pawl springs and the

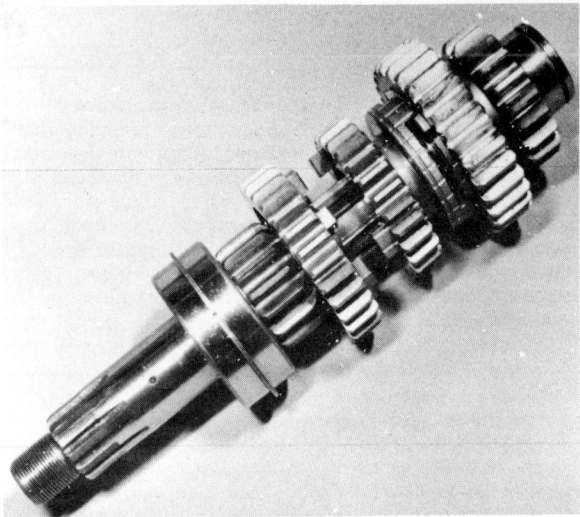
32.1a Examine the gearbox input gear train carefully, also ...

32.1b ... the gearbox output train

36.2a Fit the gear selector drum first, passing through cam plate

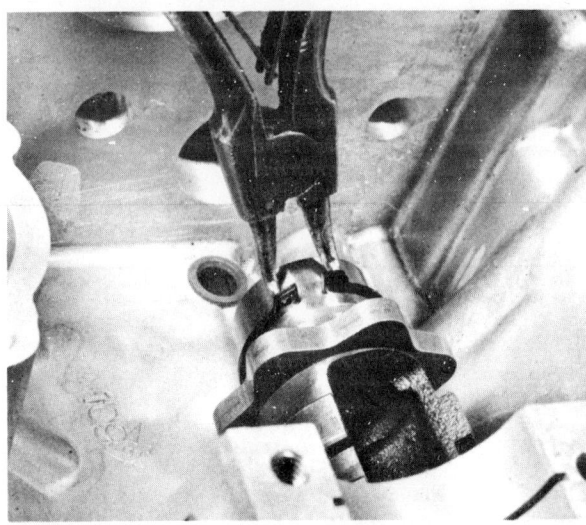
36.2b Cam plate is retained by external circlip

36.2c Plunger and spring in underside is easily forgotton

36.3 Insert forward facing selector rod and fork first

kick-starter return spring. If any of these springs fail after the engine has been rebuilt, a further complete stripdown of the engine unit will be necessary.

3 It is unlikely that the kickstart assembly will require attention, since this is likely to be used only in an emergency, most starts being accomplished with the electric starter motor. The skew splines of the pinion on the end of the kickstart shaft and also the internal matching splines of the kickstart pinion must be a good sliding fit and well lubricated.

4 An item likely to be overlooked is the detent plunger and spring that engages with the camplate on the end of the gear selector drum. This must be free to move within its housing and have a positive spring loading. If the spring weakens or breaks, gear changes will be imprecise, with an accompanying tendency for the machine to jump out of gear.

33 Gearbox bearings: examination and replacement

1 Unlike the engine bearings mentioned previously, the gearbox bearings are of either the ball journal or needle roller type, retained by half-clips. Wash the bearings free from oil, using preferably an oil solvent, and rotate them, checking for signs of roughness or sloppiness when they are rotated. If there is any question about their fitness for further service, they should be renewed without question. A further, complete stripdown will be required at a later date if any of them happen to fail prematurely.

2 Pay particular attention to the oil seal that is located immediately behind the final drive pinion of the gearbox. If this fails, serious oil leakage will occur, which may find its way on to the rear tyre and cause an accident. Now is the time to renew this seal if there is any doubt about its condition.

34 Crankshaft balancer, drive chain and sprockets: examination and replacement

1 The crankshaft balancer itself is unlikely to require attention, provided it is timed correctly on replacement. The two ball journal bearings that support the assembly should be examined carefully, and checked for wear, as described in the preceding Section.

2 Should renewal prove necessary, the drive sprocket is easily detached as described earlier in this Chapter. This also applies to the starter motor sprocket, that forms part of the chain drive assembly. When sprocket wear sets in, both sprockets and chain should be renewed. The latter, like the camshaft drive chain, is of the endless type.

3 Check the chain tensioner mounting plate, to make sure the rubber faced surface has not worn through.

35 Engine and gearbox reassembly: general

1 Before reassembly is commenced, engine and gearbox components should be thoroughly clean and placed close to the working area.

2 Make sure all traces of old gaskets have been removed and that the mating surfaces are clean and undamaged. One of the best ways to remove old gasket cement, which is needed only on the crankcase and cover joints, is to apply a rag soaked in methylated spirit. This acts as a solvent and will ensure the cement is removed without resort to scraping and the consequent risk of damage.

3 Gather all the necessary tools and have available an oil can filled with clean engine oil. Make sure that all new gaskets and oil seals are available; there is nothing more frustrating than having to stop in the middle of a reassembly sequence because a vital gasket or replacement has been overlooked.

4 Make sure the reassembly area is clean and well lit, with adequate working space. Refer to the torque and clearance settings wherever they are given. Many of the smaller bolts are easily sheared if they are over-tightened. Always use the correct size screwdriver bit for the crosshead screws and NEVER an ordinary screwdriver or punch.

5 A tube of thread sealant, such as Loctite or Torqueseal, is another essential requirement, as many of the screw threads should be treated with one or other of these proprietary aids, to prevent them from working loose when the machine is back in service.

36 Engine and gearbox reassembly: replacing the gearbox components and crankshaft assembly

1 Lay the lower crankcase half on the workbench and replace the main bearing shells, if they have been removed. They have tagged ends, so that they cannot be replaced in an incorrect position.

2 Fit the gear selector drum, inserting it into its housing from the right-hand side. Insert it approximately half way, then fit the profiled end cam and the circlip that retains it in position.

36.4a Rear selector rod and forks assembly is retained by internal 'E' clip

36.4b Pegs of selector forks must engage with channels in selector drum

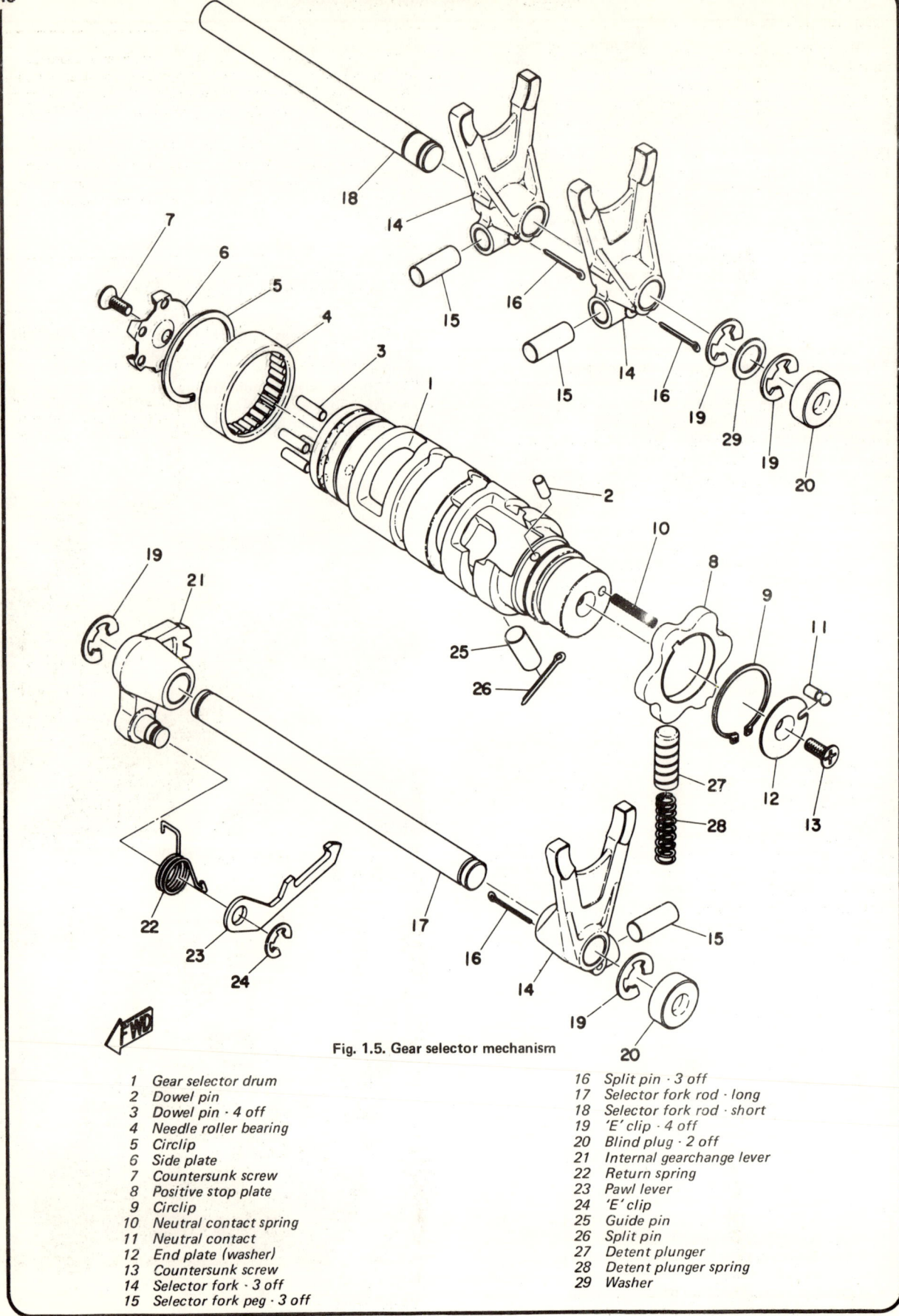

Fig. 1.5. Gear selector mechanism

1 Gear selector drum
2 Dowel pin
3 Dowel pin · 4 off
4 Needle roller bearing
5 Circlip
6 Side plate
7 Countersunk screw
8 Positive stop plate
9 Circlip
10 Neutral contact spring
11 Neutral contact
12 End plate (washer)
13 Countersunk screw
14 Selector fork · 3 off
15 Selector fork peg · 3 off
16 Split pin · 3 off
17 Selector fork rod · long
18 Selector fork rod · short
19 'E' clip · 4 off
20 Blind plug · 2 off
21 Internal gearchange lever
22 Return spring
23 Pawl lever
24 'E' clip
25 Guide pin
26 Split pin
27 Detent plunger
28 Detent plunger spring
29 Washer

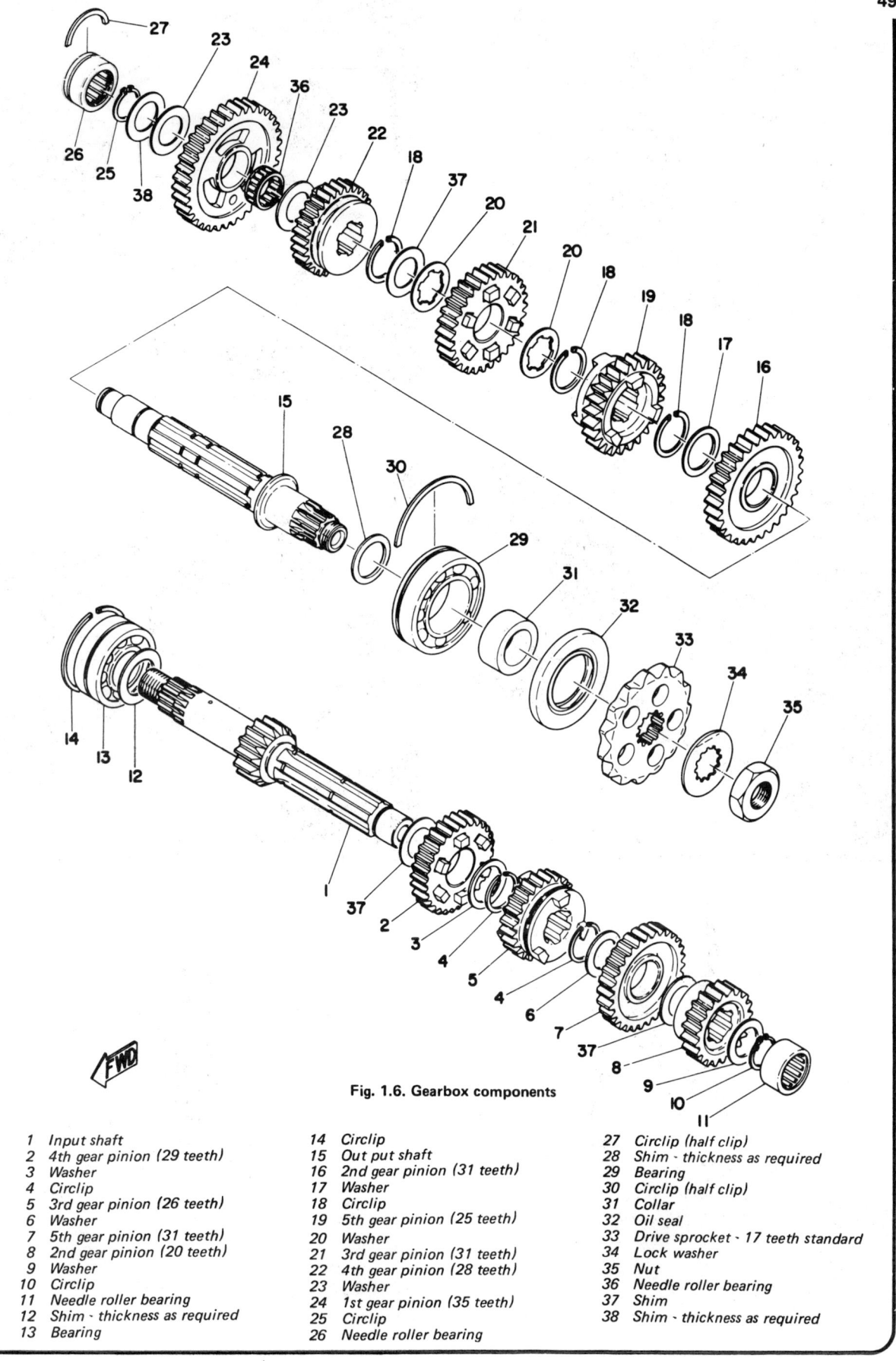

Fig. 1.6. Gearbox components

1 Input shaft	14 Circlip	27 Circlip (half clip)
2 4th gear pinion (29 teeth)	15 Out put shaft	28 Shim - thickness as required
3 Washer	16 2nd gear pinion (31 teeth)	29 Bearing
4 Circlip	17 Washer	30 Circlip (half clip)
5 3rd gear pinion (26 teeth)	18 Circlip	31 Collar
6 Washer	19 5th gear pinion (25 teeth)	32 Oil seal
7 5th gear pinion (31 teeth)	20 Washer	33 Drive sprocket - 17 teeth standard
8 2nd gear pinion (20 teeth)	21 3rd gear pinion (31 teeth)	34 Lock washer
9 Washer	22 4th gear pinion (28 teeth)	35 Nut
10 Circlip	23 Washer	36 Needle roller bearing
11 Needle roller bearing	24 1st gear pinion (35 teeth)	37 Shim
12 Shim - thickness as required	25 Circlip	38 Shim - thickness as required
13 Bearing	26 Needle roller bearing	

36.5a Internal gearchange lever is retained to selector rod by 'E' clip

36.5b Replace blind plugs that blank off selector rod ends

36.5c Insert neutral contact spring first, then ...

36.5d ... contact itself and retaining washer

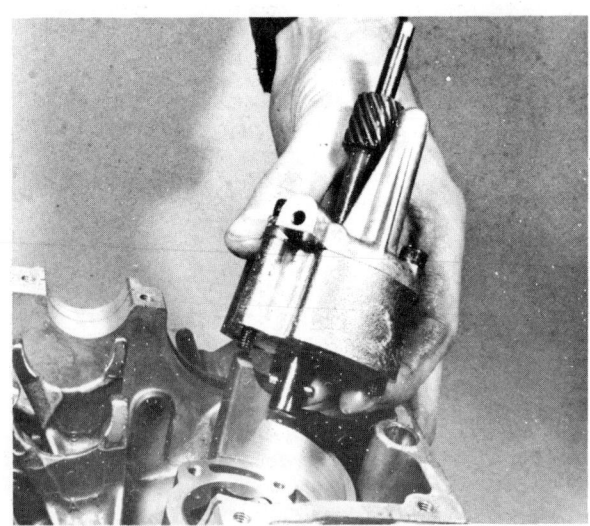
36.6a Fit oil pump body and retain with three Allen screws

36.6b Check that pump revolves freely, after tightening screws

Chapter 1: Engine, clutch and gearbox

36.6c Replace the oil pump/tachometer drive pinion, which is keyed on its shaft

36.6d Don't forget the locking plate, retained by two countersunk crosshead screws

36.7a Fit output shaft assembly after replacing bearing half clip

36.7b Input shaft can then be replaced. Check engagement of selector forks

Push the assembled drum through further, so that it is correctly positioned in both housings. It is also necessary to insert the guide pin into the lower crankcase, which locates the gearchange selector drum. Insert the pin from the underside of the crankcase and fit the split pin that retains it. This is because the end of the pin has to be splayed out INSIDE the crankcase. It can be fitted at a later stage, if overlooked, but in this case it will be necessary to retain the pin by bowing it out in the centre of the orifice.

3   Insert the forward facing selector rod from the right-hand side. This is the rod that has only a single selector fork. Replace the 'E' clip that retains it in position, and engage the peg of the selector fork with the correct channel in the gear selector drum.

4   Insert the rear facing selector rod from the right-hand side in similar fashion, this being the rod with two selector forks. Fit the inner retaining 'E' clip and engage the pegs of both selector forks with their respective channels in the selector drum.

5   Replace the gearchange lever assembly on the end of the selector rod that protrudes from the right-hand end of the crankcase. Secure it with an 'E' clip. Replace the rubber blind plugs that blank off the ends of both selector rods on the left-hand side of the crankcase. Insert the neutral contact spring and the contact itself into the left-hand end of the gear selector drum, then the centre washer and countersunk crosshead screw. The washer is grooved, to locate and hold the neutral contact. Tighten the countersunk screw.

6   Fit the lower oil pump rotors, marked surfaces upwards. Insert the pin through the drive shaft of the main oil pump assembly, align with the slot in the inner rotor that is now in position, and lower the main assembly into position, after flooding the rotors with oil. When the oil pump has seated, check that it revolves quite freely, then tighten the three allen screws that retain it in position. Re-check for freedom of movement after tightening the allen screws fully.

7   Replace the gearbox bearing half clips. Note that one bearing has its clip around its circumference, which is an integral part of the bearing itself. Fit the mainshaft first, checking that the selector fork engages correctly, then the layshaft, again making sure that the selector forks are correctly positioned. Check that the bearings have seated correctly and that the gear shafts revolve quite freely.

8   Oil the main bearing shells and refit the crankshaft assembly. Check that it has seated correctly.

9   The crankcases are now ready for joining, but before this is carried out, the cross shaft drive for the tachometer and oil pump must be inserted into the upper crankcase half. The skew pinion is splined onto the shaft, and is located by two 'E' clips, one each side. Do not omit the locking plate, secured by two crosshead screws.

Chapter 1: Engine, clutch and gearbox

36.8 Oil main bearing shells after fitting in correct locations

36.9a Crankcases are now ready for joining

36.9b Lower top half gently down holding down studs

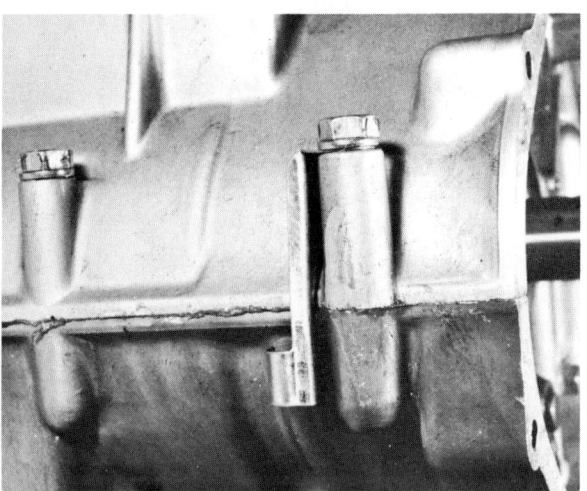

36.10a This rear bolt carries clip for contact breaker lead

36.10b Do not omit the inner main bearing nuts

10 Insert the dowels into the lower crankcase and smear the jointing surface with a thick layer of gasket cement. There is no gasket at this joint. Treat the jointing surface of the upper crankcase in similar fashion, then bring the two halves of the crankcase together. Insert the various crankcase bolts, noting that one carries the clip for the contact breaker lead. Tighten them in the order marked on the crankcase halves, in three stages, checking on each occasion that the gearbox shafts and the crankshaft revolve freely. Do not omit the two inner main bearing nuts and the four dome nuts on the underside of the crankcase assembly. The dome nuts must seat on copper washers. Refer to the torque tightening chart for the recommended settings, found in the Specifications at the beginning of this Chapter.

37 Engine and gearbox reassembly: fitting the crankcase strainer and sump

1 Invert the crankcase assembly and fit a new sump gasket. This is of the composition type and no gasket cement should be necessary. Fit the detent plunger and spring for the gear

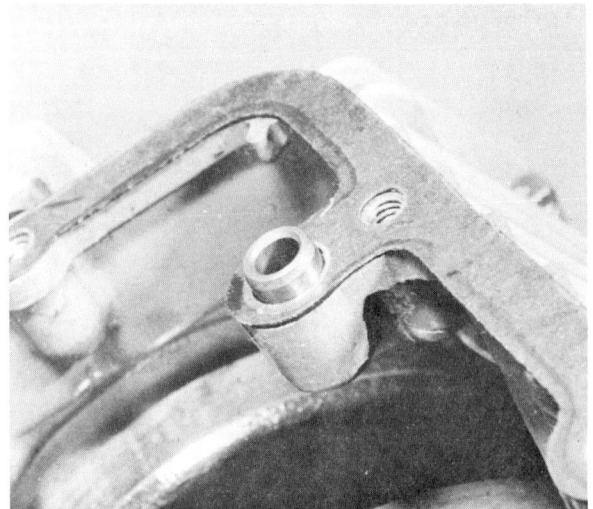
37.1a Fit a new sump gasket (dry) and the locating dowels

37.1b Gasket is of complex shape

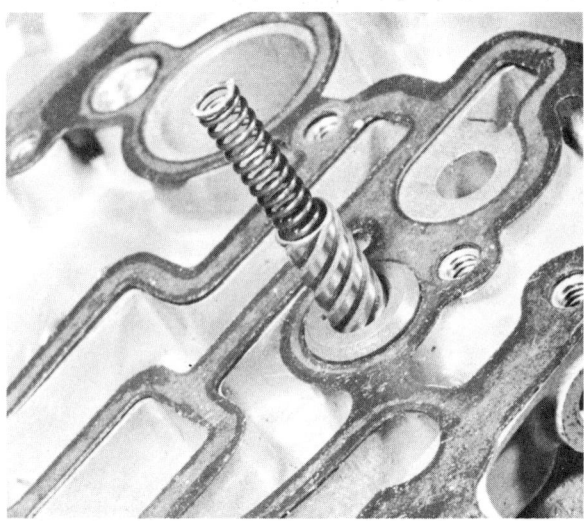
37.1c Don't forget to insert camplate plunger and spring before ...

37.1d ... replacing pressure release valve and strainer assembly

37.2a Make sure the circular magnetic filter is replaced and ...

37.2b ... the captive nuts and retaining plates for the lower crankcase mounting points

selector drum camplate, then the strainer and pressure release valve assembly, which is secured by four allen screws. Make sure the gasket is positioned correctly before these screws are tightened fully.

2 Before fitting the sump base, replace the locating dowels and make sure the circular magnetic filter is positioned within its recess. Do not omit to insert the lower crankcase mounting nuts and their holding plates, as they are held captive by the sump. Insert and tighten evenly, in a diagonal sequence, all the allen screws that retain the sump.

38 Engine and gearbox reassembly: replacing the gearchange mechanism, crankshaft balancer and kickstart assembly

1 Re-invert the crankcase assembly and insert the gearchange shaft from the left, so that it meshes correctly with the gearchange lever assembly on the end of the selector rod. The teeth that must align are clearly marked with a punch mark. A washer and an 'E' clip retain the shaft in position, at the left-hand end. Do not omit the oil seal, which will slide over

38.1a Replace the gearchange shaft and toothed claw

38.1b Teeth must engage as shown; both are marked

38.1c 'E' clip on left-hand side secures shaft in position

38.2a Insert crankshaft balancer from right and drive into position

38.2b Replace the circlip that retains the right-hand bearing

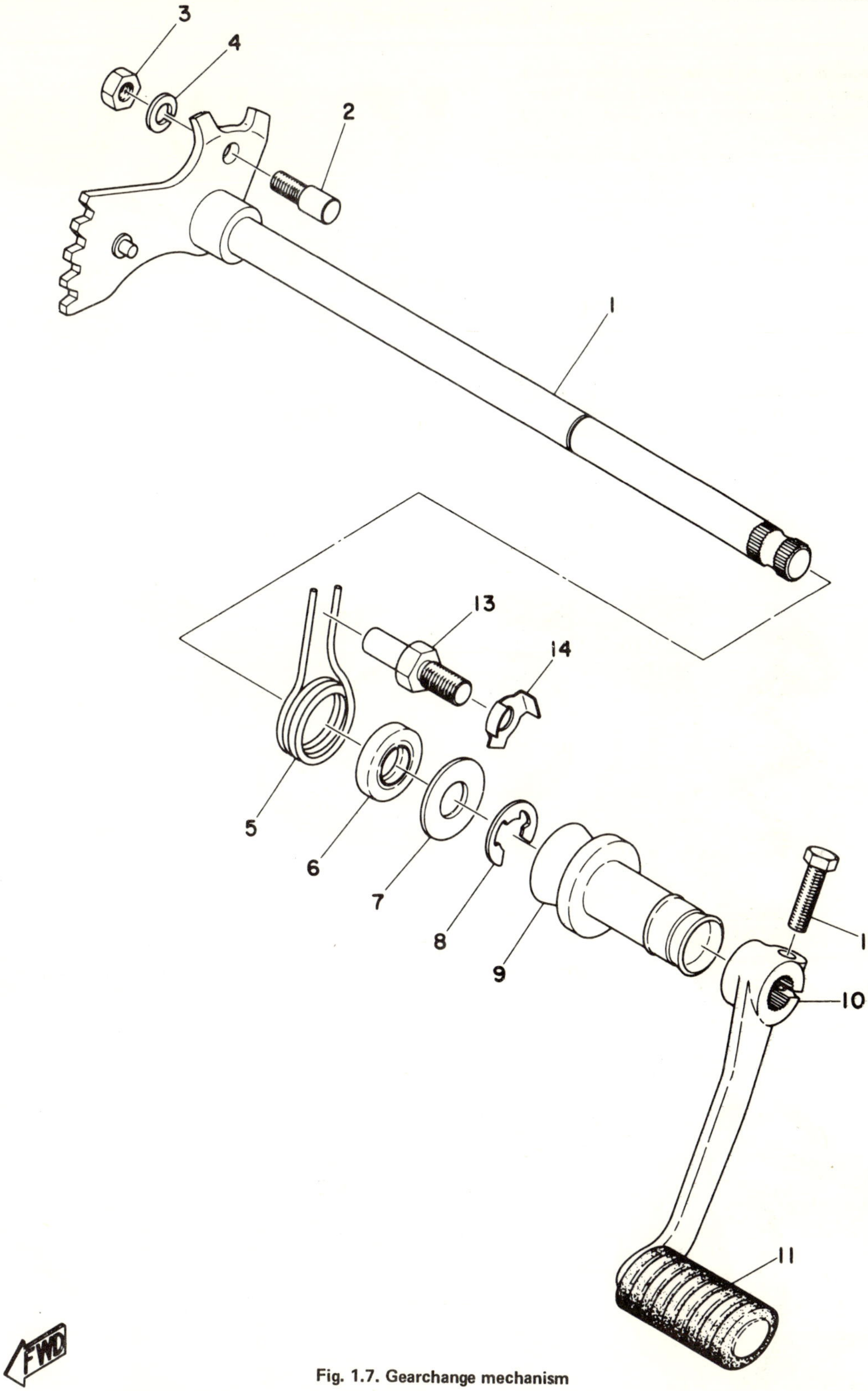

55

Fig. 1.7. Gearchange mechanism

1 Gearchange lever assembly
2 Screw
3 Nut
4 Spring washer
5 Centralising spring
6 Oil seal
7 Washer
8 'E' clip
9 Rubber boot
10 Gearchange pedal
11 Pedal rubber
12 Bolt
13 Stop screw
14 Lock washer

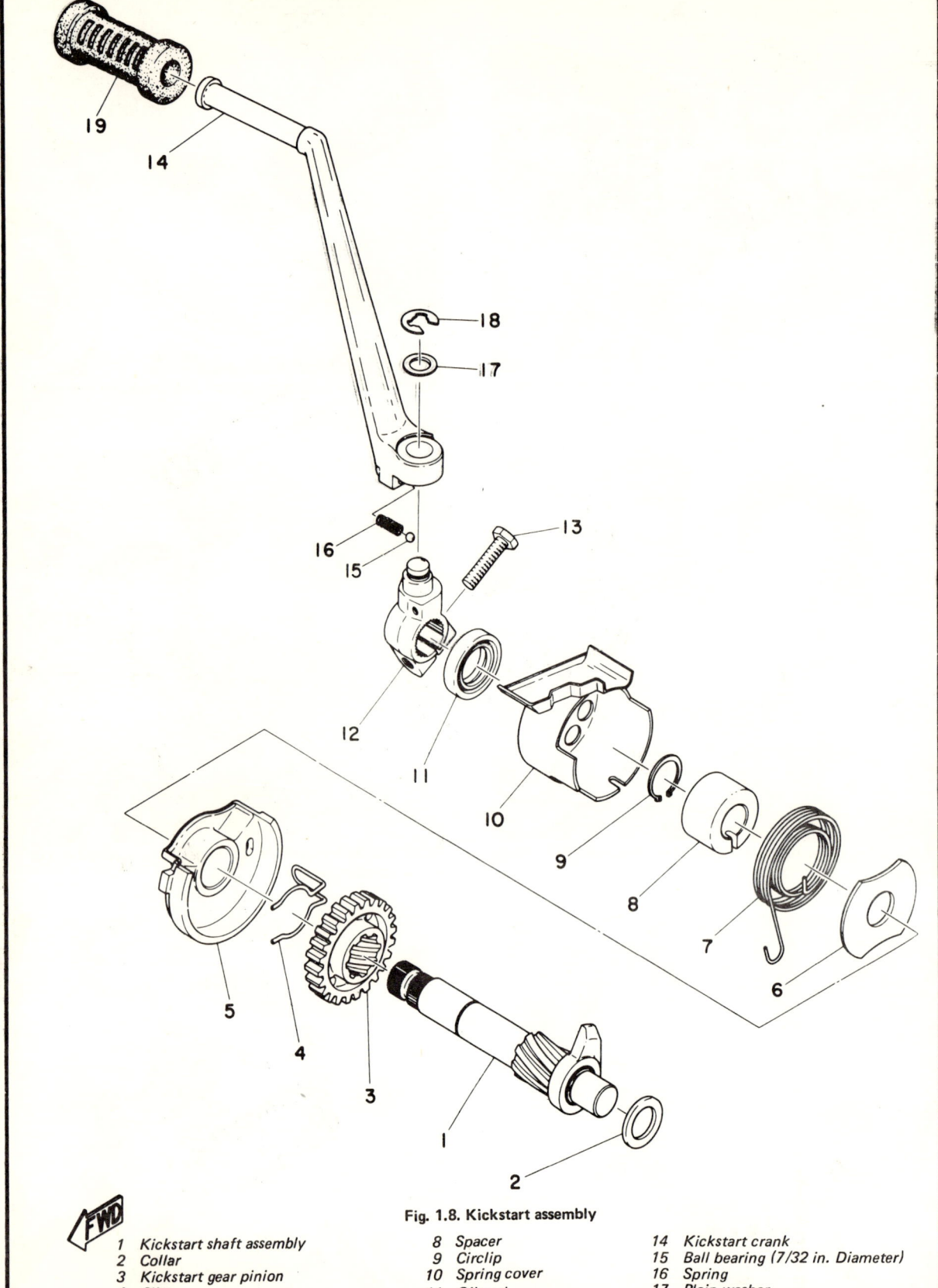

Fig. 1.8. Kickstart assembly

1 Kickstart shaft assembly
2 Collar
3 Kickstart gear pinion
4 Clip
5 Spring guide
6 Shaped metal plate
7 Return spring
8 Spacer
9 Circlip
10 Spring cover
11 Oil seal
12 Kickstart boss
13 Bolt
14 Kickstart crank
15 Ball bearing (7/32 in. Diameter)
16 Spring
17 Plain washer
18 'E' clip
19 Kickstart rubber

38.3a Use grease to retain the loose thrust washer in position

38.3b Note how projection locates with crankcase assembly

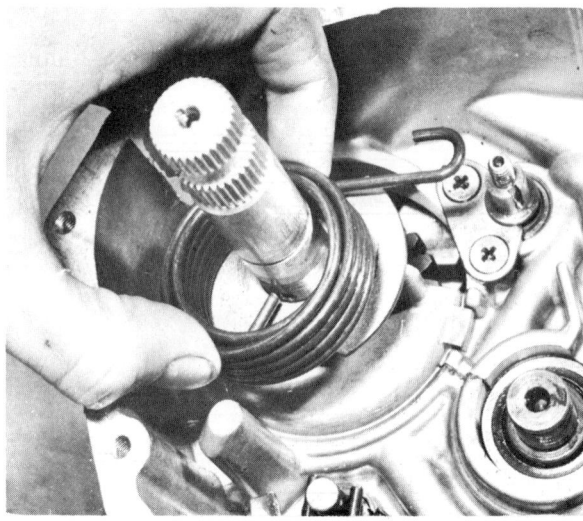
38.3c Return spring fits over shaped plate; inner end fits in shaft drilling

38.3d Turn spring clockwise to tension; loop hooked end of spring round projection

38.4a Fit oil pump/tachometer drive pinion, which is keyed on its shaft

38.4b Slide large thrust washer over end of gearbox input shaft and ...

58 Chapter 1: Engine, clutch and gearbox

38.4c ... place belville washer over end of output shaft

38.4d Idler pinion can now be fitted and retained with circlip

38.4e Position cover over kickstart spring and ...

38.4f ... catch tray over right-hand balancer bearing

this end of the shaft and should be carefully tapped into position.

2 Insert the crankshaft balancer, complete with bearing, from the right. Note that the bearing is pegged and must be introduced so that this peg clears the slot in the crankcase. Tap the bearing into position and retain it with the large diameter circlip. Replace the circlip that retains the left-hand bearing at the same time.

3 Refit the kickstart assembly, taking great care that the thick, inner thrust washer does not fall off the end of the shaft and disappear into the crankcase. Grease will help retain it. The cover plate will locate with the circular recess in the crankcase. Replace the shaped plate over the kickstart shaft, then the spring, the inner end of which will fit into a hole drilled in the shaft. Tension the spring by turning the hooked end clockwise, until it will hook over the cast projection below. Fit the alloy guide into the centre of the spring, aligning the slot with the inner end of the spring.

4 Fit the oil pump drive pinion on the drive cross shaft, which is tapered and has a woodruff key. The pinion is retained by a plain washer, a spring washer and a nut. Position the clutch thrust washer over the end of the gearbox input shaft. Replace the Belville washer on the end of the output shaft, then fit the idler pinion, which is retained by a plain washer and an 'E' clip. Fit the cover over the kickstart spring, catch tray upwards, noting how the cover locates with slots. Replace the catch tray that is retained by two crosshead screws over the end of the crankshaft balancer bearing.

39 Engine and gearbox reassembly: replacing the clutch assembly, primary drive and camshaft chain drive

1 Check that the bush has been inserted in the centre of the clutch outer drum and pinion assembly, oil it, and push the drum on to the end of the mainshaft, twisting it to engage with the idler pinion. Place the other thrust washer over the protruding end of the mainshaft and press the clutch centre over the splines. Fit the plain washer, belled washer (belled side outwards) and retaining nut on the mainshaft and tighten the nut to a torque setting of 7 - 7.5 m.kg. The inner drum will have to be spragged during this operation, as shown in the accompanying photograph. Great care is necessary, as the clutch splines are very easily damaged or fractured. It is imperative that the sprag is close up to the root of the outer drum projections, whilst tightening.

2 When the nut has been tightened fully, refit the clutch plates, commencing with a friction plate. Note that the clutch housing has a cast-in arrow and when the first plain plate is

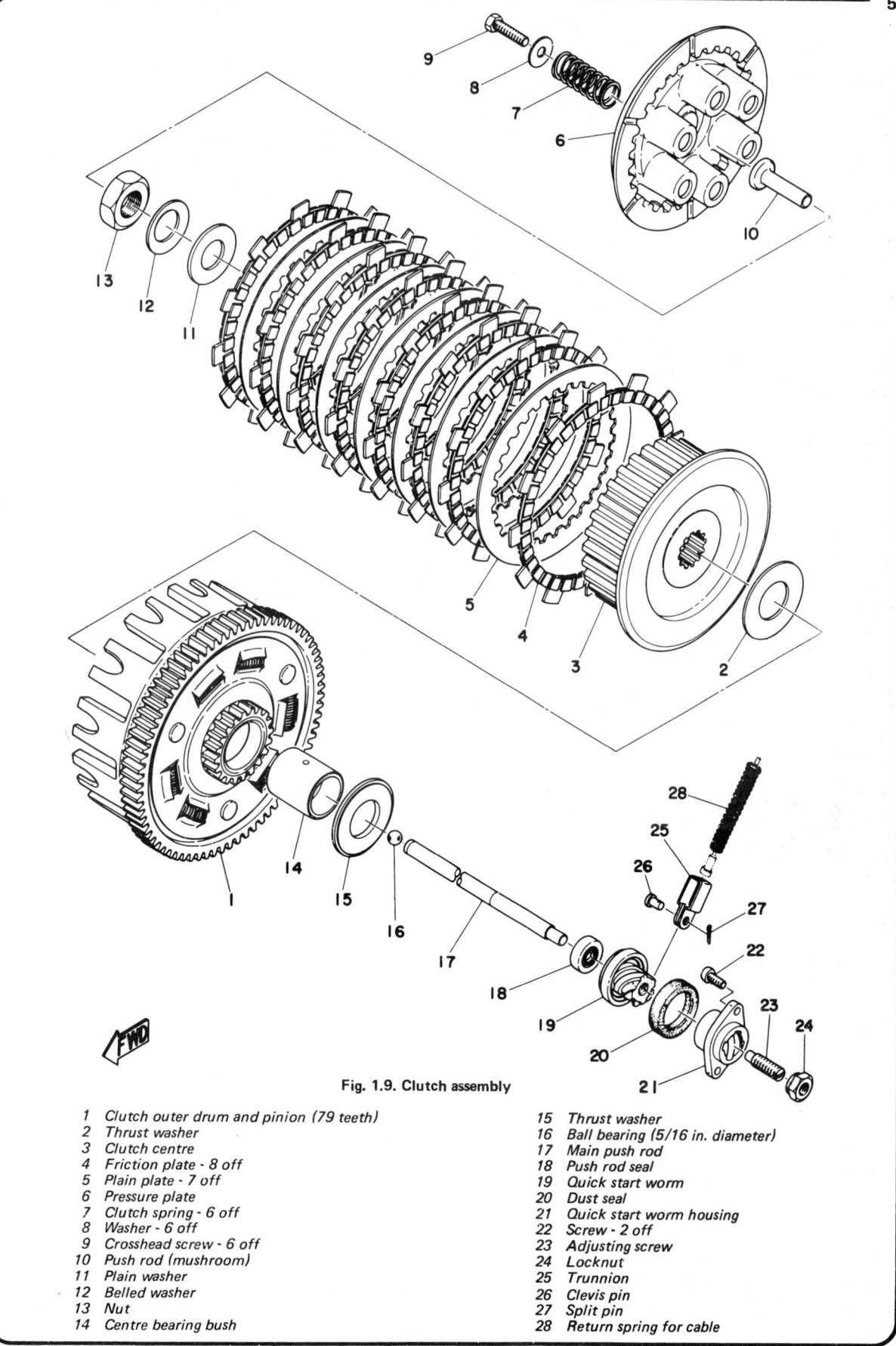

Fig. 1.9. Clutch assembly

1 Clutch outer drum and pinion (79 teeth)
2 Thrust washer
3 Clutch centre
4 Friction plate - 8 off
5 Plain plate - 7 off
6 Pressure plate
7 Clutch spring - 6 off
8 Washer - 6 off
9 Crosshead screw - 6 off
10 Push rod (mushroom)
11 Plain washer
12 Belled washer
13 Nut
14 Centre bearing bush
15 Thrust washer
16 Ball bearing (5/16 in. diameter)
17 Main push rod
18 Push rod seal
19 Quick start worm
20 Dust seal
21 Quick start worm housing
22 Screw - 2 off
23 Adjusting screw
24 Locknut
25 Trunnion
26 Clevis pin
27 Split pin
28 Return spring for cable

39.1a Clutch outer drum will slide into position over centre bush

39.1b Plain thrust washer fits next

39.1c Clutch centre will press on to splined end of shaft

39.1d Plain washer is fitted belled side outwards

39.1e Sprag clutch centre and outer drum, then torque tighten centre nut

39.2a Don't forget to insert clutch 'mushroom' prior to pressure plate addition

39.2b Note use of another sprag when tightening clutch springs

39.3a Loop chain through tunnel and refit contact breaker drive pinion

39.3b Align pinion timing marks as shown, with crankcase mark

39.4a Fit outer crankshaft pinion next

39.4b Then fit camshaft drive pinion assembly so that ...

39.4c ... timing marks coincide with outer crankshaft pinion, as shown

39.4d Replace and torque tighten crankshaft nut

39.5a Refit the outrigger bracket, then ...

39.5b ... replace and tighten the three retaining bolts, two of which have special lock plates

39.7a After replacing outer cover, replace auto-advance mechanism, followed by ...

39.7b ... contact breaker assembly. Press grommet into housing

39.7c Contact breaker lead is retained by these cable clips

Chapter 1: Engine, clutch and gearbox   63

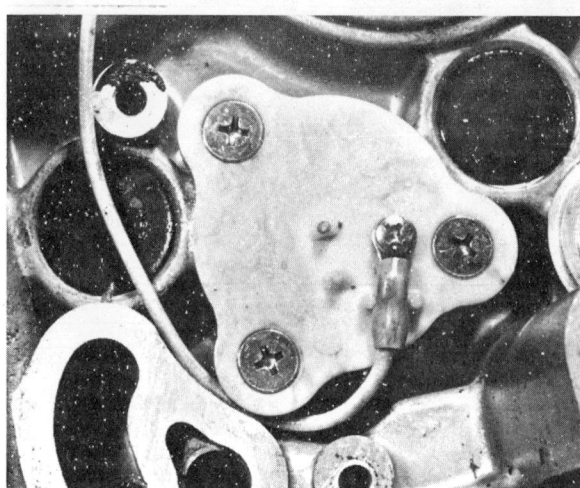
40.1a Replace plastic cover of neutral contact housing, making sure wire is tracked correctly

40.1b Push oil seal into gearbox output shaft housing

40.1c Insert the ball bearing after the long push rod

fitted, the tab must align with this arrow. To preserve clutch balance, all succeeding plain plates must be positioned so that their tabs are 50° from this original setting and 50° from each other, in clockwise rotation. Each must, of course, be separated by a friction plate. Before fitting the pressure plate, grease and insert the mushroom headed portion of the clutch push rod. One of the arrows on the pressure plate must align with the arrow on the clutch housing. Insert the springs and their retaining screws, using another sprag, as shown in the accompanying photograph, to lock the clutch whilst the springs are tightened fully.

3 Position the square-shaped key in the end of the crankshaft, and push the crankshaft drive pinion into position, chamfered side inwards, so that it will mesh with the clutch pinion. Loop the camshaft drive chain through the chain tunnel and refit the long shaft with integral pinion that drives the contact breaker assembly. There should be a thrust washer either side of the pinion. Align the mark on the pinion with the crankcase mark.

4 Fit the outer crankshaft pinion next, which fits over the same square key in the crankshaft. Then fit the camshaft drive pinion assembly, aligning the timing marks with those on the crankshaft drive pinion. There should be a washer either side of the pinion assembly prior to insertion. Refit the bolt and lockwasher to retain the crankshaft pinions in position and torque tighten the bolt to 4 - 5 m.kg. Bend over the tab washer.

5 Refit the outrigger bracket, after tapping it into position over the locating dowels. Fit and tighten the three bolts that retain it in position, noting that two of them have special washers on the underside that engage with holes in the plate.

6 The right-hand outer cover can now be refitted, after inserting the two locating dowels and fitting a new gasket (dry). Check both oil seals in the cover, before refitting, especially the oil seal in the contact breaker housing. When refitting the cover retaining screws, note that those along the bottom run have to pass through clips that carry the contact breaker lead. One passes through the contact breaker housing - the only long screw.

7 Slide the auto-advance mechanism over the contact breaker shaft and push it into position. It will locate in only one place as it is dowelled so that the position of the contact breaker cam cannot be varied. Then replace the contact breaker baseplate assembly, securing it with the two screws and washers at the edge and pushing the lead wire grommet into its housing. If its former position was marked, align the marks carefully, before tightening. Refit the centre nut and washer; do not overtighten the former. Refit the circular end cover, temporarily if necessary, retaining it with the three screws. There must be a gasket behind this cover, to keep water out of the contact breaker assembly.

40 Engine and gearbox reassembly: replacing and timing the crankshaft balancer and the starter drive chain

1 Working from the left-hand side of the crankcase unit, replace the neutral contact spring, contact retaining washer and screw, then refit the plastic end cover. It is retained by three screws. Make sure the lead wire is tracked correctly. Press the large diameter oil seal into the output shaft housing, then insert the long push rod into the push rod tunnel, after greasing the rod, followed by the ball bearing. Fit the oil adaptor plate, which should have a new gasket lightly smeared with gasket cement to preserve an oil-tight joint.

2 Tap the starter motor adaptor drive through the centre of the drive bearing. Fit the sprocket over the splined end of the balancer. It will fit in only one position, due to the recessed spline. Loop the endless chain in its approximate layout, as shown in the accompanying illustration over the balancer sprocket. Do not omit the metal oil deflector plate, which can be lodged in position. Fit the upper shaft, which will

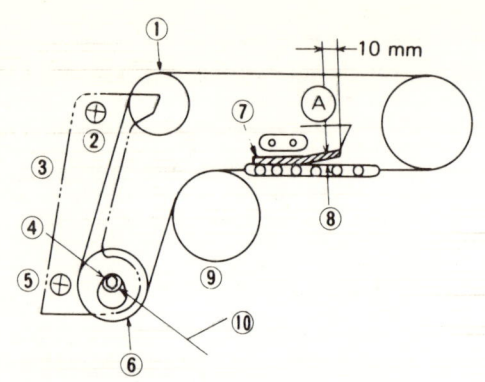

Fig. 1.10. Tensioning the balancer drive chain

1 Upper idler pinion
2 Outrigger plate screw
3 Outrigger plate
4 Serrated adjuster
5 Outrigger plate screw
6 Lower idler pinion on eccentric shaft
7 Chain guide (rubber-faced)
8 Measurement point
9 Crankshaft pinion
10 Eccentric shaft

40.1d Refit the oil adaptor plate with a new gasket fitted

40.2a Replace the balancer shaft sprocket and loop the chain in its approximate position

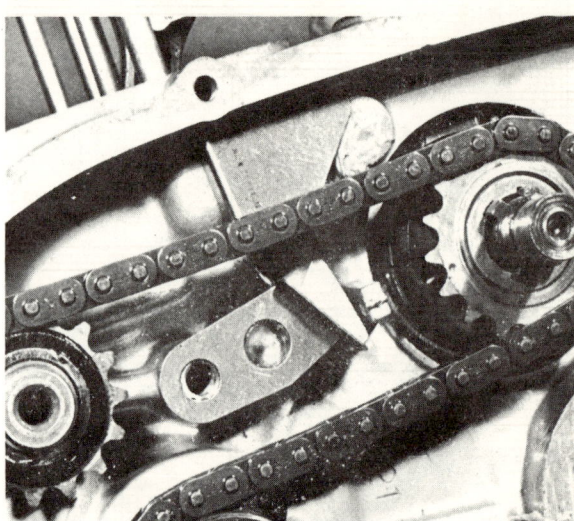

40.2b Do not omit the small oil deflector plate, which lodges in position

40.2c Fit the upper, then the lower sprockets, checking that ...

40.2d ... the balancer sprocket timing mark and ...

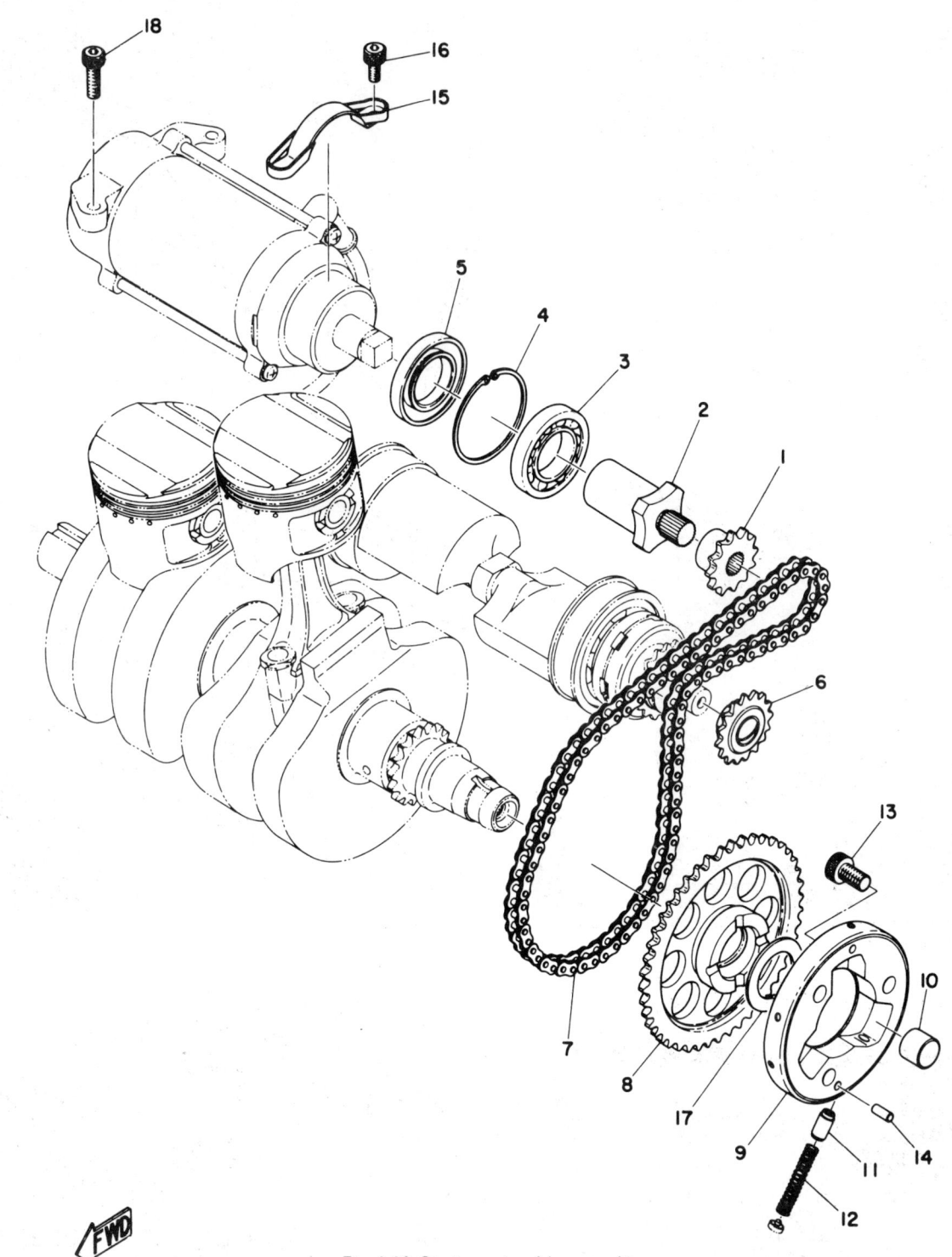

Fig. 1.11. Starter motor drive assembly

1 Starter motor sprocket
2 Shaft adaptor
3 Bearing
4 Circlip
5 Oil seal
6 Idler sprocket
7 Chain
8 Starter drive sprocket assembly
9 Free running clutch
10 Clutch roller - 3 off
11 Clutch spring cap - 3 off
12 Spring - 3 off
13 Allen screw (short) - 2 off
14 Dowel pin - 2 off
15 Starter motor clamp
16 Allen screw (short) - 2 off
17 Thrust washer
18 Allen screw (long) - 2 off

40.2e ... the crankshaft sprocket timing marks align as shown

40.3a Refit the outrigger bracket, then ...

40.3b ... the chain tensioner, adjusting the chain so that the prescribed amount of play is ...

40.3c ... measured here

40.3d Replace the retaining nut and lock washer, and tighten

40.4a Refit starter chain and sprockets in unison, as shown

push into the crankcase, then slide the sprocket over it. Fit the lower shaft so that the eccentric formation provides the least chain tension, with its own associated sprocket. Pull both these sprockets to the end of their shafts, engage them with the chain and push them home, checking first that the timing marks have aligned correctly. The mark on the balancer shaft must align with the mark on the crankcase at the same time as the mark on the crankshaft sprocket aligns with its own crankcase mark. These marks must align exactly when the complete drive is assembled, if a smooth running engine is to result.

3 Fit the outrigger bracket, tapping it into position carefully over over its locating dowels. Refit and tighten the retaining screws, one of which will hold the rear mounted oil deflector plate in position. Then adjust the chain tension by removing the allen screw that holds the adjuster and turning the lower eccentric shaft by means of an allen key inserted into its end. Adjustment is correct when there is from 5 - 7 mm (0.20 - 0.28 in) play measured at A in Fig. 1.10. Do not forget to re-lock the adjuster and re-check the setting. Fit the balancer retaining nut tab washer and nut, then tighten, bending the tab washer to secure the nut.

4 The starter chain can now be refitted after attaching the starter motor sprocket to the end of the adaptor on to which it is splined, and the second sprocket to the end of the balancer shaft, where it performs an idler function. Fit the woodruff key into the tapered end of the crankshaft and loop the chain around the large sprocket that contains the free-running clutch assembly behind the alternator rotor. With some care, all three sprockets can be entered on their respective shafts simultaneously, and pushed home. If desired, the alternator rotor can be fitted after the three sprockets have entered their shafts, without forming part of the free-running clutch assembly. When the rotor has seated correctly on the crankshaft, fit the centre bolt, flat washer and spring washer. The bolt should be torque tightened to 4 - 4.5 m.kg.

5 Before the starter motor can be fitted, it will be necessary to tap the drive adaptor forwards a little, to give sufficient clearance for the square end of the motor to be inserted and the motor itself to be lowered into its recessed housing. Retain the motor in position by the clamp and the four allen screws. Then tap the adaptor back into position on the drive shaft, without using any force.

6 The left-hand end cover can now be refitted, after inserting the locating dowels in the crankcase and fitting a new gasket. Before fitting, make sure the arm of the clutch operating

40.4b Note free-running clutch in rear of crankshaft sprocket

40.4c Make sure Woodruff key is in position, then ...

40.4d ... replace rotor on end of crankshaft

40.4e replace and torque tighten bolt to recommended setting

Chapter 1: Engine, clutch and gearbox

40.5 Refit starter motor in recess

40.6a Before fitting outer cover, check position of clutch operating arm

40.6b Operating arm works on quick thread principle. Grease well

40.6c Note how lower Allen screw retains neutral contact lead

mechanism is in the correct position. Note there is a clip for holding the neutral contact lead wire, through which one of the lower cover screws should pass. Tighten up the screws when the cover has located with the dowels and rejoin the neutral contact lead wire - in this instance a snap connector junction between the single white and blue wires.

41 Engine and gearbox reassembly: replacing the cylinder block

1 Fit the rubber strips into the channel of the cylinder block base and in the channel of the crankcase mouth, in the vicinity of the camshaft drive chain tunnel. Fit a new cylinder base gasket, dry. Pad the crankcase mouths with clean rag. Refit the pistons in their original positions oiling the gudgeon pins prior to insertion. Use new gudgeon pin circlips, NOT the originals, and make sure they have located with the piston boss grooves correctly. If they work loose whilst the engine is running, irreparable damage will be caused. The pistons must be fitted so that the arrows on each piston crown face towards the exhaust valves.

2 Space the piston rings so that their end gaps are not in line and preferably at 120° to each other. There is no need to fit piston ring clamps as there is a generous lead in chamfer to each cylinder bore.

3 Oil each cylinder bore and fit the cylinder block over the holding down studs. Lower it until it is just above the piston crowns, after turning the engine over so that both pistons are approximately at the same height. Some care will be necessary when threading the camshaft drive chain through the chain tunnel, manoeuvering it past the tensioner, which should be slackened off (if removed earlier, replace it before the block is fitted over the studs) and the idler sprocket fitted in the rear portion of the tunnel. Wire looped through each end of the chain will make this operation easier (see accompanying photograph) with a weight on the end of each wire to prevent the chain from sliding back and disappearing into the sump. The cylinder block can be rested on a tin placed edgeways between the centre studs whilst this operation is carried out (see photograph).

4 When the chain has been threaded through correctly and weighted, lower the cylinder block after removing the supporting tin. Feed the pistons and rings into the bores very carefully, taking care that none of the rings is displaced from its groove and trapped - piston rings are brittle and will snap very easily. When the rings have engaged correctly, lower the block until it seats correctly, after removing the rag padding from the

41.1a Fit rubber strips in cylinder base/crankcase joint

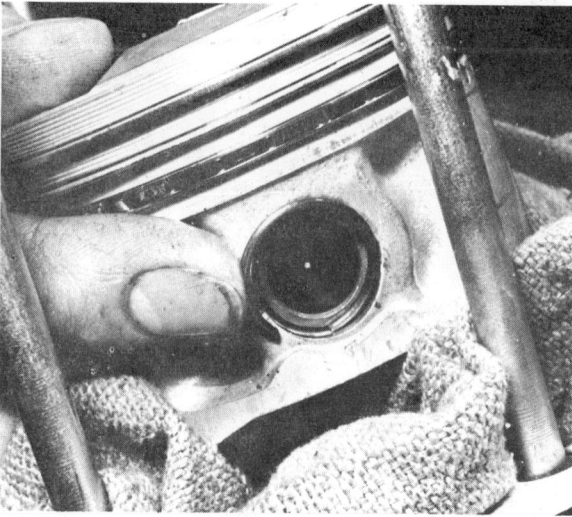
41.1b Use new circlips when refitting pistons

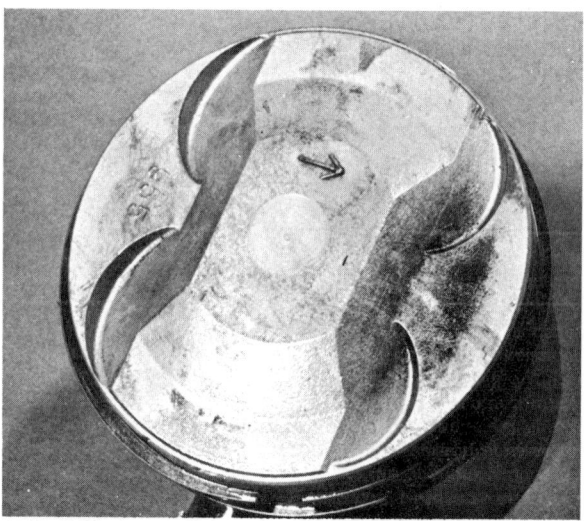
41.1c Arrows on piston crowns must face exhaust valves

41.3a If removed earlier, camshaft chain tensioner should be replaced in block

41.3b Thread chain through tunnel and weight ends to prevent slipping back. Note tin in centre, supporting block

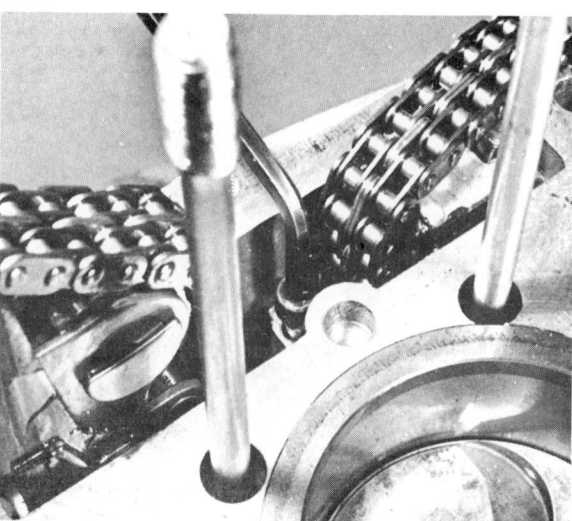
41.3c Do not forget Allen screw within camshaft chain tunnel

crankcase mouths. It is important that the camshaft chain tensioner within the tunnel is slackened off during this operation, as mentioned earlier, since it will otherwise prevent the block from seating.

5 When the block has seated correctly, replace and tighten the single allen screw within the camshaft chain tunnel. The camshaft chain tensioner can now be fully depressed and locked in this position with the dome nut at the front of the right-hand cylinder. Press down quite hard on the chain. Take precautions so that the chain does not slide back in the tunnel and disappear into the crankcase. It will prove very difficult to retrieve.

42 Engine and gearbox reassembly: replacing the cylinder head and timing the valves

1 Fit a new cylinder head gasket (dry), not omitting the additional metal insert that fits within the cutaway of the gasket, in the centre of the camshaft chain tunnel, and the dowels.

2 With one person holding the cylinder head above the holding down studs, have a second person feed the camshaft drive chain through the tunnel. This too is a somewhat tricky task, as the amount of room through which to feed the chain is very restricted. When the chain is through the tunnel and looped around the idler sprocket in the rearmost position in the tunnel, lower the head over the holding down studs until it seats correctly. Keep the wire attached to each end of the camshaft chain and the weights on the ends.

3 Align the camshaft marks so that they correspond (see Fig. 1.13) with their respective alignment marks on the end caps. There is a hexagon formed on each camshaft to permit them to be rotated by means of a spanner.

4 If refitted, remove the circular cover from the contact breaker assembly (right-hand crankcase cover) and rotate the engine clockwise until the T and F marks appear for the LEFT-HAND cylinder. Continue rotating clockwise until the following V mark aligns exactly with the timing pointer. NOTE that whilst the engine is rotated, it will be necessary to hold both ends of the camshaft drive chain so that one end does not disappear into the tunnel or that it becomes bunched and jams. When the marks align exactly, hold the camshaft drive chain loosely and by letting it loop free of the lower driving sprocket, position the ends so that they are mid-way along the top run in the cylinder head. Check that the chain has re-engaged with the drive sprocket correctly and that none of the timing marks is out of alignment. If they are, make the appropriate correction. Replace the guide strip over which the chain runs. It will press into the cylinder head.

5 The camshaft drive chain in now ready to be rejoined. Use only the correct joining link, which has pins with hollow ends that can be belled out. To secure the chain during the rivetting operation, when the wire and weights must be removed, jam the chain against each of the camshaft sprockets with slats of wood, as shown in the accompanying photograph. Again check that the alignment of the timing marks has not changed. Insert the joining link from the INSIDE of the cylinder head, not omitting the double side plates in the centre. Fit the end plate by driving it in position, whilst supporting the back of the joining link with a plate or block of metal, which will act as a small anvil. Then bell out the hollow ends of the pins with a slim centre punch, so that the side plate cannot work loose.

6 DO NOT use a spring link at this joint or attempt to re-rivet the chain without having the correct joining link. If the joint parts when the engine is running, extensive engine damage will result, quite apart from the probability of a road accident as the result of a locked engine. This cannot be overstressed.

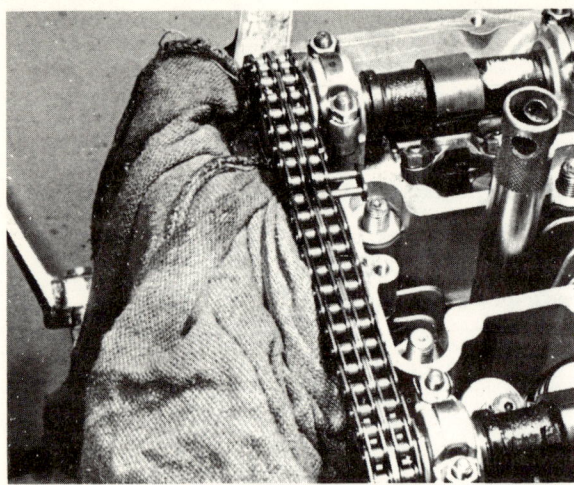

42.5a Pad tunnel with rag, to prevent parts dropping in. Note wooden wedges holding chain on sprockets

42.5b Link must pass through double inner plates

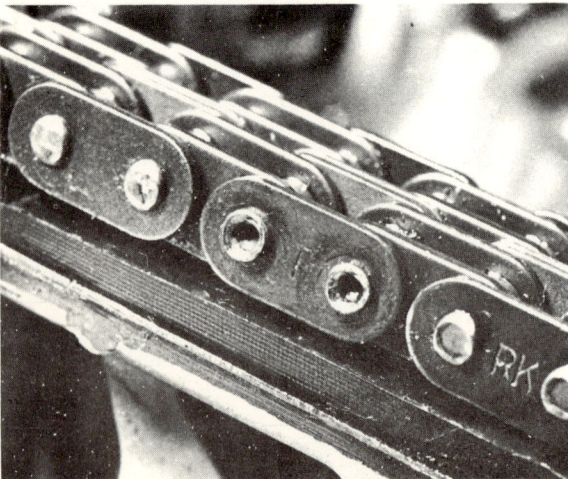

42.5c Special joining link must be used. Hollow ends of pin are splayed out, as shown, to reconnect chain

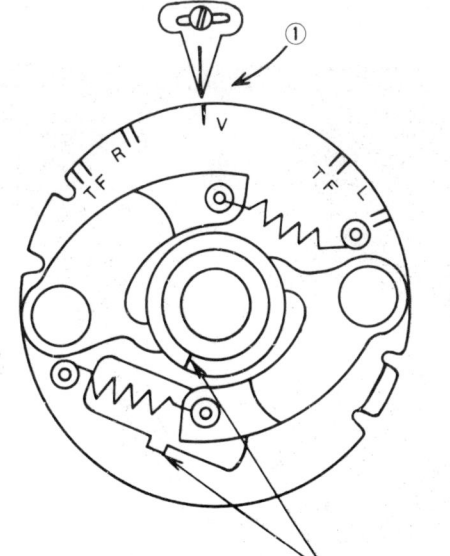

Fig. 1.12. Position of marks on auto-advance unit baseplate when timing valves

(viewed through contact breaker aperture)

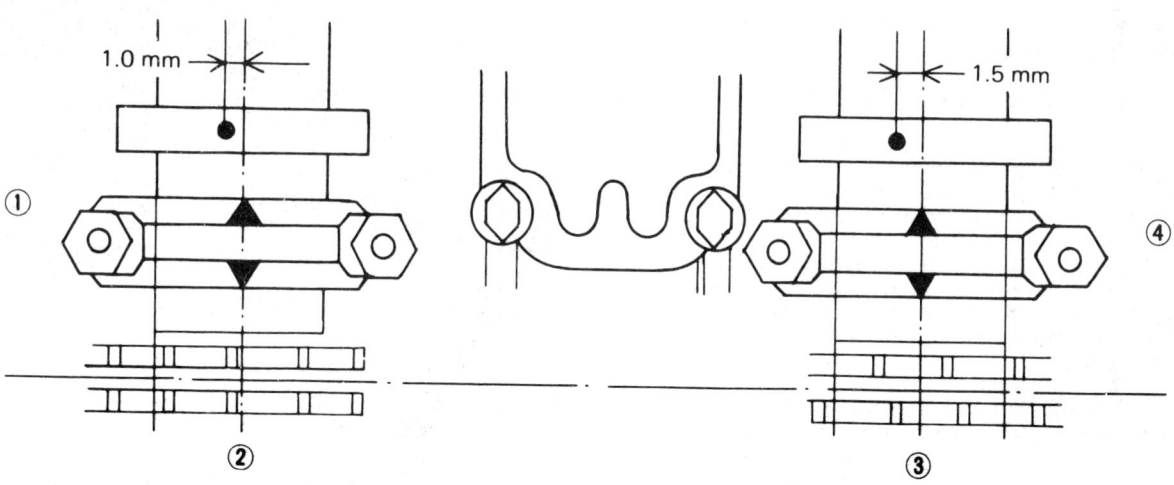

Fig. 1.13. Alignment of camshaft and end cap timing marks when timing valves

1 Carburettor side of engine unit
2 Inlet valve camshaft
3 Exhaust valve camshaft
4 Exhaust side of engine unit

Caution: If valve timing is one sprocket tooth out, the valve timing will be 21° out of phase. If the inlet valve camshaft is advanced by this amount, the piston will foul the valves on one cylinder and cause them to bend.

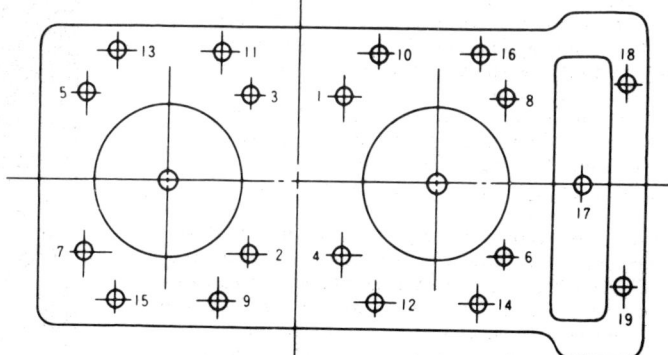

Fig. 1.14. Cylinder head and cambox bolt tightening sequence

7 Replace the cylinder head bolts and tighten them in the order shown in the accompanying illustration. Do not forget the allen screw close to the right-hand spark plug and the two knurled nuts with hexagonal centres that fit on the underside of the cylinder head, close to the camshaft chain tunnel. The bolts must be torque tightened, in the order given, to 3.0 - 3.5 m.kg.

8 Check the joint and rotate the engine by hand several times, by removing the large allen screw from the left-hand side of the contact breaker assembly and inserting an allen key into the orifice, AFTER the alignment of all the timing marks has been re-checked.

9 Using a new gasket, refit the cylinder head cover, after oiling the cams and the rocker arm skids on which they bear. It is assumed the valve clearances will have been reset whilst the engine was on the workbench, because this is possible with an engine of the DOHC type. If they require checking or resetting, refer to Section 28 of this Chapter. When all of the cylinder head cover bolts have been retightened, refit the external oil pipe at the rear of the cylinder block, using new washers at the banjo union joints. Also refit the oil pressure switch, making sure it is tight. The engine unit is now ready for lifting back into the frame.

43.1 Lift the engine unit in from the right-hand side

43 Replacing the engine unit

1 As was the case when the engine unit was removed, this is virtually a three person job, one to steady the frame and the other two to lift the heavy engine unit into position. Lift it in from the right-hand side. Most care will be needed when guiding the sump over the lower right-hand frame tube, as the clearance is minimal. Arrange the engine so that it is roughly in the correct position and insert the engine mounting bolts, whilst the engine is still supported. On no account force or drive them in, otherwise there is risk of the threads being irreparably damaged at the very least.

2 Tighten the engine mounting bolts, not forgetting these pass through the mounting plates. Remake the electrical connections, including those of the starter motor and oil pressure switch. The cover over the starter motor can now be replaced and secured. Reconnect the tachometer drive cable and the clutch cable, not forgetting the coil return spring of the latter. Check and adjust the clutch, if necessary, so that the handlebar lever has the necessary amount of free play (refer to Routine Maintenance Section). Replace the oil filter, fitting a new one if the original is due for a change. Tighten fully, with a spanner on the hexagon end.

3 Replace the final drive sprocket and torque tighten the retaining nut to 7.5 - 8.0 m.kg, bending back the tab washer afterwards. The sprocket can be prevented from turning by replacing the final drive chain, when it is positioned on the splines, the closed end of the spring link facing in the direction of travel of the chain, if it is of the detachable type. Application of the rear brake will prevent the rear wheel from turning whilst the retaining nut is tightened. Refit the final drive cover.

4 Replace the footrests, gear change lever and kickstart lever, the latter so that they are in the correct operating positions. Refit the exhaust system and make sure all the joints are leaktight. Use new gaskets at the cylinder head joint.

5 Refit the twin carburettors and their control cable(s), also the breather pipe to the cylinder head cover. Reconnect the carburettor intakes with the air cleaner and bolt the air cleaner box back into position. The battery can now be refitted and reconnected, after a final check that all the electrical connections have been remade correctly. Do not omit to reconnect the contact breaker lead wire. Do not forget to replace the small cylinder head cover duct.

43.2a Reconnect the electrical lead to the oil pressure switch and the starter motor cable

43.2b Then replace and tighten the finned starter motor cover

43.2c Replace the oil filter; make sure it is tight

43.3 Closed end of spring clip must face direction of travel

43.4 Gaskets at exhaust pipe joints ensure they are airtight

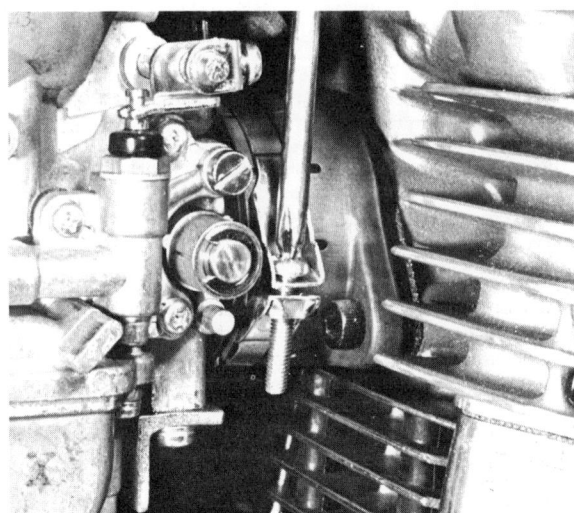
43.5a Make sure carburettor induction pipe clamps are tight

43.5b Reconnect throttle cable

43.5c Small duct must be refitted to cylinder head cover

Chapter 1: Engine, clutch and gearbox

43.7a Check security of drain plugs before

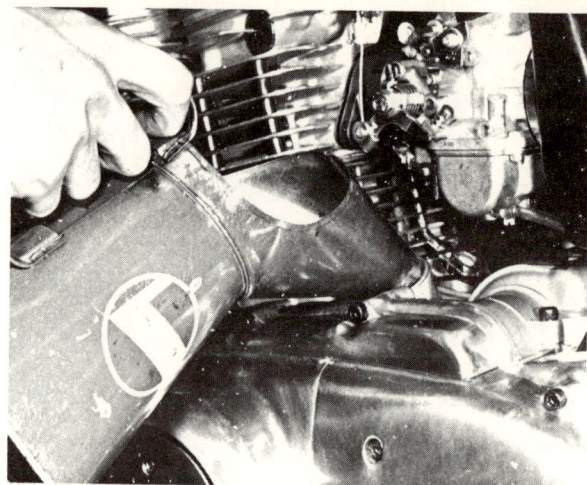

43.7b ... refilling engine unit with oil of recommended viscosity

6 Replace the fuel tank, not omitting to secure the rear end with the bolts and insulating rubbers. Reconnect the fuel pipes to the carburettors.
7 Refill the engine unit with the correct amount and grade of engine oil, after checking that both drain plugs have been replaced and tightened. 3,000 cc (5.28 pints) of SAE 20W/40 is the requirement under most normal operating temperatures. Check the level by means of the dipstick provided, which will be found immediately behind the alternator housing of the left-hand crankcase cover, close to the left-hand cylinder barrel. When checking the level, the dipstick should rest on the edge of the hole. Carry out a final check before starting the engine for the first time, to make sure that nothing remains disconnected or untightened.

44 Starting and running the rebuilt engine

1 Open the petrol tap, close the carburettor chokes and start the engine, using either the kickstart or the electric starter. Raise the chokes as soon as the engine will run evenly and keep it running at a low speed for a few minutes to allow oil pressure to build up and the oil to circulate. If the red oil pressure indicator lamp is not extinguished, stop the engine immediately and investigate the lack of oil pressure.
2 The engine may tend to smoke through the exhausts initially, due to the amount of oil used when assembling the various components. The excess of oil should gradually burn away as the engine settles down.
3 Check the exterior of the machine for oil leaks or blowing gaskets. Make sure that each gear engages correctly and that all the controls function effectively, particularly the brakes.

This is an essential last check before taking the machine on the road.

45 Taking the rebuilt machine on the road

1 Any rebuilt machine will need time to settle down, even if parts have been replaced in their original order. For this reason it is highly advisable to treat the machine gently for the first few miles to ensure oil has circulated throughout the lubrication system and that any new parts fitted have begun to bed down.
2 Even greater care is necessary if the engine has been rebored or if a new crankshaft has been fitted. In the case of a rebore, the engine will have to be run-in again, as if the machine were new. This means greater use of the gearbox and a restraining hand on the throttle until at least 500 miles have been covered. There is no point in keeping to any set speed limit; the main requirement is to keep a light loading on the engine and to gradually work up performance until the 500 mile mark is reached. These recommendations can be lessened to an extent when only a new crankshaft is fitted. Experience is the best guide since it is easy to tell when an engine is running freely.
3 If at any time a lubrication failure is suspected, stop the engine immediately, and investigate the cause. If an engine is run without oil, even for a short period, irreparable engine damage is inevitable.
4 When the engine has cooled down completely after the initial run, recheck the various settings, especially the valve clearances. During the run most of the engine components will have settled into their normal working locations.

46 Fault diagnosis - engine

Symptom	Cause	Remedy
Engine will not start	Defective spark plugs	Remove the plugs and lay on cylinder heads. Check whether spark occurs when ignition is switched on and engine rotated.
	Dirty or closed contact breaker points	Check condition of points and whether gaps are correct.
	Faulty or disconnected condenser	Check whether points arc when separated. Replace condenser if evidence of arcing.

Chapter 1: Engine, clutch and gearbox 75

Engine runs unevenly	Ignition and/or fuel system fault	Check each system independently, as though engine will not start.
	Blowing cylinder head gasket	Leak should be evident from oil leakage where gas escapes.
	Incorrect ignition timing	Check accuracy and if necessary reset.
Lack of power	Fault in fuel system or incorrect ignition timing	See above.
Heavy oil consumption	Cylinder bores in need of rebore	Check for bore wear, rebore and fit oversize pistons if required.
	Damaged oil seals	Check engine for oil leaks.
Excessive mechanical noise	Worn cylinder bores (piston slap)	Rebore and fit oversize pistons.
	Worn camshaft drive chain (rattle)	Adjust tensioner or renew chain
	Worn big end bearings (knock)	Fit replacement shells.
	Worn main bearings (rumble)	Fit new journal bearings and seals. Renew crankshaft assembly if journals are worn.
Engine overheats and fades	Lubrication failure	Stop engine immediately and check whether internal parts are receiving oil. Check oil level in crankcase.

47 Fault diagnosis - clutch

Symptom	Cause	Remedy
Engine speed increases as shown by tachometer but machine does not respond	Clutch slip	Check clutch adjustment for free play at handlebar lever. Check thickness of inserted plates.
Difficulty in engaging gears. Gear changes jerky and machine creeps forward when clutch is withdrawn. Difficulty in selecting neutral	Clutch drag	Check clutch adjustment for too much free play. Check clutch drums for indentations in slots and clutch plates for burrs on tongues. Dress with file if damage not too great.
Clutch operation stiff	Damaged, trapped or frayed control cable	Check cable and renew if necessary. Make sure the cable is lubricated and has no sharp bends.
	Bent push rod	Check for straightness.

48 Fault diagnosis - gearbox

Symptom	Cause	Remedy
Difficulty in engaging gears	Selector forks bent	Renew.
	Gear clusters not assembled correctly	Check gear cluster arrangement and position of thrust washers.
Machine jumps out of gear	Worn dogs on ends of gear pinions	Renew worn pinions.
	Stopper arm not seating correctly	Remove right-hand crankcase cover and check stopper arm action.
	Sticking detent plunger	Free in housing.
Gearchange lever does not return to original position	Broken return spring	Renew spring.
Kickstart does not return when engine is turned over or started	Broken or poorly tensioned return spring	Renew spring or re-tension.
Kickstart jams	Quick thread worm assembly worn	Remove crankcase cover and renew all worn parts.

Chapter 2 Fuel system and lubrication

Contents

General description ... 1	Air cleaner: removing, cleaning and replacing the element ... 10
Petrol tank: removal and replacement ... 2	Exhaust system ... 11
Petrol taps: removal and replacement ... 3	The lubrication system ... 12
Petrol feed pipes: examination ... 4	Crankcase sump and pressure release valve assembly:
Carburettors: removal ... 5	removal and replacement ... 13
Carburettors: dismantling, examination and reassembly ... 6	Oil pump: removal, examination and replacement ... 14
Carburettors: adjustment for tickover ... 7	Oil filter: removal and renewal ... 15
Carburettors: synchronisation ... 8	Fault diagnosis: fuel system and lubrication ... 16
Carburettor settings ... 9	

Specifications

Petrol tank:
Capacity ... 3.30 Imp gallons, 3.4 US gallons, 15 litres

Engine oil:
Capacity ... 5.28 Imp pints, 3.2 US guarts, 3.0 litres

Lubrication system ... Wet sump, pressure fed by trochoid-type oil pump. Replaceable filter element.

Carburettors:
Make ... Mikuni *
Type ... Constant velocity (BS 38)
Main jet ... 125
Needle jet ... 3.8
Pilot jet ... 45
Starter jet ... 50
Jet needle ... 302004
Float level ... 22.0 ± 2.5 mm
Air screw ... 1 3/8 turns out, ± ¼ (right-hand side)
1 turn out, ± ¼ (left-hand side)

Air cleaner:
Replacement element ... Dry, corrugated paper type

*Early models are fitted with Keihin CV32 carburettors.

1 General description

The fuel system cmprises a petrol tank from which petrol is fed by gravity, via twin petrol taps with a built-in filter, to the float chambers of the twin carburettors. A cold start lever is fitted to the left-hand carburettor, which operates a built-in cold start circuit when this lever is depressed. This provides the enriched mixture necessary for a cold start and can be released when the engine will accept full air under normal running conditions.

An opening and closing throttle cable arrangement or a single cable operates both carburettors, depending on the model, which are interconnected by a linkage system. A torsion spring system helps eliminate the heavy throttle action that is normally associated with this mode of operation. The carburettors are of the constant velocity type and share a large capacity air cleaner. Some early models have Keihin carburettors of somewhat similar design.

The lubrication system is wet sump, using a pair of trochoid-type oil pumps to deliver oil under pressure to the various engine components. One pump delivers oil to the crankshaft journals and double overhead camshafts, via an oil filter and a pressure release valve. The other pump collects the oil that has drained back into the crankcase sump, returning it to the main oil compartment, where it is recirculated. Predetermined oil levels ensure the clutch, gearbox components and primary transmission are

Chapter 2: Fuel system and lubrication

adequately lubricated from the engine oil content, which they share.

The oil pump drive has a take-off for the tachometer, providing visual evidence that the oil pump is functioning correctly at all times.

2 Petrol tank: removal and replacement

1 The petrol tank is of conventional design and sits astride the top frame tube. It is retained at the nose by two rubber buffers on the inside of the central channel, one on each side, which locate with channels formed in the vicinity of the steering head. At the rear it sits astride a rubber saddle over the frame tube and is retained by two bolts and washers that pass through rubber grommets inserted into a lip attached to the rearmost end of the tank. The bolts thread into inserts in the frame itself.
2 To remove the tank, turn off both petrol taps and detach the fuel pipe from each, which is retained by a wire clip. Remove the two bolts and washers from the lip at the rear of the tank, which will necessitate raising the seat, then raise the rear end of the tank and draw it backwards to disengage the rubber buffers from their locating channels. When they are free, the tank can be lifted clear of the machine.
3 If the tank contains petrol or petrol vapour, it will constitute a fire hazard. Make sure it is stored in a safe place, away from naked flames, until it is ready to be refitted to the machine.
4 It is always advisable to remove the petrol tank during an overhaul, even if the engine parts to be worked on are readily accessible. The tank is very easily scratched or dented and it is wise to obviate the possibility of any such risks.
5 When replacing the tank, make sure it seats correctly and does not trap any of the control cables, before refitting the two retaining bolts. It should slide back into position quite easily, if the rear end is raised initially.

3 Petrol taps: removal and replacement

1 Twin petrol taps of identical design are fitted to the rear underside of the tank, each connected to the respective float chamber of its neighbouring carburettor by a synthetic rubber feed pipe. Each tap contains a built-in filter and there is no necessity to remove the tap or drain the petrol tank if only the filter requires cleaning or attention.
2 To remove the filter screen for cleaning, turn off the tap and remove the small slotted head bolt with the fibre washer behind, from the front of the tap body. This will drain off the small petrol content from within the filter chamber itself. Then remove the three screw-slotted bolts from the rear of the tap body, to release the side plate and gasket. This will give access to the filter screen, which can be removed, cleaned and replaced.
3 Unless damaged or displaced, there is no necessity to renew the back plate sealing gasket - assuming, of course, that there has been no evidence of leakage in the past. When cleaning is complete, replace the side plate and tighten the three slotted head bolts evenly. No gasket cement is necessary at this joint. Finally, replace the drain bolt in the front of the tap, after first making sure the fibre sealing washer is in good condition.
4 If the tap lever itself tends to leak, it will be necessary to drain the tank of fuel, so that the lever and the seal behind can be removed. The lever assembly is retained by the metal plate that surrounds it, which is retained by two small crosshead screws. When these screws are removed, the lever assembly will pull out, exposing the seal. The seal should be renewed and the lever assembly replaced, not forgetting the wave washer that goes between the plate and the tap lever. This is necessary to retain pressure on the seal.

4 Petrol feed pipes: examination

1 The synthetic rubber pipes used for the connections between the carburettor float chambers and the petrol taps are of the thin walled type, and are secured by wire clips. Renewal is seldom required but they should be examined during an overhaul, to ensure there is no cracks or splits, especially in the area of the wire clips.
2 If renewal is necessary, fit an identical replacement. A transparent plastic pipe should not be used as a substitute, except in an emergency, as pipes of this latter type will eventually harden and take on a permanent shape, losing their original flexibility.

5 Carburettors: removal

1 Before removing the carburettors as a coupled-together pair, it is first necessary to disconnect them from the air cleaner and move the air cleaner assembly back enough to give sufficient clearance. The throttle cables must also be detached from the pulley attached to the right-hand instrument.

3.2 Remove plate from rear of tap for access to filter screen

3.4 Tap is retained to underside of tank by two crosshead screws

6.3 Dismantle each carburettor separately

6.4a Removal of float chamber bowl exposes twin float assembly

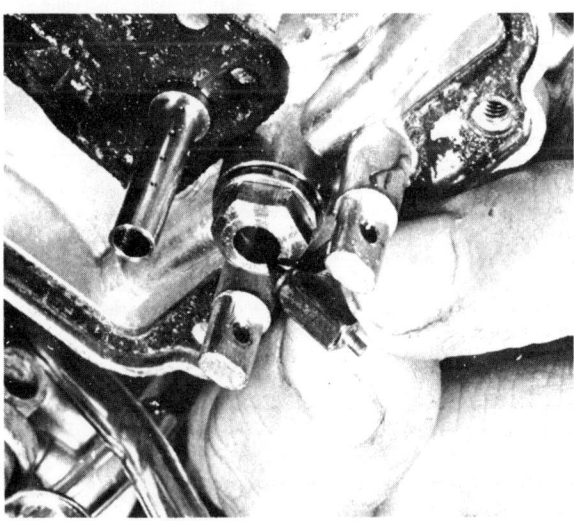
6.4b Tiny float needle is easily lost

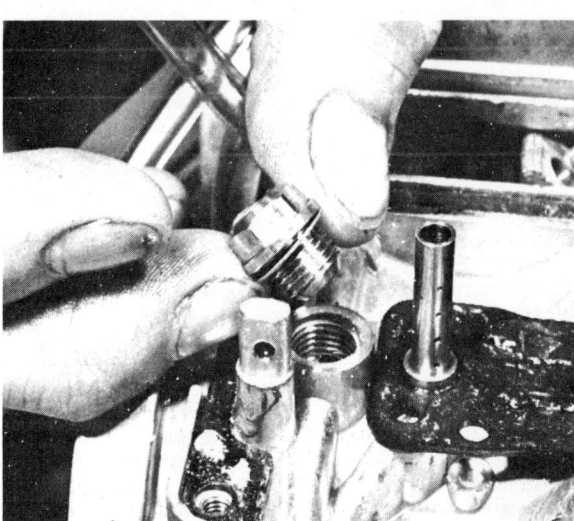
6.4c Float needle seat will unscrew from carburettor body

6.5a Push fit needle jet will pull out

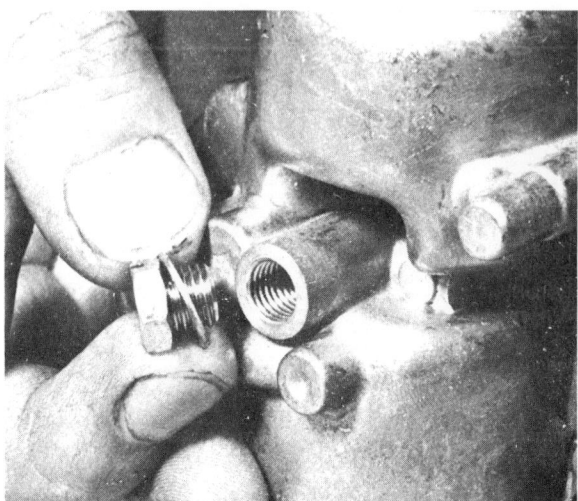
6.5b Remove plug from base of float bowl and ...

Chapter 2: Fuel system and lubrication 79

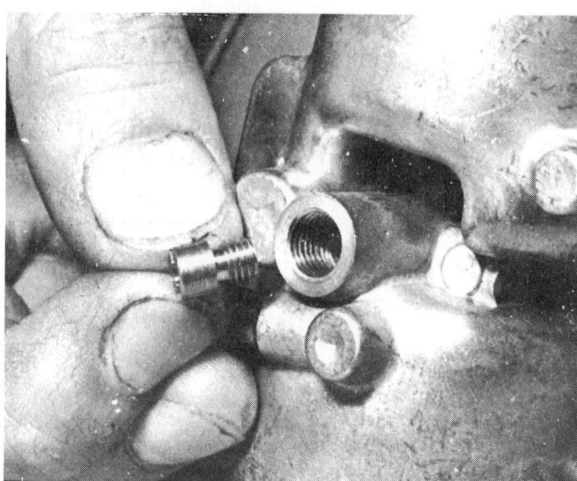
6.5c ... unscrew main jet

6.5d Pilot jet unscrews from within float bowl

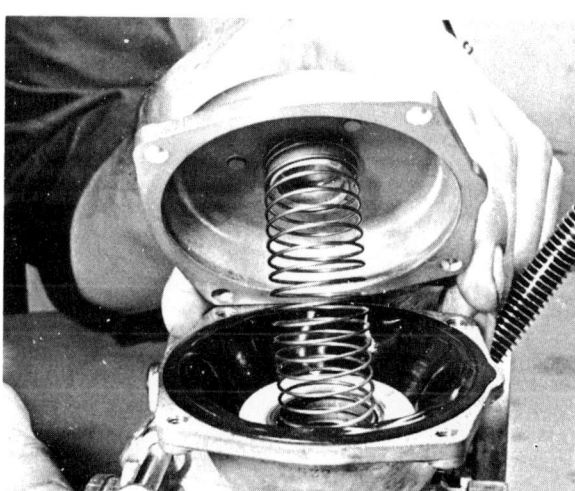
6.6a Removal of upper chamber cover exposes diaphragm, spring and piston

2 Commence by disconnecting and then removing the battery, which will be found under the nose of the dualseat. It is retained by a rubber strap. Disconnect at the battery terminals, noting the battery has a negative earth. Remove the top of the air cleaner box, which is retained by two wing nuts. Pull out the flat spring that holds the air cleaner in place and then withdraw the paper element itself. Remove the plastic side covers and loosen the air cleaner box by unscrewing the two retaining bolts, one on each side. An earthing strap is attached to one of them. Slacken the carburettor mouth hose clamps and pull off the air cleaner connections. Detach the throttle cables from the right-hand carburettor pulley. If the clamps around the carburettor induction stubs are now slackened off, the carburettors can be pulled out of these joints and eased out gently, towards the left-hand side of the machine. The reason for slackening off the air cleaner box is now obvious since it is necessary to move it backwards enough to give the minimal clearance required.

3 Before withdrawing the carburettor assembly completely, take note of how the drain pipes were tracked so that they can be replaced in the same order, during reassembly. Separation of the carburettors (if necessary) and any dismantling, should be accomplished on the workbench, where better access is available.

6 Carburettors: dismantling, examination and reassembly

1 Before complete dismantling of the carburettors can be commenced, the mounting block and pulley assembly should be removed. To dismantle the mounting block, slacken and remove the four crosshead screws that retain it to the carburettors. These screws have been treated with thread sealant and are tight. There is also an angled metal strip, secured by four crosshead screws, that holds the carburettors together in the vicinity of the float chambers. The carburettors are separated. Separation is unnecessary unless a complete stripdown is required.

2 The pulley assembly of models having a push-pull cable assembly is retained on the pivot shaft by a circlip and two washers. Note the positions and pull each component off the shaft separately.

3 It is suggested that each carburettor is dismantled and reassembled separately, to avoid mixing up the components. The carburettors are handed and therefore components should not be interchanged.

4 Invert one carburettor and remove the four (4) float chamber screws. Lift the float chamber from position. Slide the jet keeper across in its sloppy hole and lift it out. The two floats, which are interconnected, can be lifted away, after the hinge pin has been pushed out, giving access to the float needle and needle seating. Place the float needle in a safe place until reassembly commences. The float needle seat is a screw fit in the carburettor body.

5 Pull out the push fit needle jet. The main jet is in the float bowl, covered by a plug. It should be unscrewed with a screwdriver. The pilot jet will unscrew from the jet keeper plate followed by the slow running jet.

6 Remove the upper chamber screws and pull off the chamber cap and the helical spring. Pull the piston up and out of its slider. The piston needle can be removed by withdrawing the seating plate in the top of the piston. The needle will then drop out.

7 The starter plunger (choke) assembly is positioned in a tunnel to the side of the upper chamber. Unscrew the housing cap and pull the starter plunger assembly out. This consists of the plunger rod, spring and plunger piece.

8 It is not recommended that the 'butterfly' throttle valve assembly be removed as these components are not prone to wear. If wear occurs on the operating pivot a new carburettor will be required as air will find its way along the pivot bearings resulting in a weak mixture.

9 Check the condition of the floats. If they are damaged in any way, they should be renewed. The float needle and needle seating will wear after lengthy service and should be inspected carefully.

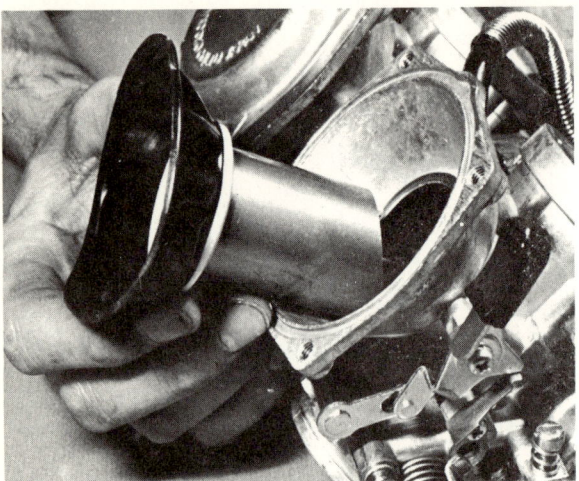
6.6b Piston and diaphragm will pull out

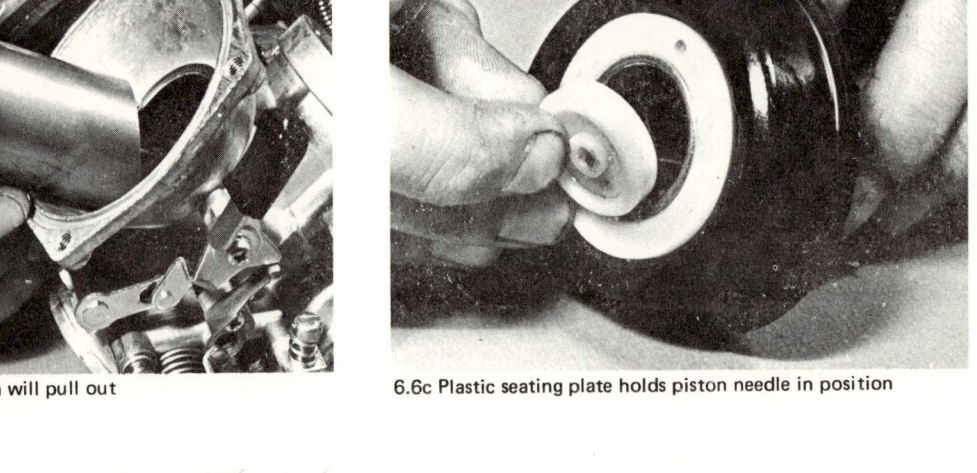
6.6c Plastic seating plate holds piston needle in position

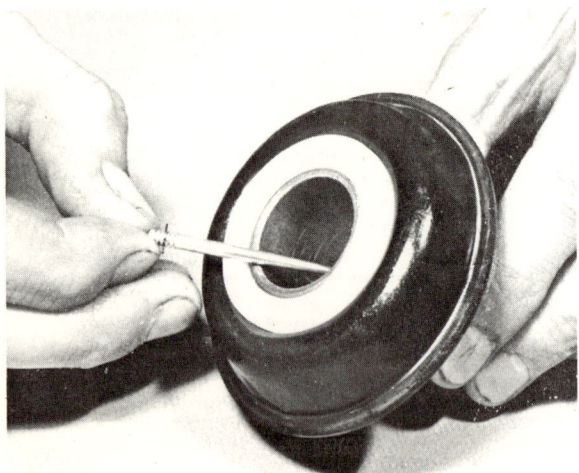
6.6d Needle and clip will lift out of piston

6.8 Butterfly assemblies should not require attention

Wear usually takes the form of a ridge or groove, which will cause the float needle to seat imperfectly. Always renew the seating and needle as a pair. An imperfection in one component will soon produce similar wear in the other.

10 After considerable service the piston needle and the needle jet in which it slides will wear, resulting in an increase in petrol consumption. Wear is caused by the passage of petrol and the two components rubbing together. It is advisable to renew the jet periodically in conjunction with the piston needle.

11 Before the carburettors are reassembled, using the reversed dismantling procedure, each should be cleaned out thoroughly using compressed air. Avoid using a piece of rag since there is always risk of particles of lint obstructing the internal passageways or the jet orifices.

12 Never use a piece of wire or any pointed metal object to clear a blocked jet. It is only too easy to enlarge the jet under these circumstances and increase the rate of petrol consumption. If compressed air is not available, a blast of air from a tyre pump will usually suffice.

13 Do not use excessive force when reassembling a carburettor because it is easy to shear a jet or some of the smaller screws. Furthermore, the carburettors are cast in a zinc-based alloy which itself does not have a high tensile strength. Take particular care when replacing the throttle valves to ensure the needles align with the jet seats.

14 Avoid overtightening the screws which retain the carburettors to the mounting plate. Overtightening will cause the flanges to bow, giving rise to mysterious air leaks and a permanently weak mixture. If the flange is bowed, it can be rubbed down until it is flat once again using a rotary motion and a sheet of emery cloth wrapped around a sheet of glass. Make sure no particles of emery grit enter the carburettors and that the 'O' ring in the centre of each flange is replaced when the grinding operation is complete.

15 Do NOT remove either the throttle stop screw or the pilot jet screw without first making note of their exact positions. Failure to observe this precaution will make it necessary to resynchronise both carburettors on reassembly.

7 Carburettors: adjustment for tickover

1 Before adjusting the carburettors, a check should be made to ensure that the following settings are correct: contact breaker

Fig. 2.1. Carburettor (Keihin type)

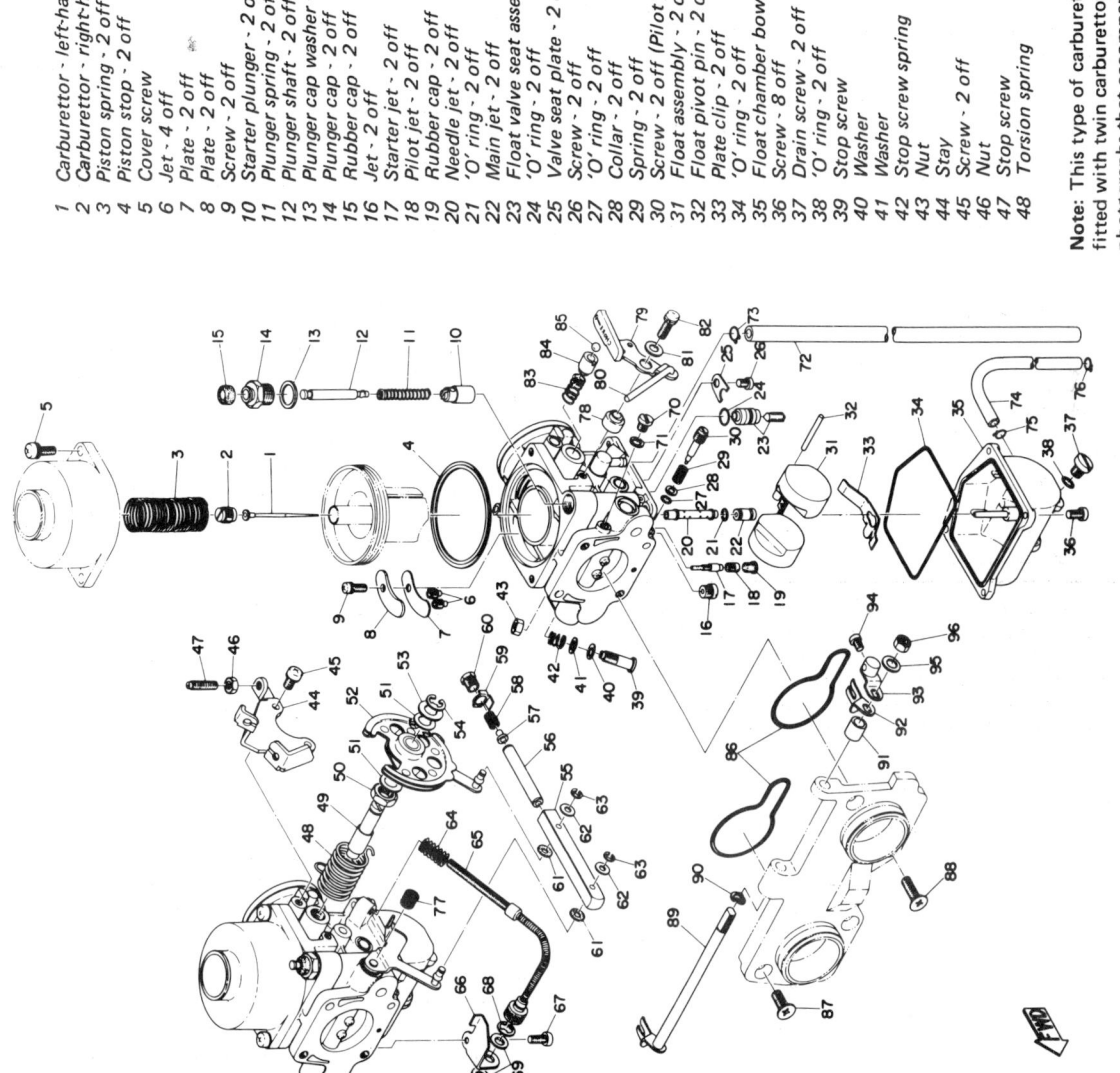

#	Part	#	Part
1	Carburettor - left-hand	49	Shaft link
2	Carburettor - right-hand	50	Nut
3	Piston spring - 2 off	51	Washer - 2 off
4	Piston stop - 2 off	52	Throttle lever
5	Cover screw	53	Washer
6	Jet - 4 off	54	'E' clip
7	Plate - 2 off	55	Adjuster holder
8	Plate - 2 off	56	Adjusting rod
9	Screw - 2 off	57	Spring seat
10	Starter plunger - 2 off	58	Spring
11	Plunger spring - 2 off	59	Lock washer
12	Plunger shaft - 2 off	60	Retaining bolt
13	Plunger cap washer - 2 off	61	Seal - 2 off
14	Plunger cap - 2 off	62	Washer - 2 off
15	Rubber cap - 2 off	63	Bar clip - 2 off
16	Jet - 2 off	64	Spring
17	Starter jet - 2 off	65	Stop screw
18	Pilot jet - 2 off	66	Stay plate
19	Rubber cap - 2 off	67	Screw
20	Needle jet - 2 off	68	'E' clip
21	'O' ring - 2 off	69	Washer - 2 off
22	Main jet - 2 off	70	Plug screw - 2 off (for vacuum gauge)
23	Float valve seat assembly - 2 off	71	Washer - 2 off
24	'O' ring - 2 off	72	Drain pipe - 2 off
25	Valve seat plate - 2 off	73	Pipe clip - 2 off
26	Screw - 8 off	74	Drain pipe (float chamber) - 2 off
27	'O' ring - 2 off	75	Pipe clip
28	Collar - 2 off	76	Pipe clip
29	Spring - 2 off (Pilot jet adjuster)	77	Spring
30	Screw - 2 off (Pilot jet adjuster)	78	Collar
31	Float assembly - 2 off	79	Starter (choke) lever
32	Float pivot pin - 2 off	80	Rod
33	Plate clip - 2 off	81	Washer
34	'O' ring - 2 off	82	Screw
35	Float chamber bowl - left-hand	83	Spring
36	Screw - 8 off	84	Spring seat
37	Drain screw - 2 off	85	Ball bearing
38	'O' ring - 2 off	86	'O' ring
39	Stop screw	87	Screw
40	Washer	88	Shaft link
41	Washer	89	Wave washer
42	Stop screw spring	90	Collar
43	Nut	91	Lever
44	Stay	92	Lever
45	Screw - 2 off	93	Screw
46	Nut	94	Lock washer
47	Stop screw	95	Nut
48	Torsion spring	96	

Note: This type of carburettor is fitted to the earlier models. The later XS500C models are fitted with twin carburettors of Mikuni manufacture, the component parts of which are shown in the photographs that accompany the text of this Chapter.

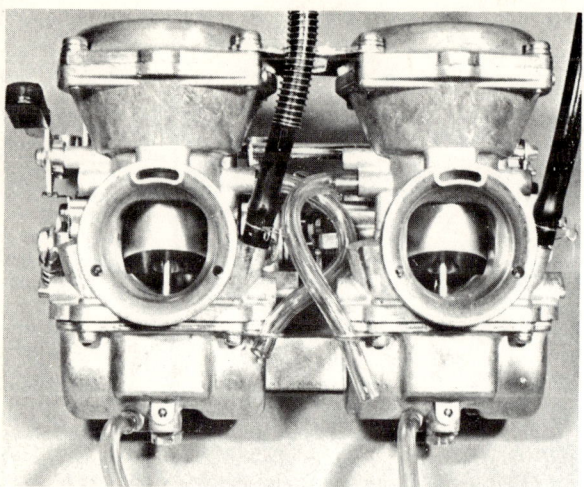

8.1 When synchronised correctly, both carburettors must open an identical amount

gap, ignition timing, valve clearance, spark plug gaps, crankcase oil level. It is also important that the engine is at normal running temperature. From cold the engine will take between 5 - 10 minutes to warm up satisfactorily.
2 Check that when the throttle is fully opened both 'butterfly' valves are in their fully open position (ie; parallel to the carburettor bore). This check can best be done when the carburettors are off the machine. A stop screw on the pulley bracket gives adjustment to the stop position.
3 Start the engine and bring it up to normal running temperature. Unscrew the throttle stop screw, which is synchronised to both carburettors and is mounted on a bracket on the right-hand carburettor, until the engine turns over at the slowest smooth speed obtainable. Turn each pilot screw an equal amount each until the engine, reaches the highest rpm obtainable. Adjust the engine speed, using the throttle screw, until the engine is turning over at 1.100 - 1.300 as shown by tachometer.
4 Alter the position of the pilot screws an equal amount to check whether the engine speed rises. If this is the case repeat the procedure in the previous paragraph.
5 With the idling speed (tickover) correct, screw each pilot screw in 1/16 turn.

8 Carburettors: synchronisation

1 For the best possible performance it is imperative that the carburettors are working in perfect harmony with each other. At any given throttle opening if the carburettors are not synchronised, not only will one cylinder be doing less work but it will also in effect have to be 'carried' by the other cylinder. This effect will reduce the performance considerably.
2 It is essential to use a vacuum guage set consisting of two separate dial guages, one of each being connected to each carburettor by means of a special adaptor tube. The adaptor pipe screws into the outside edge of each carburettor, the orifice of which is normally blocked by a crosshead screw. Most owners are unlikely to possess the necessary vacuum guage set, which is somewhat expensive and is normally held by Yamaha service agents who will carry out the synchronising operation for a nominal sum.
3 If the vacuum guage set is available, the guage reading at tick-over (1.100 - 1.200) should be 15 - 20 cm Hg with a variation of less than 3 cm Hg. If the variation is greater than 3 cm Hg the fuel tank must be removed and the balancer adjusting screw turned. Adjustment for the reading 15- 20 cm Hg can be made on the pilot air screw.

9 Carburettor settings

1 Some of the carburettor settings, such as the sizes of the needle jets, main jets and needle positions, etc are predetermined by the manufacturer. Under normal circumstances it is unlikely that these settings will require modification, even though there is provision made. If a change appears necessary, it can often be attributed to a developing engine fault.
2 Always err slightly on the side of a rich mixture, since a weak mixture will cause the engine to overheat. Reference to Chapter 3 will show how the condition of the spark plugs can be interpreted with some experience as a reliable guide to carburettor mixture strength. Flat spots in the carburation can usually be traced to a defective timing advancer. If the advancer action is suspect, it can be detected by checking the ignition timing with a stroboscope.

10 Air cleaner: removing, cleaning and replacing the element

1 As mentioned previously, the air cleaner assembly takes the form of a metal box, immediately in front of the battery container, access to which is available after raising the seat. The element, which is of the paper type, can be raised from position after the top of the air cleaner box is lifted from position. It is retained by two wing nuts.
2 The element is retained in position by a flat spring, or in the case of earlier models, by a shaped wire clip. Remove the spring or clip and lift the complete element assembly from position.
3 Being of the corrugated paper type, the element must not be cleaned with any solvent. It should be blown clean, using an air line applied to the inside. Loose particles of grit or dust clinging to the exterior can be removed with a soft brush. Care is necessary when handling the element as it will tear very readily, necessitating renewal.
4 If the paper element is torn, damp or oily, it should be renewed without question. Never run the machine without the element in position or with the air cleaner box disconnected from the carburettors. The carburettors are specially jetted to compensate for the attachment of the air cleaner and the mixture will be permanently weakened if this condition is changed in any way. It follows that any cracks or splits in the air cleaner box, or in the interconnections must be remedied, immediately they are noticed.
5 The air cleaner must be serviced every 2000 miles (3,200 kilometres) or monthly, whichever is soonest.
6 When replacing the air cleaner element, make sure the element is retained in position by the spring or clip and that the two wing nuts which hold the top of the air cleaner box are tightened.

11 Exhaust system

1 Unlike a two-stroke, the exhaust system does not require such frequent attention because the exhaust gases are usually of a less oily nature.
2 Do not run the machine with the exhaust baffles removed, or with a quite different type of silencer fitted. The standard production silencers have been designed to give the best possible performance, whilst subduing the exhaust note to an acceptable level. Although a modified exhaust system or one without baffles, may give the illusion of greater speed as a result of the changed exhaust note, the chances are that performance will have suffered accordingly.

12 The lubrication system

1 A particularly good, reliable lubrication system is required in an engine of the type fitted to the Yamaha 500 Twins, in which shell bearings are used in the crankshaft and big-end assemblies. A

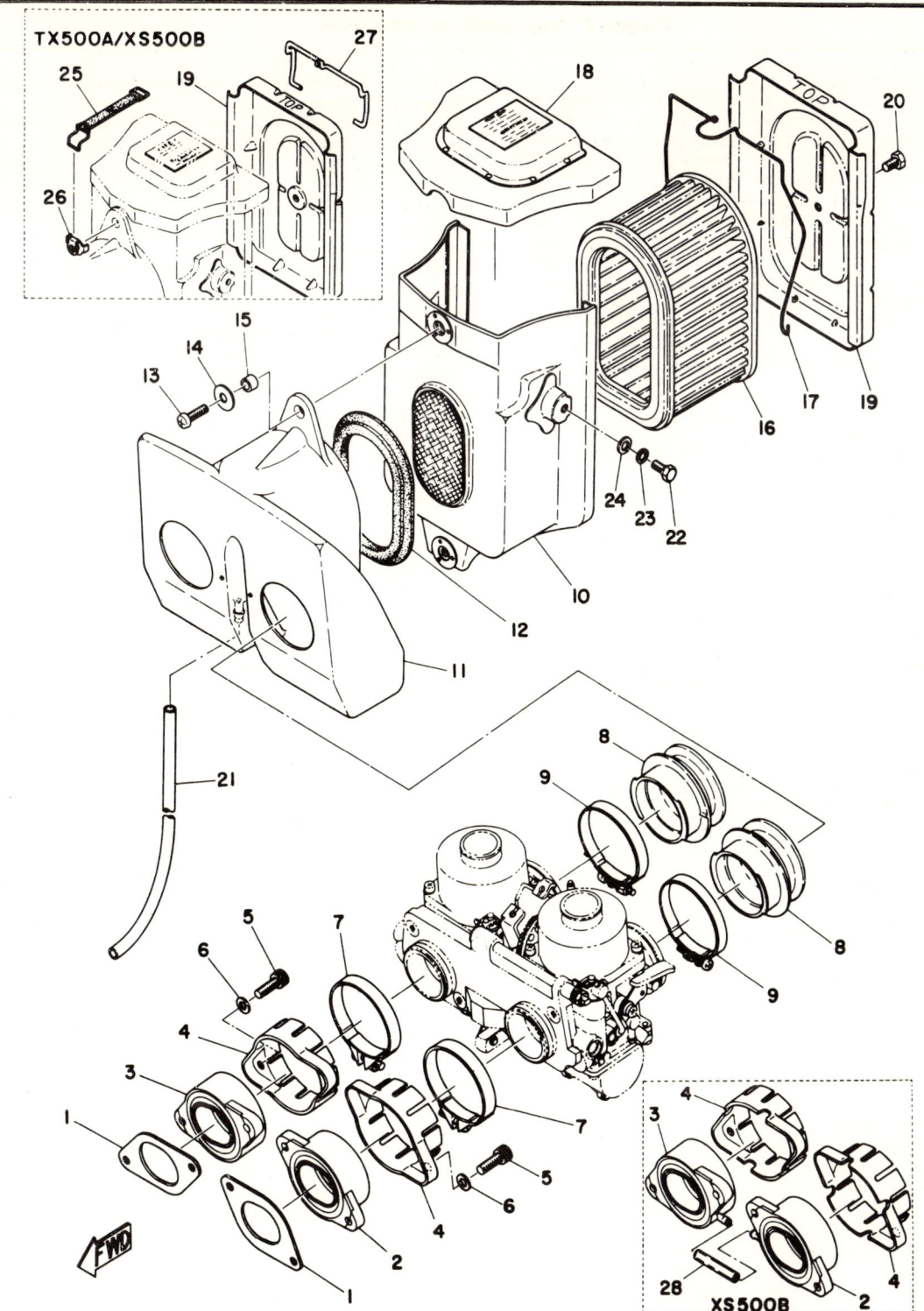

Fig. 2.2. Air cleaner assembly

1 Induction manifold gasket - 2 off
2 Carburettor stub joint - left-hand
3 Carburettor stub joint - right-hand
4 Joint cover - 2 off
5 Allen screw - 4 off
6 Spring washer - 4 off
7 Air cleaner clip - 2 off
8 Air cleaner joint - 2 off
9 Hose clamp - 2 off
10 Air cleaner inner case
11 Air cleaner
12 Air cleaner outer case
13 Crosshead screw - 2 off
14 Plain washer - 2 off
15 Collar - 2 off
16 Air cleaner element
17 Element retaining spring
18 Air cleaner top cover
19 Outer end cover
20 Bolt
21 Hose
22 Bolt - 2 off
23 Spring washer - 2 off
24 Spring washer - 2 off
25 Element holder
26 Stay
27 Element retaining spring (alternative type)
28 Carburettor balance pipe

pressurised lubrication system to feed bearings of this type is a vital necessity and it is for this reason that twin oil pumps of the trochoid type have been fitted - one to deliver oil under pressure and the other to return the oil that has drained into the crankcase sump to the main oil compartment, for recirculation. The clutch, primary transmission and gearbox use the same lubricant, through a system of oil levels that are predetermined.

2 To protect the system from any impurities that may find their way into the oil stream, a filter is included in the delivery side of the main oil pump. Following car practice, this has a replaceable filter element, that must be renewed at recommended mileages, a simple task. There is also a built-in gauze strainer attached to the input of the pump and a circular magnet retained within a recess in the sump itself, to attract any ferrous metal particles that may otherwise find their way into either pump and cause damage to the rotors.

13 Crankcase sump and oil pressure release valve assembly: removal and replacement

1 It is possible to remove the crankcase sump and the oil pressure release valve assembly from the underside of the machine, without lifting the engine unit out of the frame, provided the oil content is first drained off. Two drain plugs are fitted, both of which must be removed when draining the oil. One drains the sump itself and the other the oil compartment. The engine oil content is approximately 3 litres, making it necessary to use a large capacity catch tray. If the engine is run prior to the removal of both drain plugs, the warmth imparted to the oil will make it drain off much more easily.

2 The sump is retained to the lower crankcase half by eleven allen screws. Two of these bolts pass through locking plates that locate engine mounting bolts. Lift off the sump noting the circular magnet within a recess inside the sump casting. This should be cleaned of all ferrous metal particles before the sump casting is replaced.

3 The pressure release valve and strainer assembly can be detached after removing an additional four allen screws. Pull out the pressure release plunger and spring, after removing the retainer plug. It is necessary to remove the pressure release valve and strainer assembly if the sump gasket has to be renewed, as part of it passes underneath. It is advisable to renew this gasket when the sump is replaced, to avoid oil leaks, unless the original is still in perfect condition.

4 Clean the strainer gauze and also the pressure release plunger and spring. Check that the plunger slides quite freely in its housing. The by-pass plug and spring should be checked at the same time.

14.1 The dismantalled oil pump assembly

This assembly will be found in a vertical position, within the main release valve casting.

5 When replacing the sump, make sure the jointing surfaces are perfectly clean and use a light smearing of gasket cement to maintain an oiltight joint. Tighten the eleven allen screws evenly, in a diagonal sequence, to make sure the sump casting is not distorted during tightening down.

14 Oil pump: removal, examination and replacement

1 The oil pump assembly can be removed only after the crankcase assembly has been dismantled and the upper and lower crankcase halves separated. It is retained to the lower crankcase half, to the rear of the gear cluster, by four Allen screws. When the four screws are detached, the assembly can be lifted upwards, out of its housing, complete with drive shaft and pinion. It follows that removal of the oil pump can take place only after the engine unit has been removed from the frame.

2 When the oil pump assembly is raised upwards, it is possible that the lower pump components will remain in the lower crankcase and have to be lifted out. There is no possibility of inadvertently interchanging the parts of either pump, as they are of differing heights. Drive to the inner rotors is imparted by means of dowel pins that pass through the main drive shaft.

3 Examination of the rotors will show whether they are fit for further service, as any damage to their polished surfaces will be obvious. Score marks, caused by metallic particles being drawn into the pump will necessitate renewal of the complete rotor assembly, inner and outer. The assembly must always be renewed as a matched pair of components, to ensure the working clearances remain within the acceptable tolerances.

4 It is also important to check that the dowel pins that transmit the drive are not worn or damaged or that there is any backlash in the drive, If necessary, renew both the drive shaft and the pins. The drive pinion on the end of the drive shaft should also be examined. If damaged, the whole shaft will have to be renewed, since the pinion is integral with it. There is a thrust washer above and below this pinion.

5 When reassembling, oil the rotors and check that the pump spindle revolves quite freely, before reassembling the crankcase halves. Because the tachometer drive is taken from the cross shaft that drives the oil pump, failure of the drive will be immediately obvious.

15 Oil filter: removal and renewal

1 The oil filter element fitted to the left-hand side of the machine, immediately behind the final drive cover, is of the disposable type. Its purpose is to filter out any impurities in the oil stream that would otherwise find their way into the bearings or other working parts of the engine, causing damage and premature failure of the parts concerned. In consequence, the oil filter has to be renewed at set mileage readings, a simple but none the less essential operation.

2 The oil filter should be changed at the same time as an engine oil change, in accordance with the routine maintenance schedule prescribed by the manufacturer. In practice, this means the oil filter should be renewed during *every other* oil change, following the completion of the full initial running-in period, ie every 2,000 miles after the first 2,000 miles has been recorded.

3 To renew the oil filter, first drain off all the old engine oil, preferably whilst the engine is still warm. Both drain plugs must be removed from the underside of the engine, so that the oil compartment and the crankcase sump have their oil content released. The catch tray placed beneath the sump should have a capacity in excess of 3 litres, which is the approximate oil capacity of the engine unit.

4 Remove the small cover over the final drive sprocket. This is found on the left-hand side of the machine and is retained by five Allen screws. Access is then available to the circular oil filter

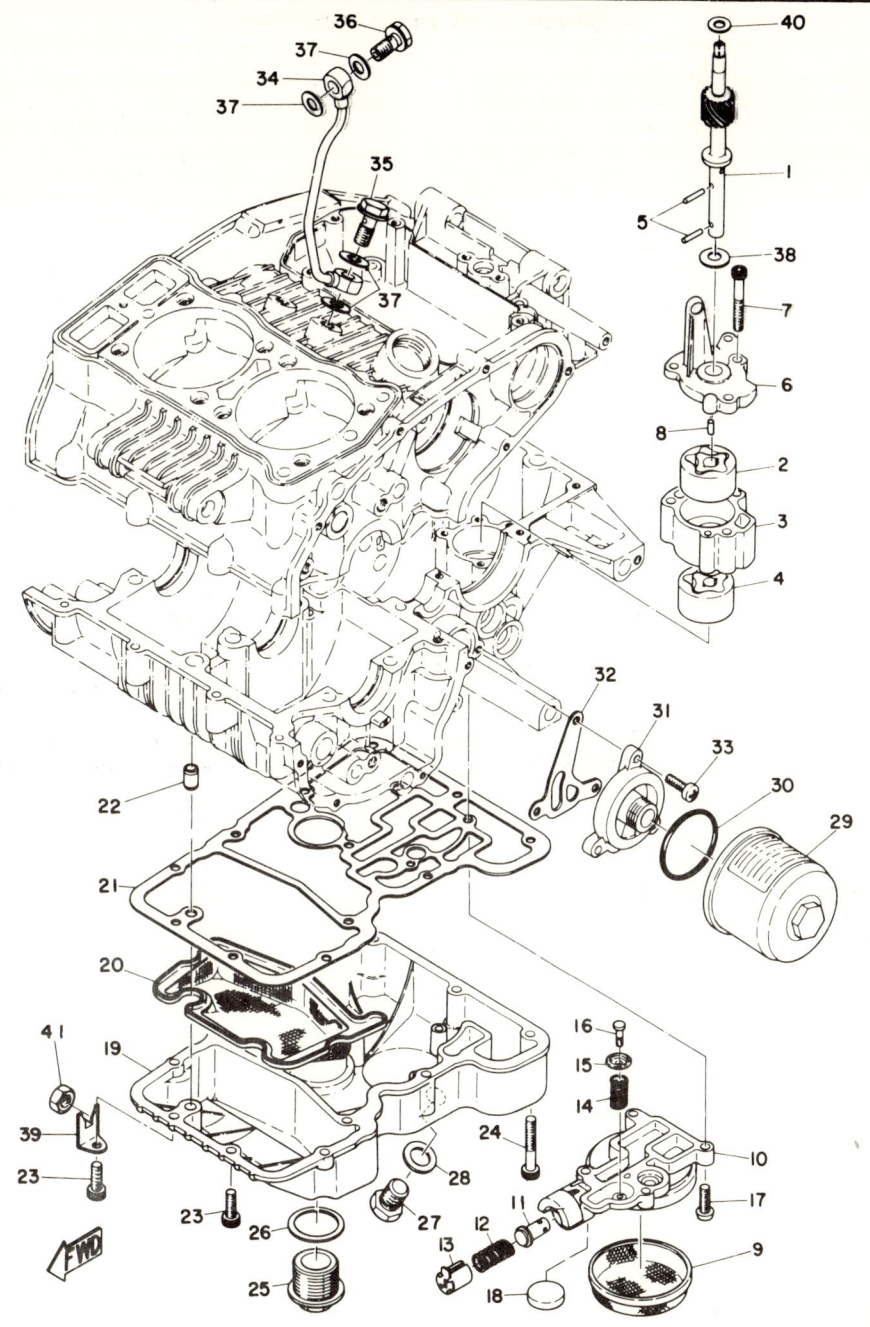

Fig. 2.3. Oil pump, strainer and pressure release assembly

1 Oil pump shaft
2 Upper rotor
3 Rotor housing
4 Lower rotor
5 Dowel pin - 2 off
6 Pump cover
7 Allen screw - 3 off
8 Dowel pin - 4 off
9 Strainer
10 Strainer housing
11 Pressure release plunger
12 Compression spring
13 Release valve retainer
14 Bypass spring
15 Bypass plug
16 Pin
17 Allen screw - 4 off
18 Magnet
19 Sump cover
20 Secondary strainer
21 Sump cover gasket
22 Dowel pin
23 Allen screw - 4 off
24 Allen screw - 7 off
25 Drain plug (sump)
26 Drain plug gasket
27 Drain plug (oil compartment)
28 Drain plug gasket
29 Oil filter unit
30 'O' ring
31 Oil filter adaptor plate
32 Adaptor plate gasket
33 Crosshead screw - 3 off
34 Oil delivery pipe
35 Union bolt
36 Union bolt
37 Washer - 4 off
38 Washer
39 Retaining plate - 2 off
40 Washer
41 Nut - 2 off

element found immediately below the final drive sprocket. It has a hexagon formed on the end and can be unscrewed in an anti-clockwise direction, using a ring spanner.

5   When fitting the replacement filter, note that there is an 'O' ring that forms the oil tight joint. Always fit a new 'O' ring and give it a light coating of grease, prior to installation. Tighten, but do not overtighten, the filter element, and replace the final drive cover. After the first run, check the filter element for oil leaks.

16 Fault diagnosis

Symptom	Cause	Remedy
Engine gradually fades and stops	Fuel starvation	Check vent hole in filler cap. Sediment in filter bowl or float chamber. Dismantle and clean.
Engine runs badly. Black smoke from exhausts	Carburettor(s) flooding	Dismantle and clean carburettor(s). Check for punctured float or sticking float needle.
Engine lacks response and overheats	Weak mixture Air cleaner disconnected or hose split Modified silencer has upset carburation	Check for partial block in carburettors. Reconnect or renew hose. Replace with original design.
Oil pressure warning light comes on	Lubrication system failure	Stop engine immediately. Trace and rectify fault before re-starting.
Engine gets noisy	Failure to change engine oil when recommended	Drain off old oil and refit with new oil of correct grade. Renew oil filter element.

Chapter 3 Ignition system

Contents

General description ... 1	Ignition switch ... 7
Alternator: checking the output ... 2	Ignition timing: checking and setting ... 8
Contact breakers: adjustment ... 3	Automatic ignition advance unit: examination ... 9
Contact breaker points: removal, renovation and replacement ... 4	Timing mark pointer ... 10
Condenser: location and testing ... 5	Spark plugs: checking and resetting the gap ... 11
Ignition coil: location and testing ... 6	Fault diagnosis: ignition system ... 12

Specifications

Alternator:
Make ... Hitachi
Type ... LD115 - 04
Output ... 14.5 volts, 13 amps

Regulator unit:
Make ... Hitachi
Type ... TR1Z-17 encapsulated solid state

Rectifier:
Make ... Hitachi
Type ... SB6B-15

Ignition system:
Type ... Coil, powered by battery
Ignition coil ... Hitachi, type CM11-50B
Ignition timing ... 5° BTDC static (fully retarded), 41° automatic timing unit fully advanced
Contact breaker points gap ... 0.30 - 0.45 mm (0.012 - 0.018 in)
Ignition advance commences ... 2,100 rpm
Ignition fully advanced ... 3,700 rpm

Spark plugs:
Make ... NGK
Type ... D8ES
Gap ... 0.6 - 0.7 mm (0.024 - 0.028 in)

1 General description

1 The spark necessary to ignite the petrol/air mixture in the combustion chambers is derived from an alternator attached to the left-hand end of the crankshaft and a separate ignition coil(s). A twin contact breaker assembly, one set of points for each cylinder, determines the exact moment at which the spark will occur, in the cylinder that is due to fire. As the points separate, the low tension circuit is interrupted and a high tension voltage is developed across the points of the spark plug. This jumps the air gap and ignites the mixture under compression.

2 When the engine is running, the surplus current generated by the alternator is used to provide a regulated 12 volt supply for charging the battery, after it has been converted to direct current by a rectifier. If the battery is fully charged and the demand from the ignition and lighting circuits is low, the excess current is used to reduce the output from the alternator by the appropriate amount.

2 Alternator: checking the output

1 The usual sign of reduced output from the alternator or possibly even complete failure is a battery that is in a permanently low state of charge. Before investigating the alternator, verify that the battery itself is in good order and is capable of holding its charge. Refer to Section 3 of Chapter 6 for further information in this respect. Another factor that can affect alternator output is

88   Chapter 3: Ignition system

3.3a Check contact breaker gaps with a feeler gauge

3.3b Screwdriver slot is provided to aid adjustment

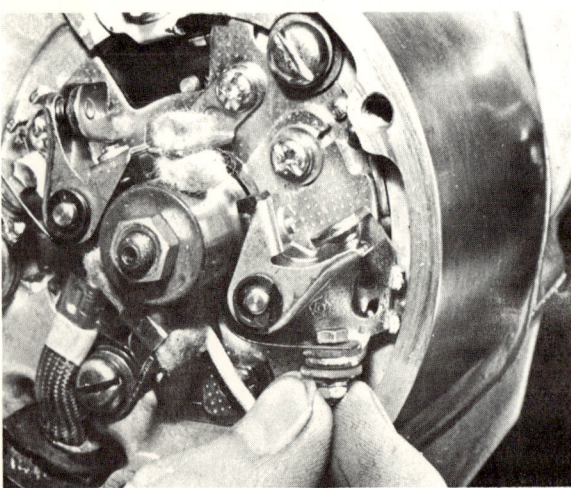

4.2 Remove screw and nut from terminal post. Note insulating washers

the use of bulbs of higher rating than standard, or an increase in the lighting load by the addition of spotlamps.

2 Without sophisticated electrical test equipment and instruction in its use, only relatively simple tests can be carried out by the average rider. None the less, they should indicate whether or not the alternator is at fault so that the machine can be taken to a local Yamaha repair specialist or an auto-electrician, who should be entrusted with the necessary repair work.

3 The initial check should be made with the battery in a fully-charged condition, connected as it would be under normal running conditions. Connect a voltmeter across the battery terminals and check the reading with the engine running. The reading should be less than 14.5 volts $\pm$ 0.3 volt at 2,000 rpm. Do not run the battery disconnected, as the much higher open circuit voltage will damage the rectifier.

4 Check the resistance of the field coil, using an ohmmeter. The resistance across the coil should be 4.04 ohms $\pm$ 10%. Check also for continuity between the coil and earth. If continuity exists, the coil is shorted out.

5 The stator coil should be tested in similar fashion, after first checking for any evidence of broken wires. In this case, a reading of 0.7 ohms $\pm$ 10% should be obtained.

6 If, after carrying out the preceding checks, the results are inconclusive, or if there is definite evidence of a fault, the machine should be entrusted to a Yamaha repair specialist or an auto-electrician for more comprehensive testing and, if necessary, for the appropriate repairs to be made.

3 Contact breakers: adjustment

1 To gain access to the contact breaker assembly, remove the three screws that retain the circular cover to the right-hand primary transmission cover. The cover will then lift off, complete with the sealing gasket, to expose the contact breaker assembly.
2 Rotate the engine slowly by placing a spanner on the nut on the end of the crankshaft, until one set of points is fully open. Examine the faces of the contacts. If they are dirty, pitted or burnt, it will be necessary to remove them for further attention, as described in Section 4 of this Chapter. Repeat this operation for the second set of points.
3 The correct contact breaker gap, when the points are fully open, is 0.35 mm (0.014 in). Adjustment is effected by slackening the screws that retain the fixed point in position and moving the fixed point either nearer to or further away from the moving point, with a screwdriver in the adjustment slot provided. Make sure the points are fully open when this adjustment is made, or false readings will result. When the gap is correct, as measured with a feeler gauge, tighten the screw and re-check.
4 Repeat the procedure with the other set of points.

4 Contact breaker points: removal, renovation and replacement

1 If the contact breaker points are burned, pitted or badly worn, they should be removed for dressing. If it is necessary to remove a substantial amount of material before the faces can be restored, new contacts should be fitted.
2 To remove the moving contact, slacken the screw and nut at the end of the return spring and remove the circlip from the post on which the contact pivots. The moving contact can now be lifted away complete with the return spring and the fibre heel bearing on the contact breaker cam.
3 To remove the fixed contact, remove the screw and nut that has already been slackened, so that the wires can be detached from the end of the mounting plate. Remove the screws that hold the mounting plate in position and lift away the plate complete with fixed contact.
4 When removing the wires from the fixed contact mounting plate, take particular note of the arrangement of the insulating washers. If they are replaced incorrectly, the points will be isolated electrically causing the ignition circuit to fail completely.
5 The points should be dressed with an oilstone or fine emery

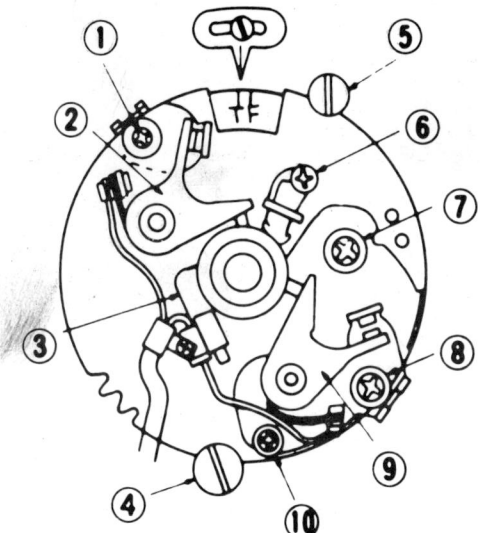

Fig. 3.1. Contact breaker

1 Points gap adjusting screw (left-hand cylinder)
2 Points for left-hand cylinder
3 Lubricator
4 Baseplate locking screw
5 Baseplate locking screw
6 Lubricator
7 Adjusting screw for right-hand cylinder points*
8 Points gap adjusting screw (right-hand cylinder)
9 Points for right-hand cylinder
10 Adjusting screw for right-hand cylinder points*

* This set of points can be moved independently of the baseplate

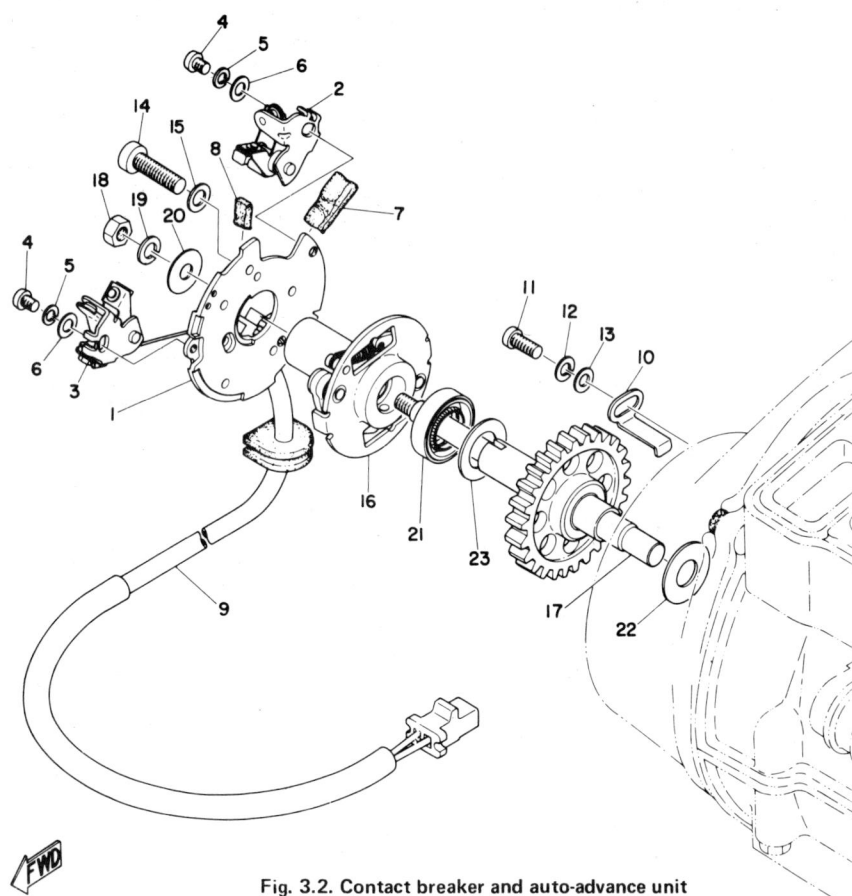

Fig. 3.2. Contact breaker and auto-advance unit

1 Contact breaker base plate assembly
2 Contact breaker assembly - left-hand cylinder
3 Contact breaker assembly - right-hand cylinder
4 Retaining screw - 4 off
5 Spring washer - 2 off
6 Plain washer - 2 off
7 Lubrication wick
8 Lubricator
9 Lead wire assembly
10 Timing plate indicator
11 Screw
12 Spring washer
13 Plain washer
14 Screw - 2 off
15 Plain washer
16 Auto-advance unit
17 Contact breaker drive shaft assembly
18 Nut
19 Spring washer
20 Washer
21 Oil seal
22 Washer
23 Washer

cloth. Keep them absolutely square during the dressing operation, otherwise they will make angular contact when they are replaced and will burn away rapidly as a result.

6 Replace the contacts by reversing the dismantling procedure, taking care to position the insulating washers in the correct sequence. Lightly grease the pivot post before replacing the moving contact and check that there is no oil or grease on the surface of the points. Place a few drops of oil on the lubricating wick that bears on the contact breaker cam, so that the surface is kept lubricated.

7 Re-adjust the contact breaker gap to the recommended setting, after verifying that the points are in their fully-open position.

8 Repeat the whole procedure for the other set of contact breaker points.

5 Condenser: location and testing

1 A condenser is connected into the primary circuit of the contact breaker assembly, to prevent arcing across each set of contact breaker points as they separate. It also helps increase the intensity of the spark as it occurs across the points of each spark plug. It is connected in parallel with each set of points and if a fault develops, ignition failure is likely to occur.

2 The condenser is located within the electrical compartment under the dualseat, and is readily available when the left-hand side cover is detached. It is retained by a bracket through which a single crosshead screw and washer passes, this forming the earth connection.
  If the engine is difficult to start, or if misfiring occurs, it is possible that the condenser is at fault. To check whether the condenser has failed, observe the points whilst the engine is running, after removing the circular portion of the left-hand crankcase cover. If excessive sparking occurs across points and they have a blackened or burnt appearance, it may be assumed the condenser is no longer serviceable

3 An insulation tester is necessary to check the condenser, since any internal breakdown usually results in an internal puncture and shorting out. If the condenser is in satisfactory condition, the pointer of the tester will normally give an initial kick as the condenser discharges, then return to its original position. A high reading will indicate renewal is essential; a defective condenser cannot be repaired.

4 The capacity of the condenser should be checked at the same time, using a capacity tester. The capacity should be 0.22 uF ± 10%. If there is any significant change, the condenser must be renewed.

5 Most owners will not have access to the condenser testing equipment mentioned, or instruction in its use. Under these circumstances, a check is best made by direct replacement, fitting a new condenser in place of the original and observing the effect. A condenser is a relatively low cost part, which should be available from most Yamaha spare part stockists.

6 When the replacement is fitted, make sure the electrical connections are good and that the condenser itself is firmly secured. Poor connections will give the effect of a failed condenser.

6 Ignition coil: location and testing

1 A single ignition coil is fitted to the Yamaha 500 Twins, bolted to the top frame tube, underneath the petrol tank. It is a completely sealed unit and in the event of failure, a new replacement will have to be fitted. A defective ignition coil cannot be repaired. Some models have twin coils, one for each cylinder.

2 Each cylinder has its own ignition circuit and if one cylinder misfires, one half of the complete ignition circuit can be eliminated immediately. The components most likely to fail in the circuit that is defective are the spark plug or the condenser, since contact breaker faults should be obvious on examination. Replacement of the existing condenser will show whether the condenser is at fault, leaving by elimination, the ignition coil. Note that if total ignition failure occurs, it is highly improbable that both ignition circuits will have broken down simultaneously.

3 To check whether the ignition coil is at fault, unscrew the spark plug from the cylinder head and lay it across the fins with the insulating plug cap still attached to the coil. Switch on the ignition and check whether a spark occurs at the plug points when the engine is turned over. If no spark is evident, connect the positive lead of a dc voltmeter with a 0-20 volt range to the brown coloured lead to the coil and earth the negative lead. The voltmeter needle should 'kick' as the engine is rotated, as the contact breaker points open and close and interrupt the low tension circuit. If there is no such response, the fault lies in the coil. If the test is satisfactory, disconnect the positive voltmeter lead from the brown lead of the coil and connect it to the orange or white lead of the coil. The grey lead will provide the check for the left-hand cylinder and the white for the right-hand cylinder. A similar 'kick' should be observed if there is electrical continuity through the coil. If a spark is still not evident across the spark plug points as the engine is rotated, either the spark plug is faulty or there is a break in the high tension windings of the coil itself.

4 If a spark tester is available, the coil can be wired up with a fully charged 12 volt battery and a measurement made of the length of the spark jump. If the coil is in good condition, it should be capable of producing a spark at least 7 mm in length.

7 Ignition switch

1 The ignition switch is bolted from the underside of the top yoke of the forks and is located immediately in front of the handlebars.

2 The switch is unlikely to malfunction during normal service life of the machine and does not require any maintainance. If an ignition failure occurs and it would appear the switch may be responsible, the voltmeter test described in Section 6.3 will confirm whether the switch is at fault. If the voltmeter does not give a reading when it is connected to the brown lead, with the ignition switched on and the contact breaker points closed, the switch is the source of the trouble, assuming the fuse in the electrical circuit has not blown. Replacement of the switch is the only remedy. Reconnection is easy. on account of the junction box connector used.

8 Ignition timing: checking and setting

1 On any high performance machine, the accuracy with which the ignition timing is set is of paramount importance if full performance is to be achieved. Over-advanced timing will cause the engine to knock and will eventually result in damage to the internal working parts of the engine. If the setting is retarded, there will be a noticeable fall off in acceleration, accompanied by overheating. Here again, damage will be caused to the internal working parts of the engine, if the cause is not diagnosed correctly and remedied.

2 To check the ignition timing, first detach the circular cover of the primary transmission cover, found on the right-hand side of the machine. Lift the cover away, complete with sealing gasket. Check the set of points for the left-hand cylinder first; these are the points in the 10 o'clock position.

3 Rotate the engine in a clockwise direction by removing the large allen screw in the lower left-hand side of the contact breaker housing and inserting an allen key into the hexagon in the centre of this nut. Turn the engine until the points are in the fully open position and check that the contact breaker gap is correct. If not, adjust it as described in Section 3 of this Chapter. The gap must be correct before the ignition timing is checked or reset, since adjustments made afterwards will affect the accuracy of the timing.

4 Continue rotating the engine in a clockwise direction until the points have closed and the F mark viewed through the aperture in the top of the housing is approaching the timing plate pointer.

Chapter 3: Ignition system

91

5.2 Condenser is located in electrical compartment, under dualseat

6.1 The ignition coil is located under fuel tank

8.4a When pointer and 'F' mark align exactly, points for left-hand cylinder should be about to separate

8.4b 'T' mark aligns when piston is at top-dead-centre

Connect the positive lead of a voltmeter to the moving contact and the negative lead to a convenient earth point on the engine. Switch on the ignition and continue turning the engine clockwise very slowly until the reading on the voltmeter ceases and the pointer returns to zero. If the ignition timing is correct, the F mark should coincide exactly with the timing plate pointer tip.

5 Make any adjustments by removing the allen screws that lock the contact breaker base plate in position and turn the base plate in the direction required, until the marks line up exactly. Lock the base plate by replacing the two allen screws and tightening them both, then re-check to ensure the setting is correct. It is best to turn the engine over several times, before re-checking, as backlash in the engine itself may account for minor inaccuracies. It is very important that the timing marks coincide exactly.

6 Repeat the procedure for the right-hand cylinder. In this instance, the contact breaker points can be moved independently of the base plate, to correct any inaccuracies in setting. Any movement of the base plate itself will immediately upset the accuracy of the timing of the left-hand cylinder, which has just been achieved, so it must be left undisturbed on this occasion. An elongated hole in the mounting of the second set of contact breaker points permits their movement within a limited arc. Replace and tighten the large allen screw, to avoid oil loss.

7 When both cylinders have had their timing verified or reset by the method described, start the engine and make a final check with a strobe lamp. Before switching off and disconnecting, increase the engine speed to 4 – 5,000 rpm very briefly, to check whether the ignition is advanced sufficiently on both cylinders, as the automatic ignition advance unit comes into operation. If the unit is functioning correctly, the pointer should align with the first of the two special timing marks. If the marks do not align correctly, refer to the following Section.

9 Automatic ignition advance unit: examination

1 The automatic ignition advance unit is located below the contact breaker baseplate, which will have to be removed in order to gain access. Mark the exact position of the baseplate first, in relation to the surrounding housing, so that it can be replaced in identical position. This will save having to retime the engine. A scribe line will suffice.

2 To remove the automatic ignition advance unit, unscrew the small hexagonal nut on the end of the crankshaft. This has a normal right-hand thread. When this nut, the spring washer and the plain washer below have been removed, the automatic advance unit can be drawn off the crankshaft, complete with contact breaker cam. Its exact position is determined by a dowel pin,

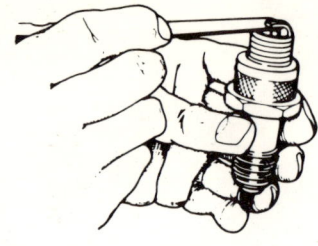
Checking plug gap with feeler gauges

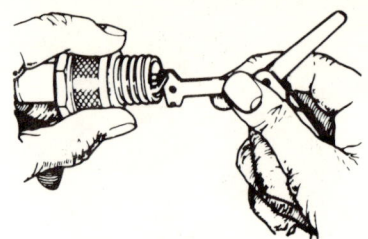
Altering the plug gap. Note use of correct tool

Fig. 3.3a. Spark plug maintenance

White deposits and damaged porcelain insulation indicating overheating

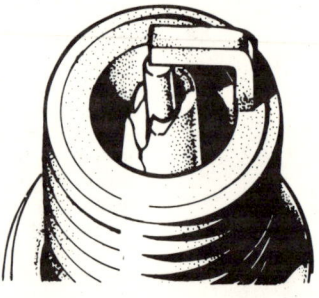
Broken porcelain insulation due to bent central electrode

Electrodes burnt away due to wrong heat value or chronic pre-ignition (pinking)

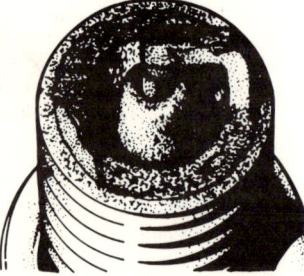
Excessive black deposits caused by over-rich mixture or wrong heat value

Milde white deposits and electrode burnt indicating too weak a fuel mixture

Plug in sound condition with light grey brown deposits

Fig. 3.3b. Spark plug electrode conditions

Chapter 3: Ignition system

which locates with a cutaway in the crankshaft. In consequence, it cannot be replaced in any but the correct position.

3 The unit operates on the centrifugal principal. Spring-loaded bobweights are on the ends of short arms which extend outwards as engine speed increases. As these arms are attached to the baseplate of the unit, with which the contact breaker cam is an intergral part, the ignition is advanced quite automatically as engine speed increases.

4 If the unit fails, the usual causes are broken or binding springs, seized pivots or general rusting of the unit as a result of condensation within the engine. In many cases, the unit can be restored to full working efficiency by a general clean up and lubrication, but if there is any doubt whatsoever about its condition, renewal is preferable. A unit that malfunctions will have a very marked effect on engine performance and fuel consumption. Wear connot be taken up and the unit reclaimed in a satisfactory manner.

10 Timing mark pointer

1 The timing mark pointer is attached to the contact breaker housing by a single crosshead screw, with a spring washer and a plain washer underneath. It is set correctly at the factory during the manufacture of the machine and should not, under any circumstances, be removed or moved in position. Although the plate has an elongated slot to permit adjustment, this is for factory use only.

2 If for any reason the setting of the point is disturbed, it must be reset with great accuracy. Remove the left-hand spark plug and insert a dial gauge. Rotate the engine in a clockwise direction by turning the crankshaft, until the piston is exactly at top dead centre on the compression stroke (both valves of the left-hand cylinder closed). Align the timing plate tip with the 'F' mark through the aperture in the contact breaker baseplate, making sure it matches up with the 'F' mark for the left-hand cylinder (marked L). When the marks coincide exactly, apply thread sealant to the pointer retaining screw and tighten it fully, checking that the marks are still exactly in register. Remove the dial gauge, rotate the engine a few times, then re-check. This setting must be really accurate, as it will affect all future checks and adjustments of the ignition timing.

11 Spark plugs: checking and resetting the gap

1 Two NGK type D8ES spark plugs are fitted as standard equipment. This is the grade recommended by the manufacturer after extensive tests and no benefit will be gained from changing the type, except under very exceptional operating conditions. In most cases, the effect of a change will be detrimental in the long run.

2 The spark plugs should each have a gap of 0.6 - 0.7 mm (0.024 - 0.028 in). Check the gap during every 2,000 mile (1,600 km) service after the initial running-in period. To reset the gap, bend the outer electrode to bring it closer to the centre electrode and check that a 0.6 mm (0.024 in) feeler gauge can be inserted. Never bend the central electrode or the insulator will crack, causing extensive damage if particles fall in whilst the engine is running.

3 With some experience the condition of the spark plug electrodes and insulator can be used as a reliable guide to engine operating conditions. See the accompanying diagram.

4 Always carry a spare pair of spark plugs of the recommended grade. In the rare event of plug failure, they will enable the engine to be restarted.

5 Beware of over-tightening the spark plugs, otherwise there is risk of stripping the threads from the aluminium alloy cylinder heads. The plugs should be sufficiently tight to seat firmly on their copper sealing washers, and no more. Use a spanner which is a good fit to prevent the spanner from slipping and breaking the insulator.

6 If the threads in the cylinder head strip as a result of over-tightening the spark plugs, it is possible to reclaim the head by the use of a Helicoil thread insert. This is a cheap and convenient method of replacing the threads; most motorcycle dealers operate a service of this nature at an economic price.

7 Make sure the plug insulating caps are a good fit and have their rubber seals. They should also be kept clean to prevent tracking. These caps contain the suppressors that eliminate both radio and TV interference.

12 Fault diagnosis: ignition system

Symptom	Cause	Remedy
Engine will not start	Faulty ignition switch	Operate switch several times in case contacts are dirty. If ignition circuit is still not activated, switch may need renewal.
	Starter motor not working	Discharged battery. Use kickstart until battery is recharged.
	Short circuit in wiring	Check whether fuse is intact. Eliminate fault before switching on again.
	Completely discharged battery	If lights do not work, remove battery and recharge.
Engine misfires	Faulty condenser in ignition circuit	Renew condenser and re-test.
	Fouled spark plug	Renew plug and have original cleaned.
	Poor spark due to generator failure and dishcarged battery	Check output from generator. Remove and recharge battery.
Engine lacks power and overheats	Retarded ignition timing	Check timing and also contact breaker gap. Check whether auto-advance mechanism has jammed.
Engine 'fades' when under load	Pre-ignition	Check grade of plugs fitted; use recommended grades only.

Chapter 4 Frame and forks

Contents

General description ... 1	Prop stand: examination ... 12
Front forks: removal from frame ... 2	Footrests: examination and renovation ... 13
Front forks: dismantling ... 3	Rear brake pedal: examination and renovation ... 14
Front forks: examination and renovation ... 4	Dualseat: removal and replacement ... 15
Steering head bearings: examination and renovation ... 5	Speedometer and tachometer heads: removal and replacement ... 16
Front forks: reassembly ... 6	
Steering head lock ... 7	Speedometer and tachometer drive cables: examination and maintenance ... 17
Frame: examination and renovation ... 8	
Swinging arm rear fork: dismantling, examination and renovation ... 9	Speedometer and tachometer drives: location and examination ... 18
Rear suspension units: examination ... 10	Cleaning the machine ... 19
Centre stand: examination ... 11	Fault diagnosis: frame and forks ... 20

Specifications

Frame:
Type ... Duplex cradle type, made of steel tubing
Rear suspension ... Swinging arm type, controlled by hydraulically damped suspension units

Forks:
Caster ... 62° 30'
Trail ... 117 mm
Oil content per leg ... 147 cc, SAE 10W/30

1 General description

The Yamaha 500 twin has a full cradle frame of the duplex tube type, fitted with a heavily gusseted steering head that provides the degree of rigidity necessary for high speed riding. Rear suspension is of swinging arm type, using conventional rear suspension units of the sealed, oil-damped type. They are adjustable, to suit varying riding conditions.

The front forks are of the telescopic type, having internal, oil-filled one way dampers. The fork springs are contained within the stanchions and each fork leg can be detached from the machine as a complete unit, without having to dismantle the steering head assembly.

2 Front forks: removal from the frame

1 It is unlikely that the front forks will have to be removed from the frame as a complete unit, unless the steering head assembly requires attention, or the machine suffers frontal damage. If such action is necessary, the following procedure should be adopted.
2 Commence by removing the master cylinder body of the hydraulic front brake which is secured to the handlebars by two bolts. Then disconnect the clutch cable from the clutch lever.
3 Remove the combined starter, lighting and ignition switch assembly on the right-hand end of the handlebars, AFTER first disconnecting the positive lead from the battery. The switch assembly is retained by two screws on the underside. Detach the twist grip cable.
4 Detach the front of the headlamp and disconnect the electrical wiring at the snap connectors. The wires leading to the handlebars can be pulled through the orifice in the rear of the headlamp, complete with their connectors.
5 Remove the four allen screws which retain the two handlebar split clamps in position, and lift the handlebars away. Slacken the bracket which retains the tachometer and speedometer heads and remove these instruments from the fork top yoke.
6 Slacken the pinch bolts at the top of the upper yoke, to release the grip on the individual fork legs. Remove the domed nut in the centre of the fork stem and the pinch bolt at the rear of the upper yoke. The yoke can then be lifted off the top of the fork assembly.
7 Place a sturdy support under the engine unit so that the front wheel is raised clear of the ground. Detach the speedometer drive cable from the drive gearbox on the front wheel hub; it is retained by a single nut. Remove the split pin through the castellated nut of the front wheel spindle, then remove the nut and washer. Slacken the nuts and washers of the spindle clamp at the base of the lower left-hand fork leg and withdraw the wheel spindle. This will release the front wheel from the forks.
8 Remove the lower and upper bolts that retain the front

2.6 Slacken the pinch bolts at the top of each fork leg

2.7a Detach drive cable from speedometer drive gearbox

2.7b Slacken clamp nuts at base of left-hand fork leg

2.8a Remove bolts that retain caliper unit to tight-hand fork leg

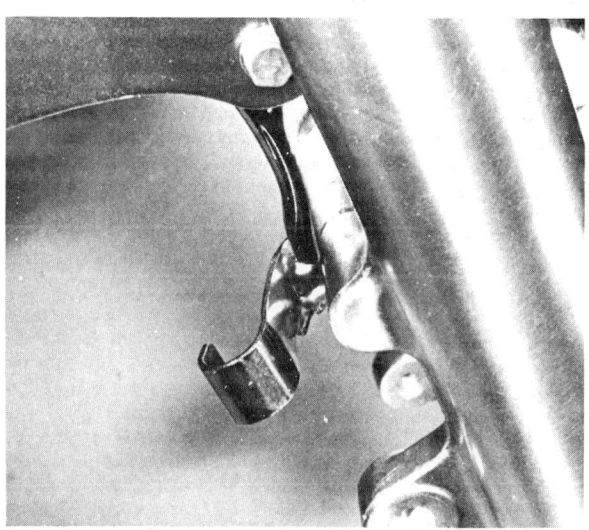
2.8b Detach clip that restrains hydraulic brake hose

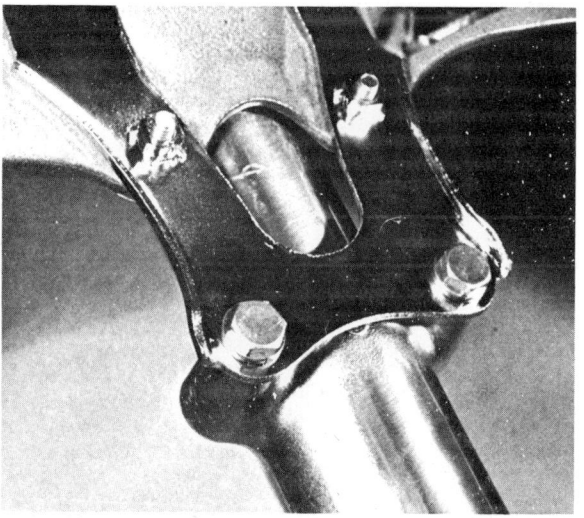
2.10 Mudguard is retained by two bolts inside each fork leg

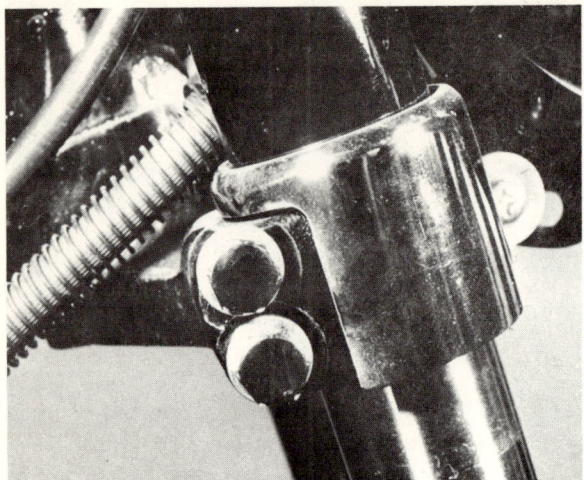

2.11a Slacken pinch bolts in lower fork yoke and ...

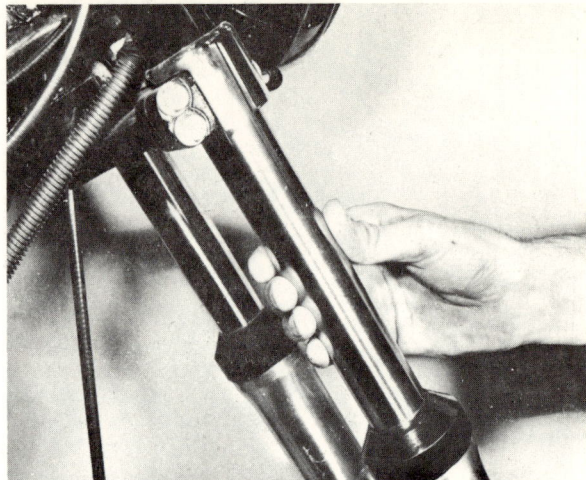

2.11b ... pull fork legs downwards, clear of lower yoke

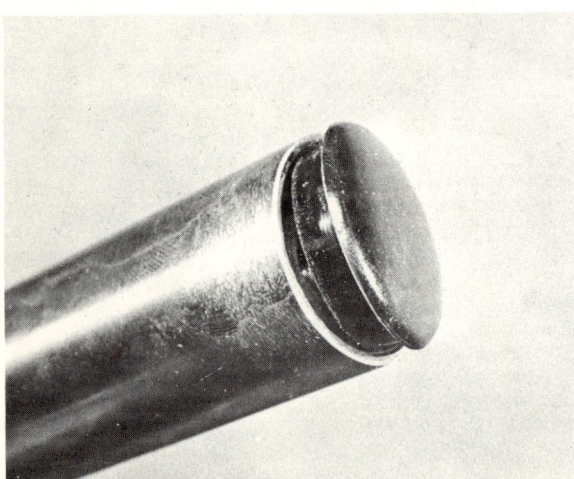

3.1 Prise out rubber cap in top of fork leg

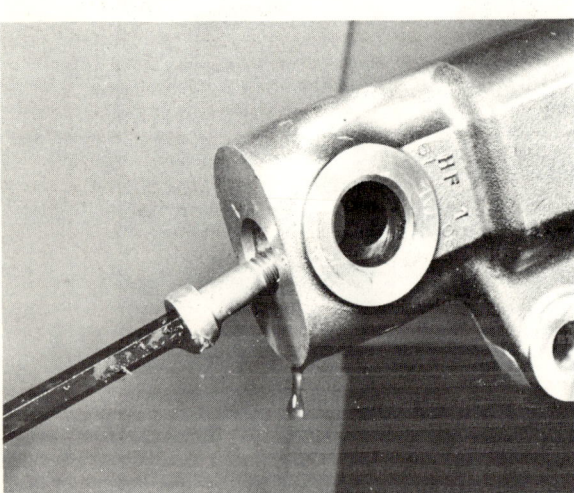

3.2a Remove recessed socket screw to free damper unit

disc brake caliper unit to the right-hand lower fork leg. The complete caliper unit can then be lifted clear of the forks, after removing the clip that retains the hydraulic system. Make arrangements to support the caliper assembly, so that the strain is not taken by the hose pipe.

9 Beware of kinking either the hose or the pipe and under no circumstances operate the front brake lever as there is risk of forcing the caliper pistons out of the caliper unit, with the resulting loss of fluid. Should this happen, the brake assembly must be bled of air after it has been replaced and the front wheel is again in position.

10 Remove the front mudguard, which is retained by two bolts at the lower end of each fork leg, and by two additional bolts on the inside of each fork leg (inside bolts only on the late models). Remove the mudguard complete with the centre bridge and stays. It will be necessary to squeeze the plastic mudguard before it can be extracted from between the fork legs.

11 Unscrew the pinch bolts through the lower fork yoke, and pull the individual fork legs downwards so that each is released from the yoke as a complete unit. It may be necessary to spring the clamp apart with a screwdriver blade to release the grip on the fork stanchions. Note that the headlamp shell and upper fork shrouds will remain in position and can be lifted off when the fork legs are withdrawn.

12 To release the lower yoke and steering head stem, unscrew the slotted sleeve nut at the top of the steering head column, using a 'C' spanner or a punch. As the steering head column is released, the uncaged ball bearings from the lower race will be released and care should be taken to catch them by wrapping a rag around the bearing area. The bearings in the upper race will almost certainly remain in position.

13 It follows that much of this procedure can be avoided if it is necessary to remove the individual fork legs without disturbing the steering head assembly or bearings. Under the circumstances, commence dismantling as described in paragraphs 7 to 10 then slacken the pinch bolts in the lower fork yoke, so that the fork legs can be withdrawn as complete units.

3 Front forks - dismantling

1 It is advisable to dismantle each fork leg separately, using an identical procedure. There is less chance of unwittingly exchanging parts if this approach is adopted. Commence by draining the fork legs; there is a drain plug in each lower leg, above and to the rear of the wheel spindle housing. Remove the cap at the top of the fork leg first, by lifting out the rubber plug and pressing

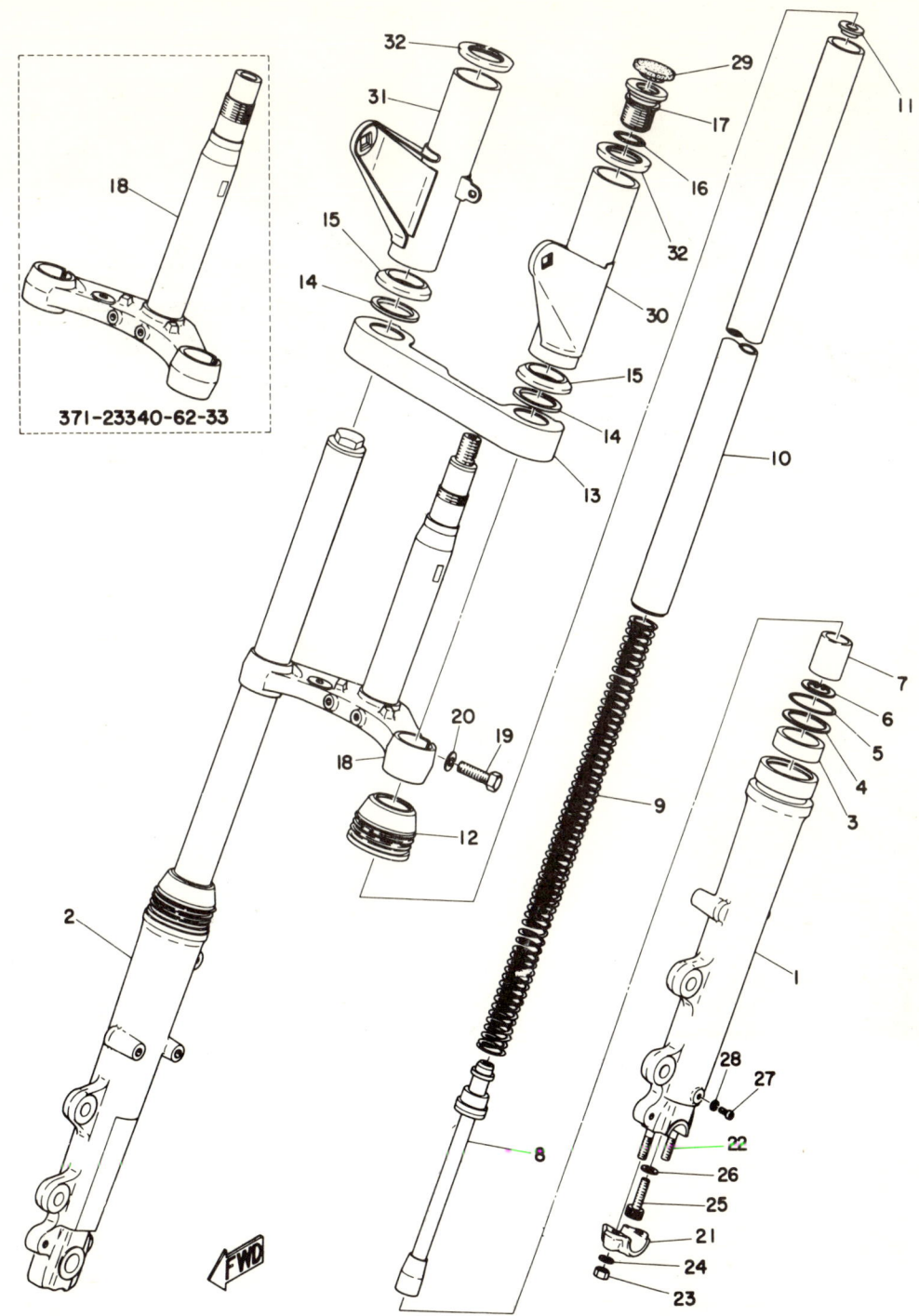

Fig. 4.1. Front fork assembly

1 Lower fork leg - left-hand
2 Lower fork leg - right-hand
3 Oil seal - 2 off
4 Oil seal washer - 2 off
5 Oil seal clip - 2 off
6 Circlip - 2 off
7 Damper piston - 2 off
8 Damper assembly - 2 off
9 Fork spring - 2 off
10 Stanchion - 2 off
11 Fork spring upper cap - 2 off
12 Dust seal - 2 off
13 Outer cover for lower yoke
14 Gasket - 2 off
15 Guide - 2 off
16 Gasket - 2 off
17 Cap bolt - 2 off
18 Steering head stem and fork lower yoke
19 Fork lower yoke pinch bolt - 4 off
20 Spring washer - 4 off
21 Fork spindle cap
22 Stud - 2 off
23 Nut - 2 off
24 Spring washer - 2 off
25 Socket head bolt - 2 off
26 Sealing washer - 2 off
27 Drain plug - 2 off
28 Drain plug sealing washer
29 Blanking off cap - 2 off
30 Upper left-hand fork shroud
31 Upper right-hand fork shroud
32 Upper guide - 2 off

Note: The front fork assembly fitted to the XS500C models differs in certain minor respect from the above illustration

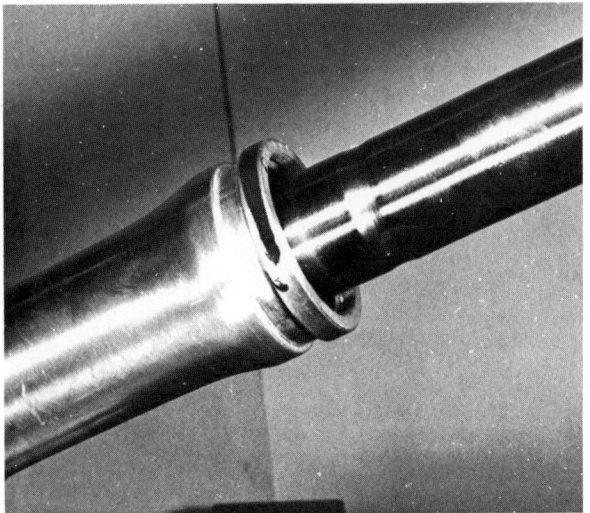

3.2b Grip lower fork leg and withdraw stanchion sharply

3.2c Press down on inner metal cap, to free internal circlip

3.2d Lift out cap, followed by ...

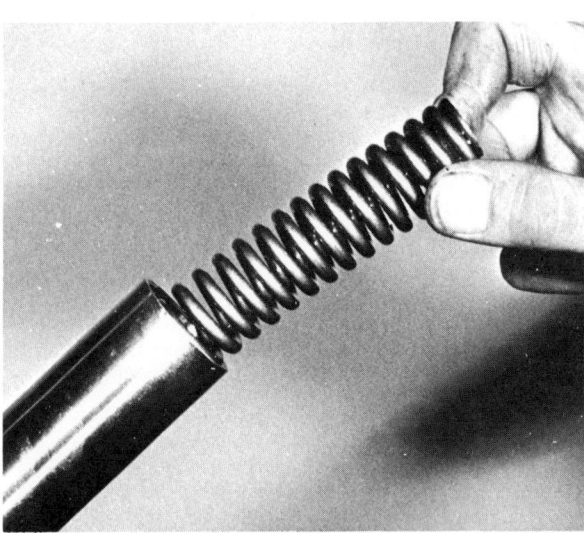

3.2e ... internal fork spring

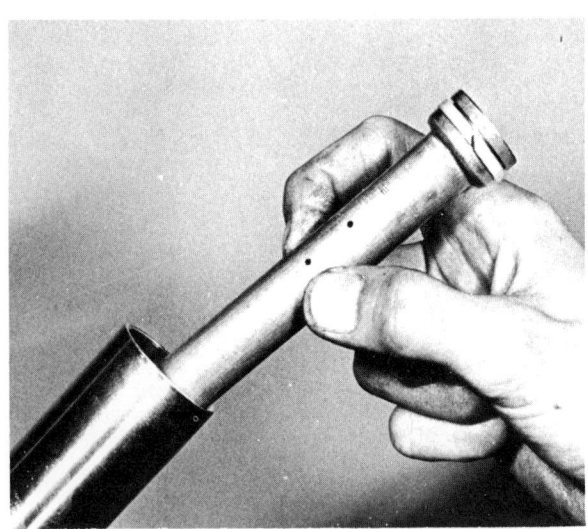

3.2f Damper unit will now lift out. Care with nylon piston ring

3.3 Oil seal is retained in lower fork leg by an internal circlip

Chapter 4: Frame and forks

down on the metal cap so that its retaining clip can be removed. This will free the cap. Some models are fitted with a cap that has a hexagon insert, which will have to be unscrewed with a large Allen Key.

2 Clamp the lower fork leg in a vice fitted with soft clamps and unscrew the socket screw recessed into the housing which carries the wheel spindle. If the fork stanchion tube is now gripped firmly and pulled sharply outward, it will come away from the lower fork leg complete. The fork spring can now be withdrawn, followed by the damper assembly. Note the spring has its closed ends towards the top.

3 Whenever the fork legs are dismantled, it will be necessary to renew the oil seal in the top of each lower fork leg, regardless of its condition. The oil seal is retained by a circlip and can be prised out of position when this circlip is removed.

4 Front forks: examination and renovation

1 After an extended period of service, wear will develop between the fork stanchion and the lower fork leg, in which it slides. The usual sign of advanced wear of this kind is fork judder, whenever the front brake is applied hard. As a cross-check, wear can be verified by pulling and pushing on the handlebars when the front brake is applied hard. Make sure, however, that slack steering head bearings are not responsible for the play, as the symptoms will be almost identical.

2 There is no provision for renovating worn forks, as forks of the type fitted to the Yamaha 500 Twins do not have renewable bushes. The fork stanchions and the lower fork legs will have to be renewed. If there is no evidence of serious wear, check the surface of each fork stanchion to ensure the portion that slides within the lower fork leg is not scored or otherwise damaged in any way. Damage of this nature will greatly reduce the serviceable life of the forks and it is therefore important that renewals are made at an early stage. This also applies to the inside surface of the lower fork legs, which should be checked in similar fashion.

3 In view of the foregoing, it is important that the dust seals are in good condition. If there is any doubt about them, they should be renewed without question. A damaged dust seal will permit grit and other debris from the road to find its way into the forks, damaging the oil seals and generally accelerating the rate of wear.

4 As mentioned earlier, the oil seals will have to be renewed whenever the forks are dismantled. Take great care when fitting the new seals to the lower fork legs and make sure they are located correctly before the retaining circlips are fitted.

5 The fork springs will compress after a lengthy period of service and the time will eventually occur when both will need renewing. Check them against the length of a new fork spring and if either has compressed a significant amount, renew BOTH, as a matched pair.

6 The damper unit is unlikely to require attention, as it is permanently immersed in oil, the damping medium. The nylon sealing ring is most probably the only item likely to require renewal; here again, treat both units in an identical manner.

7 It is rarely possible to straighten forks which have been badly damaged in an accident, especially if the correct jigs are not available. It is always best to err on the side of safety and fit new ones, especially since there is no easy means of detecting whether the forks have been overstressed and the metal fatigued. Fork stanchions can be checked for straightness by stripping them and rolling them on a flat surface. Any misalignment will immediately be obvious.

8 If the fork stanchions are rusty, they should be cleaned up very carefully, prior to reassembly, taking special care that abrasive does not find its way on to the sliding areas, which will remain clean and polished. Apart from causing damage to the oil seal, when refitted, a rusty stanchion will also prove difficult to feed through the lower fork yoke clamp.

5 Steering head bearings: examination and renovation

1 Before commencing reassembly of the forks, examine the steering head races. The ball bearing tracks of the respective cup and cone bearings should be polished and free from indentations and cracks. If signs of wear or damage are evident, the cups and cones must be renewed. They are a tight push fit and should be drifted out of position.

2 Ball bearings are relatively cheap. If the originals are marked or discoloured, they should be renewed. To hold the steel balls in position during re-attachment of the forks, pack the bearings with grease. Note that each race should contain a total of nineteen ¼ inch diameter ball bearings. Although space will be left to include one extra ball, it is necessary to prevent the bearings from skidding on each other and accelerating the rate of wear.

6 Front forks: reassembly

1 Replace the front forks by following in reverse the dismantling procedures described in Sections 2 and 3 of this Chapter. Before fully tightening the front wheel spindle clamp and the fork yoke pinch bolts, bounce the forks several times to ensure they work freely and are clamped in their original settings. Complete the final tightening from the wheel spindle clamp upwards.

2 Do not forget to add the recommended quantity of fork damping oil to each leg before the caps in the top of each fork leg are replaced. Check that the drain plugs have been re-inserted and tightened before the oil is added. The correct quantity is 147 cc of SAE 10W/30 oil per leg.

3 If the fork stanchions prove difficult to re-locate through the fork yokes, make sure their outer surfaces are clean and polished so that they will slide more easily. It is advantageous to use a screwdriver blade to open up the clamps as the stanchions are pushed upward into position. Remember that the fork springs must be replaced with their close together coils facing upwards.

4 Before the machine is used on the road, check the adjustment of the steering head bearings. If they are too slack, judder will occur. There should be no detectable play in the head races when the handlebars are pulled and pushed, with the front brake applied hard.

5 Overtight head races are equally undesirable. It is possible to unwittingly apply a loading of several tons on the head bearings by overtightening, even though the handlebars appear to turn quite freely. Overtight bearings will cause the machine to roll at low speeds and give generally imprecise handling with a tendency to weave. Adjustment is correct if there is no perceptible play in the bearings and the handlebars will swing to full lock in either direction, when the machine is on the centre stand with the front wheel clear of the ground. Only a slight tap should cause the handlebars to swing.

7 Steering head lock

1 The steering head lock is attached to the underside of the lower yoke of the forks by a single screw and washer. When in a locked position, a tongue extends from the body of the lock when the handlebars are on full lock in either direction and abuts against a plate welded to the base of the steering head. In consequence, the handlebars cannot be straightened until the lock is released.

2 If the lock malfunctions, it must be renewed. A repair is impracticable. When the lock is changed the key must be changed too, to match the new lock. No maintenance is necessary; when not in use the lock is protected by a spring-loaded cover plate.

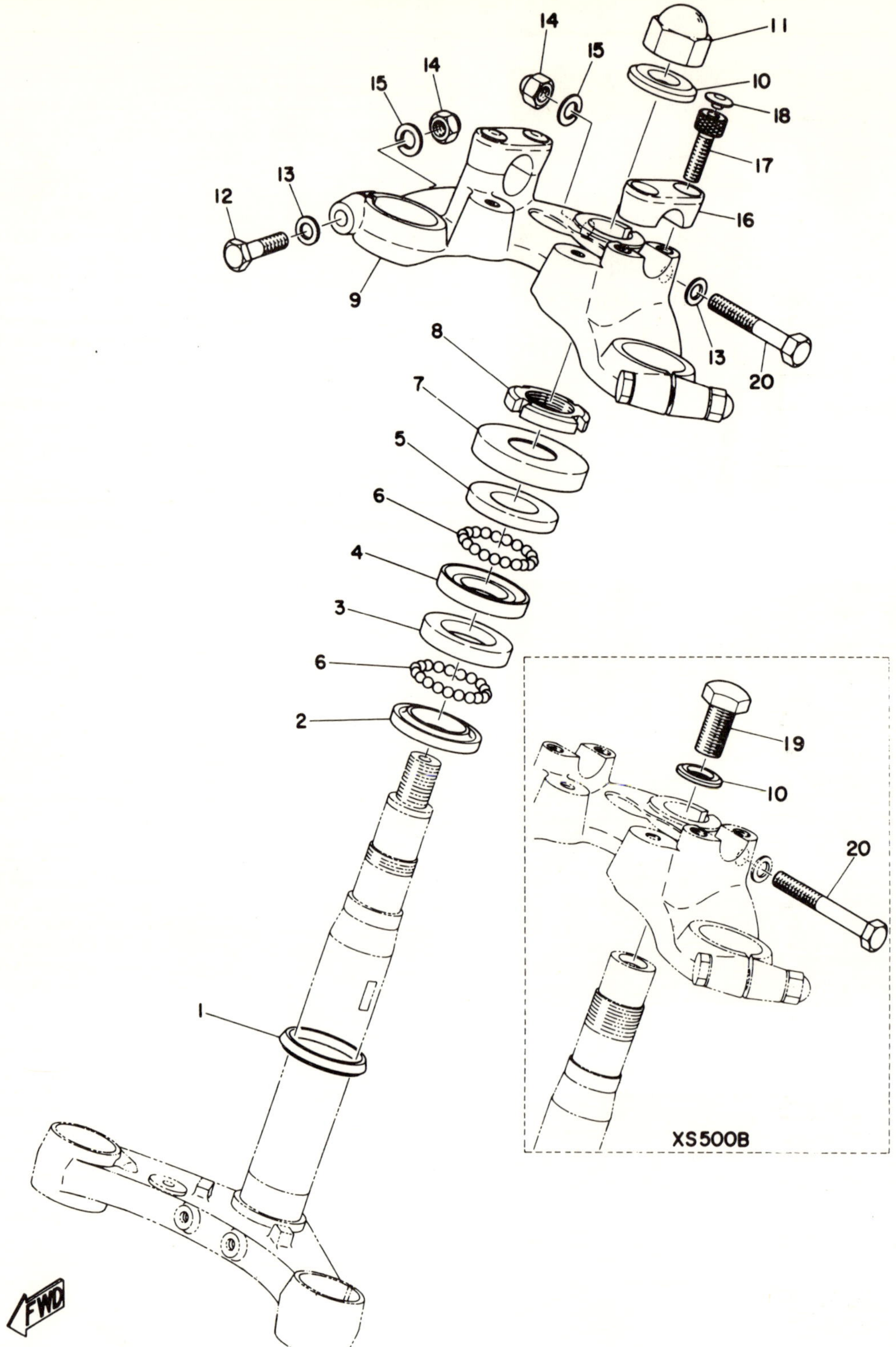

Fig. 4.2. Steering head assembly

1 Dust seal
2 Lower beaing cup
3 Lower bearing cone
4 Upper bearing cup
5 Upper bearing cone
6 Ball bearing (¼ in. diameter) - 38 off
7 Ball race cover
8 Nut - 2 off
9 Fork upper yoke
10 Washer
11 Domed nut
12 Pinch bolt - 2 off
13 Washer - 3 off
14 Domed nut - 3 off
15 Spring washer - 3 off
16 Handlebar clamp - 2 off
17 Allen screw - 4 off
18 Cap bolt - 4 off
19 Bolt
20 Bolt

Chapter 4: Frame and forks 101

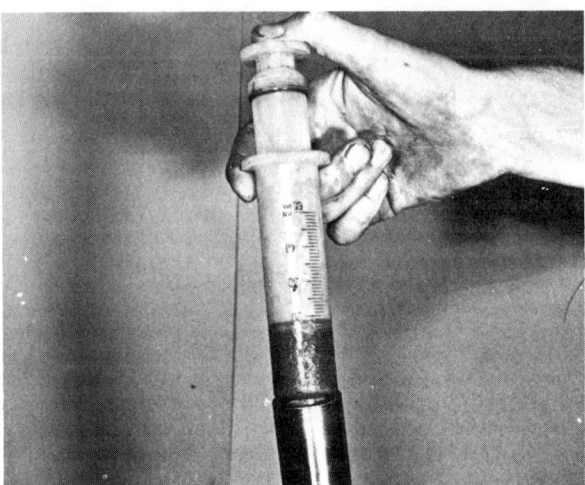

6.2 Refill fork legs with correct quantity of fluid before refitting end caps

7.2 If steering head lock malfunctions, it must be renewed

9.4a Unscrew nut of rear torque arm bolt

8 Frame: examination and renovation

1 The frame is unlikely to require attention unless accident damage has occurred. In some cases, replacement of the frame is the only satisfactory course of action, if it is badly out of alignment. Only a few frame repair specialists have the jigs and mandrels necessary for resetting the frame to the required standard of accuracy and even then there is no easy means of assessing to what extent the frame may have been overstressed.
2 After the machine has covered a considerable mileage, it is advisable to examine the frame closely for signs of cracking or splitting at the welded joints. Rust can also cause weakness at these joints. Minor damage can be repaired by welding or brazing, depending on the extent and nature of the damage.
3 Remember that a frame which is out of alignment will cause handling problems and may even promote 'speed wobbles'. If misalignment is suspected, as the result of an accident, it will be necessary to strip the machine completely so that the frame can be checked and, if necessary, renewed.

9 Swinging arm rear fork: dismantling, examination and renovation

1 The rear fork of the frame assembly pivots on a detachable bush within each end of the fork crossmember and a pivot shaft which itself is surrounded by a long detachable bush. The pivot shaft passes through frame lugs on each side of the engine unit and the centre of the long detachable bush, so that the inner and outer bushes form the bearing surfaces. It is quite easy to renovate the swinging arm when wear necessitates attention.
2 Remove the swinging arm fork; first position the machine on the centre stand, then detach the plastic chainguard which is retained to three crosshead screws, one of them on the swinging arm crossbrace. Detach the final drive chain from the rear wheel sprocket by removing the spring link or, if the chain is of the endless type, move the wheel spindle to a point at which it is at its slackest, and remove the chain when convenient.
3 On drum brake models, detach the rear brake torque arm from the brake plate on the right-hand side of the machine, by removing the split pin, nut, washer and bolt. Remove the rear brake operating rod by unscrewing the adjuster from the end and pulling the rod through the trunnion in the end of the brake operating arm. Take care not to lose the trunnion, which is no now free. Remove the split pin from the end of the rear wheel spindle and unscrew the castellated nut. The rear wheel spindle can now be withdrawn. Take care not to misplace the spacer between the brake plate and the inside of the swinging arm fork, which is released, possibly with the right-hand chain adjuster. Remove the brake plate, complete with the brake assembly, which will lift away from the wheel. Then remove the rear wheel, complete with the sprocket (lift off the endless chain if fitted), by tilting it to clear the mudguard so that it can be eased away from the machine.
4 On the disc brake model (XS500C), the torque arm must be removed from the rear disc brake assembly by pulling out the split pin, unscrewing the nut and removing the bolt and washer. The bolt itself cannot be turned, as there are locating flats milled on its shank. Remove the fluted cover over the disc pads, which is retained by a single crosshead screw and lift out the pads. The caliper unit will be freed when the rear wheel spindle is withdrawn. Remove the split pin from the castellated rear wheel spindle nut, unscrew the nut and remove it, together with the washer underneath. The spindle can now be withdrawn from the right-hand side of the machine, which will free the caliper assembly and the spacer between the wheel hub and the inside of the swinging arm fork, on the right-hand side. There is now sufficient space to tilt the wheel to the left (lift off the endless chain if fitted), so that it will clear the mudguard and can be eased away from the machine.
5 Slacken the upper mounting nuts of the rear suspension units and remove completely the nuts that retain the lower ends. If

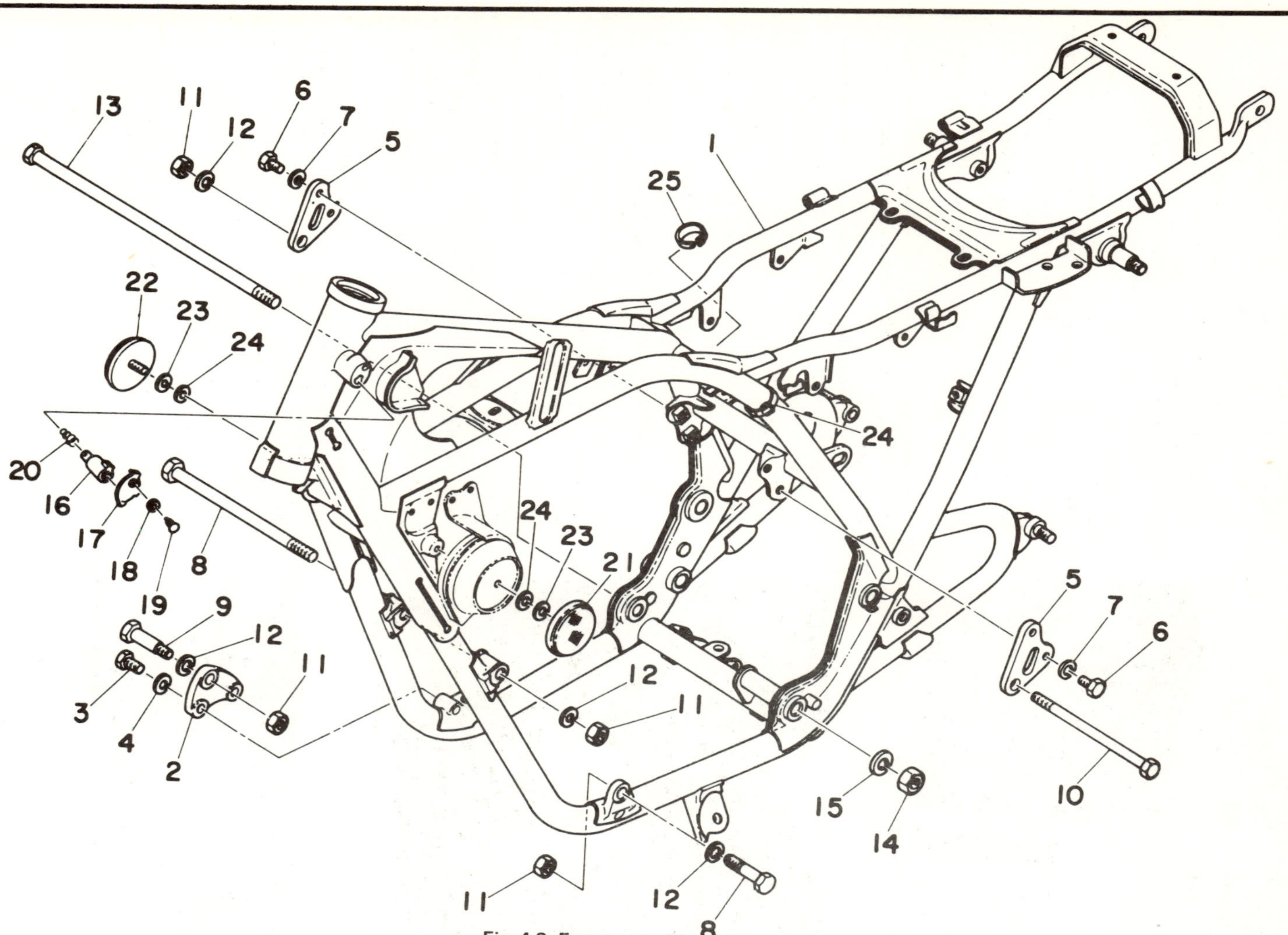

Fig. 4.3. Frame assembly

1 Frame assembly complete
2 Lower front engine plate
3 Bolt - 2 off
4 Spring washer - 2 off
5 Upper rear engine plate
6 Bolt - 4 off
7 Spring washer - 4 off
8 Bolt
9 Bolt - 2 off
10 Bolt
11 Nut - 4 off
12 Spring washer - 4 off
13 Bolt
14 Nut
15 Spring washer
16 Steering head lock assembly
17 Flap for lock
18 Wave washer
19 Rivet
20 Conical spring
21 Left-hand reflector
22 Right-hand reflector
23 Spring washer - 2 off
24 Plain washer - 2 off
25 Cable clip - 7 off

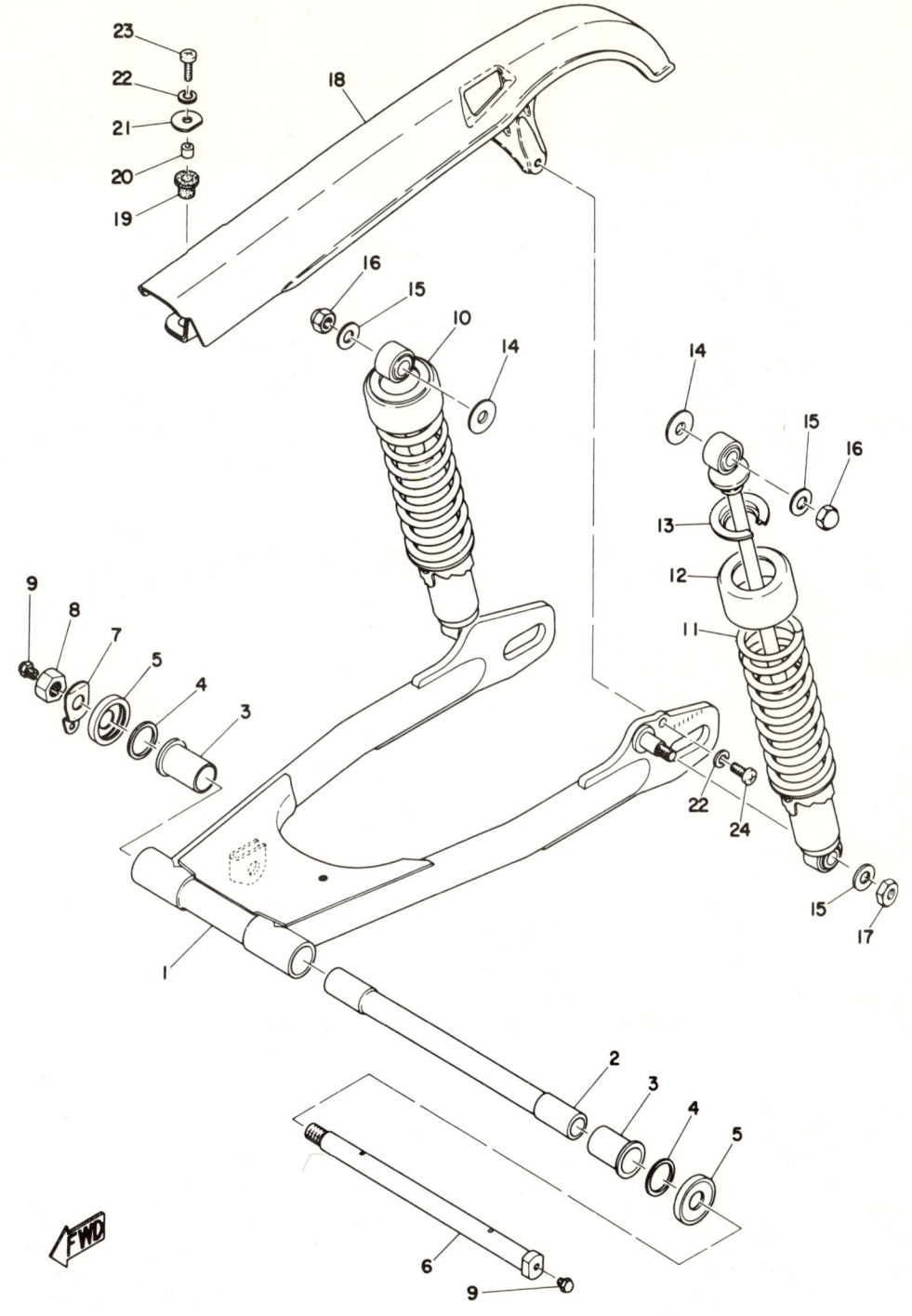

Fig. 4.4. Swinging arm rear suspension

1 Swinging arm fork
2 Swinging arm bush - centre
3 Swinging arm bush - end (2 off)
4 Shim - thickness as required
5 Dust cover - 2 off
6 Pivot shaft
7 Lock washer
8 Nut
9 Grease nipple
10 Rear suspension unit - 2 off
11 Rear suspension unit spring - 2 off
12 Upper shroud - 2 off
13 Upper spring seat - 2 off
14 Washer - 2 off
15 Washer - 4 off
16 Domed nut - 2 off
17 Nut - 2 off
18 Chainguard
19 Flexible mounting
20 Collar
21 Washer
22 Spring washer - 2 off
23 Screw
24 Screw

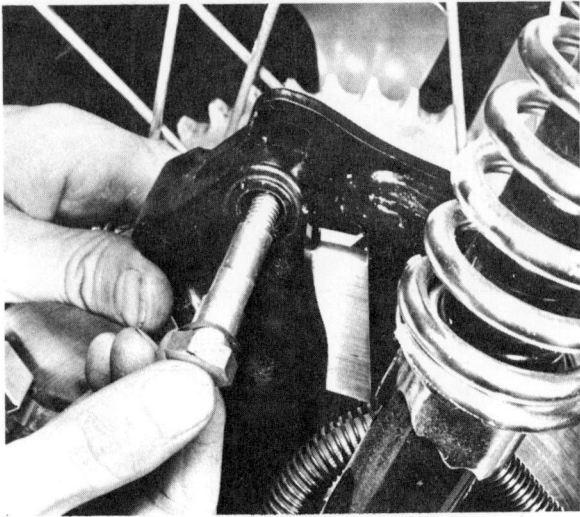
9.4b Bolt will not unscrew as it has locating flats on shank

9.4c Fluted cover over pads is held by one crosshead screw

9.4d Remove split pin and unscrew castellated nut

9.4e Removal of rear wheel spindle will free ...

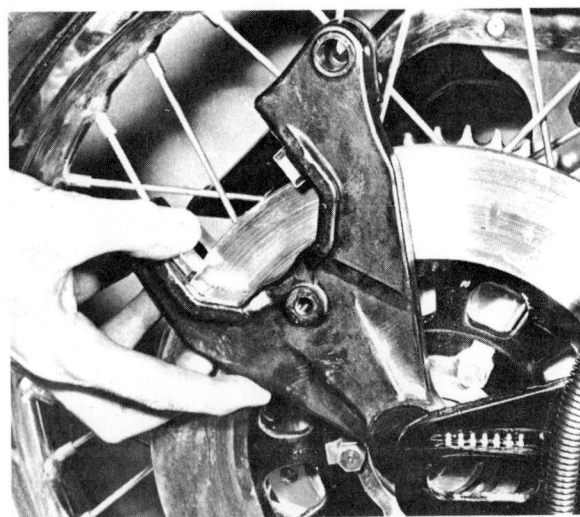
9.4f ... rear caliper unit, shown with pads removed

9.5a Remove nut from end of each rear suspension unit

Chapter 4: Frame and forks

9.5b Unscrew nut and remove, with washer, from end of pivot shaft

9.6 Raise and push forward first, to free fork from frame assembly

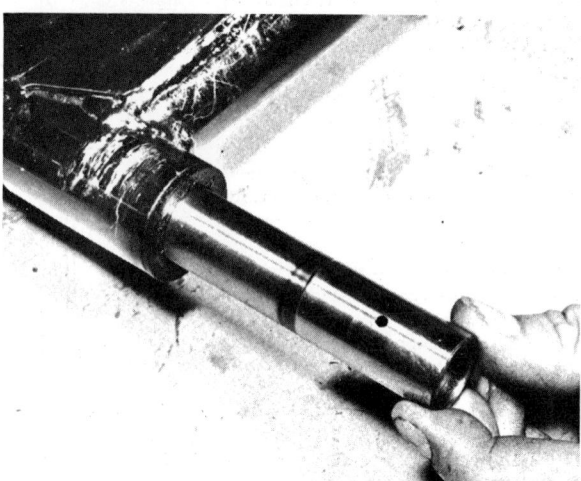
9.7 This long, outer bush surrounds pivot shaft

9.8a Check 'O' ring seal inside each dust cap

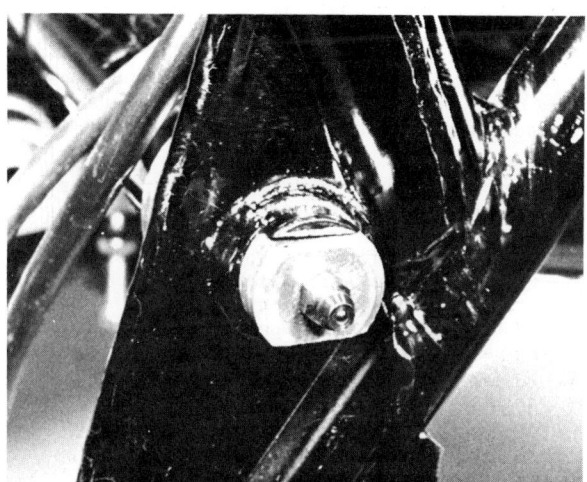
9.8b Pump grease through this nipple, after reassembly

desired, the rear suspension units can be removed completely. On drum brake models only, remove the rear brake torque arm, which is retained by a single bolt at the forward end, then remove the nut and lockwasher from the end of the pivot shaft and withdraw the shaft itself. The swinging arm fork is now free to be withdrawn from the frame.

6 Removal is made easier if the fork is first raised and then pushed forward so that the dust covers can be removed from each end of the pivot housing. They pull off quite easily. Then draw the fork backwards again and tilt the left-hand end upward. It should then clear the frame without difficulty.

7 The two pivot bushes should press out of the ends of the fork crossmember with ease. The inner bush which surrounds the pivot shaft will also be released at the same time. Wash the bearings and the pivot shaft with a petrol/paraffin mix, then check the amount of play between them. If the clearance exceeds 0.5 mm (0.020 in) the bearings and the pivot shaft should be renewed as a set. If renewal is not necessary, check the pivot shaft for straightness. If it is bent, it must be renewed.

8 Reassemble the swinging arm fork by reversing the dismantling procedure. Grease the pivot shaft and bearings liberally prior to reassembly and check that the seals within the dust covers are in good order.

9 Worn swinging arm pivot bearings will give imprecise handling

with a tendency for the rear end of the machine to twitch or hop. The play can be detected by placing the machine on its centre stand and with the rear wheel clear of the ground, pulling and pushing on the fork ends in a horizontal direction. Any play will be greatly magnified by the leverage effect.

10 On some machines, the rear chain is of the endless type. Under these circumstances, the chain will have to be cut and re-rivetted on reassembly, or the rear wheel moved as far forward as possible prior to removal from the frame, so that the chain can be unlooped from the rear wheel sprocket.

10 Rear suspension units: examination

1 The rear suspension units are of the hydraulically-damped three position type, in which the spring ratings can be adjusted to give three different settings to suit the requirements of the rider and the nature of the terrain over which the machine is ridden. A 'C' spanner, or screwdriver or rod inserted into the peg hole immediately above the adjusting notches is used to turn the spring seatings in the direction desired. Rotate clockwise to increase the spring tension and stiffen up the suspension. The recommended settings are as follows:

Position 1 (least tension)	Normal running, without a pillion passenger
Position 2 (middle position)	High speed touring
Position 3 (most tension)	Very high speed or with pillion passenger and/or heavy loads

2 There is no means of draining the units or topping up, because the dampers are built as a sealed unit. If the damping fails or if the units commence to leak, the complete damper assembly must be renewed.
3 The compression springs can be removed by detaching the damper units from the machine and holding each one upright on the workbench whilst the outer top shroud is pressed downward in opposition to the spring pressure. This will permit a second person to remove the split collets from the top of the shroud so that the shroud and spring can be withdrawn over the upper end of the unit.
4 To check whether the damping is functioning correctly, press downwards on the end of the detached unit until it is fully compressed. When released slowly, the unit should extend rapidly to approximately half way, and slowly for the final 10 mm, if it is still in serviceable condition.
5 When renewing the units, always do so as a matched pair, to preserve good roadholding. This also applies if the springs alone have to be changed. It follows that the units should be always adjusted so that both have an identical setting position.

11 Centre stand: examination

1 The centre stand pivots on short lugs, welded to the underside of a crossbrace between the lower frame tubes. A shouldered bolt passes through each leg of the stand and is secured by a nut and spring washer. Periodically, these bolts should be checked, to ensure the retaining nut is still tight.
2 An extension spring is used to keep the stand in the fully retracted position when the weight of the machine is taken off it. Check that the spring is in good condition at the same time, and that it is not overstretched. An accident is almost certain to occur if the stand drops whilst the machine is on the move.

12 Prop stand: examination

1 The prop stand bolts to a lug attached to the rear of the left-hand lower frame tube, An extension spring ensures that the stand is retracted when the weight of the machine is taken off the stand.
2 Check that the pivot bolt is secure and that the extension spring is in good condition and not over-stretched. An accident is almost inevitable if the stand extends whilst the machine is on the move.

13 Footrests: examination and renovation

1 Footrests bolt to a rod which passes through the frame gussets on either side of the machine, at the point where the lower frame tubes commence to curve upward. The footrests pivot upwards and are spring-loaded to keep them in the normal horizontal position. If an obstacle is struck, they will fold upwards, obviating the risk of injury to the rider's foot or damage to the frame.
2 If the footrests are damaged in an accident, it is possible to dismantle the assembly into its component parts by detaching each footrest from the rod and separating the folding rubber from the main support on which it pivots by withdrawing the split pin and releasing the clevis pin through the pivot. It is preferable to renew the damaged parts, but if necessary they can be bent straight by clamping them in a vice and heating to a dull red with a blow lamp whilst the appropriate pressure is applied. Never attempt to bend the footrests straight whilst they are still attached to the frame.
3 If heat is applied to the main footrest support during any straightening operation, it follows that the footrest rubber must be removed temporarily to prevent damage from heat conduction.

14 Rear brake pedal: examination and renovation

1 The rear brake pedal is attached to a splined pivot which passes through a tube, immediately below the swinging arm pivot. A short arm welded to the other end of the pivot forms the pivot point of attachment for the rod which operates the rear brake. The pivot is fitted with a strong return spring coiled around its boss, to provide the brake pedal with positive action.
2 If the brake pedal is bent or twisted, it can be drawn off the splined pivot and straightened by adopting the same technique as recommended for bent footrests. It is held in position by a single clamp bolt. Mark the position of the pedal in relation to the pivot splines before removal, so that it is replaced in the same position.
3 Check the return spring periodically and renew it if it shows signs of weakening.

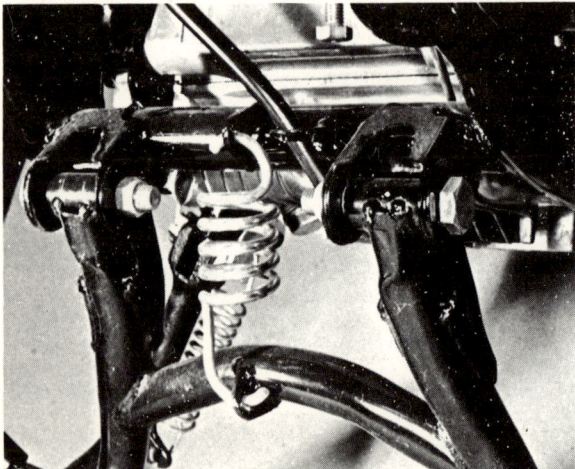

11.2 A stout spring is used to retract the centre stand. Note pivot arrangement

15 Dualseat: removal and replacement

1 The seat is attached to small lugs on the right-hand side of the subframe and pivots on two long clevis pins which pass through these lugs. It opens from the left, and locks in position to safeguard the battery and safety helmets attached to hooks covered by the seat.
2 Although it is seldom necessary to detach the seat, it can be lifted away as a complete unit if the split pins through the ends of the clevis pins are withdrawn, and then the clevis pins themselves.

16 Speedometer and tachometer heads: removal and replacement

1 The speedometer and tachometer heads are freed quite readily by removing the single dome nut, spring washer and plain washer under each base, then the base itself, so that they can be lifted upward. Detach the drive cables at the screwed couplings and withdraw the bulb holders from the base of each head.
2 Apart from defects in either the drive or drive cables, a speedometer or tachometer which malfunctions is difficult to repair. Fit a replacement or alternatively entrust the repair to a competent instrument repair specialist.
3 Remember that a speedometer in correct working order is a statutory requirement in the UK. Apart from the legal necessity, reference to the odometer readings is the most satisfactory means of keeping pase with the maintenance schedules.

17 Speedometer and tachometer drive cables: examination and maintenance

1 It is advisable to detach the drive cable(s) from time to time in order to check whether they are lubricated adequately, and whether the outer coverings are damaged or compressed at any point along their run. Jerky or sluggish movements can often be traced to a damaged drive cable.
2 For greasing, withdraw the inner cable. After removing all the old grease, clean with a petrol-soaked rag and examine the cable for broken strands or other damage.
3 Regrease the cable with high melting point grease, taking care not to grease the last six inches at the point where the cable enters the instrument head. If this precaution is not observed, grease will work into the head and immobilise the instrument movement.
4 If any instrument head stops working suspect a broken drive cable unless the odometer readings continue. Inspection will show whether the inner cable has broken; if so, the inner cable alone can be replaced and re-inserted in the outer casing, after greasing. Never fit a new inner cable alone if the outer covering is damaged or compressed at any point along its run

18 Speedometer and tachometer drives: location and examination

1 The speedometer drive gearbox forms part of the front hub assembly and can be pulled away from the wheel hub after the wheel is removed from the forks and the wheel spindle withdrawn The drive rarely gives trouble; it is prepacked with grease and should be relubricated when the front wheel bearings receive attention.
2 The tachometer drive is taken from a cross-shaft in the upper crankcase, driven from an idler pinion on the end of the gearbox output shaft. The drive operates the oil pump and tachometer, by means of skew-cut pinions, the latter via a flexible cable to the tachometer head. It is unlikely that the drive will give trouble during the normal service life of the machine, especially since it is fully enclosed and effectively lubricated.

19 Cleaning the machine

1 After removing all surface dirt with a rag or sponge which is washed frequently in clean water, the machine should be allowed to dry thoroughly. Application of car polish or wax to the cycle parts will give a good finish, particularly if the machine receives this attention at regular intervals.
2 The plated parts should require only a wipe with a damp rag, but if they are badly corroded, as may occur during winter when the roads are salted, it is permissible to use one of the proprietary chrome cleaners. These often have an oily base which will help to prevent corrosion from recurring.
3 If the engine parts are particularly oily, use a cleaning compound such as Gunk or Jizer. Apply the compound whilst the parts are dry and work it in with a brush so that it has an opportunity to penetrate and soak into the film of oil and grease. Finish off by washing down liberally, taking care that water does not enter the carburettors, air cleaner or the electrics. If desired, the now clean aluminium alloy parts can be enhanced still further when they are dry by using a special polish such as Solvol Autosol. This will restore the full lustre.
4 If possible, the machine should be wiped down immediately after it has been used in the wet, so that it is not garaged under damp conditions which will promote rusting. Make sure that the chain is wiped and re-oiled, to prevent water from entering the rollers and causing harshness with an accompanying rapid rate of wear. Remember there is less chance of water entering the control cables and causing stiffness if they are lubricated regularly as described in the Routine Maintenance Section.

Fault diagnosis overleaf

20 Fault diagnosis

Symptom	Cause	Remedy
Machine veers to the left or right with hands off handlebars	Incorrect wheel alignment Bent forks Twisted frame	Check and re-align. Check and renew. Check and renew.
Machine rolls at low speeds	Overtight steering head bearings	Slacken and re-test.
Machine judders when front brake is applied	Slack steering head bearings Worn forks	Tighten until all play is taken up. Renew all worn parts
Machine pitches badly on uneven surfaces	Ineffective fork dampers Ineffective rear suspension units	Check oil content. Check damping action.
Fork action stiff	Fork legs out of alignment (twisted yokes)	Slacken yoke clamps, front wheel spindle and fork top bolts. Pump forks several times, then tighten from bottom upwards.
Machine wanders. Steering imprecise, rear wheel tends to hop	Worn swinging arm pivot	Dismantle and renew bushes and pivot shaft.

Chapter 5 Wheels, brakes and tyres

Contents

General description ... 1	Rear wheel: examination, removal and renovation ... 9
Front wheel: examination and renovation ... 2	Rear brake assembly: examination, renovation and reassembly 10
Front wheel disc brake: examination and bleeding the hydraulic system ... 3	Adjusting the rear brake pedal ... 11
	Cush drive assembly: examination and renovation ... 12
Replacing the brake pads and overhauling the caliper unit ... 4	Rear wheel sprocket: removal, examination and replacement 13
Removing and replacing the brake disc ... 5	Final drive chain: examination, lubrication and replacement 14
Master cylinder: examination and renovation (front brake) ... 6	Tyres: removal and replacement ... 15
Front wheel bearings: examination and replacement ... 7	Front wheel: balancing ... 16
Front wheel: replacement ... 8	Fault diagnosis: wheels, brakes and tyres ... 17

Specifications

Wheels ... 19 inch diameter front, 18 inch diameter rear, of conventional spoked type, with alloy hubs and cush drive in rear hub
Cast aluminium alloy wheels available as optional extra on XS500C model only

Brakes ... Front wheel disc brake of hydraulically-operated type *
Rear wheel drum brake of single leading shoe type
XS500C model only has rear wheel disc brake of hydraulically-operated type

Tyres:
Front tyre... 3.25 x 19 4PR
Rear tyre ... 3.50 x 18 4PR (4.00 x H18 4PR - XS500C model)

Tyre pressures:
Front ... 23 psi   28 psi
1.6 kg/cm^2 normal riding   2.0 kg/cm^2 high speed riding
Rear ... 28 psi   33 psi
2.0 kg/cm^2 normal riding   2.3 kg/cm^2 high speed riding

Optional twin front disc brake available.

1 General description

The Yamaha 500 twin has a 19 inch diameter front wheel and an 18 inch diameter rear wheel. The front tyre is of 3.25 inch section and normally has a ribbed tread pattern, with blocks in the centremost portion. The rear tyre is of 3.50 or 4.00 inch sections, and has a more general block tread pattern.

The front wheel is fitted with a single hydraulically-operated disc brake and the rear wheel has either a conventional drum brake of the single leading shoe type, or an hydraulically-operated disc brake (XS 500 C model). The rear wheel is not of the quickly detachable type. It is necessary to remove the final drive chain, which may or may not be of the endless type, before the wheel can be detached from the frame.

2 Front wheel: examination and renovation

1 Place the machine on the centre stand so that the front wheel is raised clear of the ground. Spin the wheel and check the rim alignment. Small irregularities can be corrected by tightening the spokes in the affected area although a certain amount of experience is necessary to prevent over-correction. Any flats in the wheel rim will be evident at the same time. These are more difficult to remove and in most cases it will be necessary to have the wheel rebuilt on a new rim. Apart from the effect on stability, a flat will expose the tyre bead and walls to greater risk of damage if the machine is run with a deformed wheel.

2 Check for loose and broken spokes. Tapping the spokes is the best guide to tension. A loose spoke will produce a quite different sound and should be tightened by turning the nipple in an anticlockwise direction. Always check for run out by spinning the wheel again. If the spokes have to be tightened by an excessive amount, it is advisable to remove the tyre and tube as detailed in Section 15 of this Chapter. This will enable the protruding ends of the spokes to be ground off, thus preventing them from chafing the inner tube and causing punctures.

Chapter 5: Wheels, brakes and tyres

3.5 Attach tube to bleed nipple, other end immersed in brake fluid

3 Some models are fitted with cast alloy wheels, which should be checked for run out and any cracks or other damage, especially where the spokes join the hub and rim.

3 Front wheel disc brake - examination, renovation and bleeding the hydraulic system

1 Check the front brake master cylinder, hose and caliper unit for signs of fluid leakage. Pay particular attention to the condition of the hose, which should be renewed without question if there are signs of cracking, splitting or other exterior damage.
2 Check the level of hydraulic fluid by removing the cap on the brake fluid reservoir, diaphragm plate and diaphragm. This is one of the regular maintenance tasks, which should never be neglected. If the fluid is below the level mark, brake fluid of the correct grade must be added. NEVER USE ENGINE OIL or anything other than the recommended fluid. Other fluids have unsatisfactory characteristics and will rapidly destroy the seals.
3 The brake pads should be inspected for wear. Each has a red line around its periphery, which marks the limit of the friction material. When this limit has been reached, BOTH pads must be renewed, even if only one has reached the limit line. Check by applying the brake so that the pads engage with the disc. They will lift out of the caliper unit when the front wheel is removed and the caliper unit is separated. See Section 4 of this Chapter.
4 If brake action becomes spongy, or if any part of the hydraulic system is dismantled (such as when the hose is renewed) it is necessary to bleed the system in order to remove all traces of air. The following procedure should be followed:
5 Attach a tube to the bleed valve at the top of the caliper unit, after removing the dust cap. It is preferable to use a transparent plastic tube, so that the presence of air bubbles is seen more readily.
6 The far end of the tube should rest in a small bottle so that it is submerged in hydraulic fluid. This is essential, to prevent air from passing back into the system. In consequence, the end of the tube must remain submerged at all times.
7 Check that the reservoir on the handlebars is full of fluid and replace the cap to keep the fluid clean.
8 If spongy brake action necessitates the bleeding operation, squeeze and release the brake lever several times in rapid succession, to allow the pressure in the system to build up. Then open the bleed valve by unscrewing it one complete turn whilst maintaining pressure on the lever. This is a two-person operation. Squeeze the lever fully until it meets the handlebar, then close the bleed valve. If parts of the system have been renewed, the bleed valve can be opened from the beginning and the brake lever worked until fluid issues from the bleed tube. Note that it may be necessary to top up the reservoir during this operation; if it empties, air will enter the system and the whole operation will have to be repeated.
9 Repeat operation 8 until bubbles disappear from the bleed tube. Close the bleed valve fully, remove the bleed tube and replace the dust cap.
10 Check the level in the reservoir and top up if necessary. Never use the fluid which has drained into the bottle at the end of the bleed tube because this contains air bubbles which will re-introduce air into the system. It must stand for 24 hours before it can be re-used.
11 Refit the diaphragm and diaphragm plate and tighten the reservoir cap securely.
12 Do not spill hydraulic fluid on the cycle parts. It is a very effective paint stripper! The plastic 'glasses' in the speedometer and tachometer heads will be obscured badly if hydraulic fluid is spilt on them.

4 Replacing the brake pads and overhauling the caliper unit

1 Remove the front wheel by following the procedure described in Chapter 4, Section 2.7. Before the brake pads can be removed, it will be necessary to separate the caliper unit by unscrewing the dome nut and the lower bolt that retain the unit to the right-hand fork leg, then the third bolt that passes right through the unit. Note there is a tagged, anti-rattle shim behind each pad. On no account disturb the piston unless it has to be examined, in which case special care is necessary after the hydraulic system has been drained of fluid. Refer to paragraph 6 of this Section. This also applies to the front brake lever, which must not be operated whilst the caliper unit is separated and removed from its normal operating position. If these precautions are overlooked, the fluid will drain from the system, necessitating bleeding off the air that accumulates as a result.
2 As an alternative to removing the front wheel, the brake pipe can be detached from the top of the caliper unit and wrapped in clean plastic sheeting. Keep the front brake lever pulled in throughout the operation, to prevent fluid from dripping. If the bolt is removed from the lower fork anchorage and the upper acorn nut slackened, the caliper unit can be tilted upwards to clear the brake disc. Under these circumstances, the brake pads can be extracted more easily and the new replacements fitted, without need to separate the unit.
3 Inspect the friction pads closely and renew them both if the limit level of wear is approached, as described in paragraph 3 of the preceding Section. If there is any doubt whatsoever about their condition, they should be renewed as a pair.
4 Clean the recesses into which the pads fit and the exposed ends of the pistons which actuate the pads. Use only a small, soft brush and NOT solvent or a wire brush. Smear the piston faces and the brake pad recesses with hydraulic fluid, to act as a lubricant. Only sparing lubrication is required.
5 Remove the reservoir cap, diaphragm plate and diaphragm to check whether the level of fluid rises as the piston is pushed back into the recess. It may be necessary to syphon some fluid out of the reservoir prior to this operation, to prevent over-flowing. If the pistons do not move freely, the caliper must be removed from the machine and overhauled. Because damage of some kind is inevitable to cause piston seizure, it is best to entrust the repair or replacement of the unit to a Yamaha agent.
6 If it is considered necessary to examine the pistons, or if the pistons have stuck or move only sluggishly, it is necessary to disconnect the brake pipe as described in paragraph 2, and use a compressed air line to displace the pistons from their housings. On no account use a screwdriver or any other sharp instrument to prise a piston from its housing as irreparable damage will be

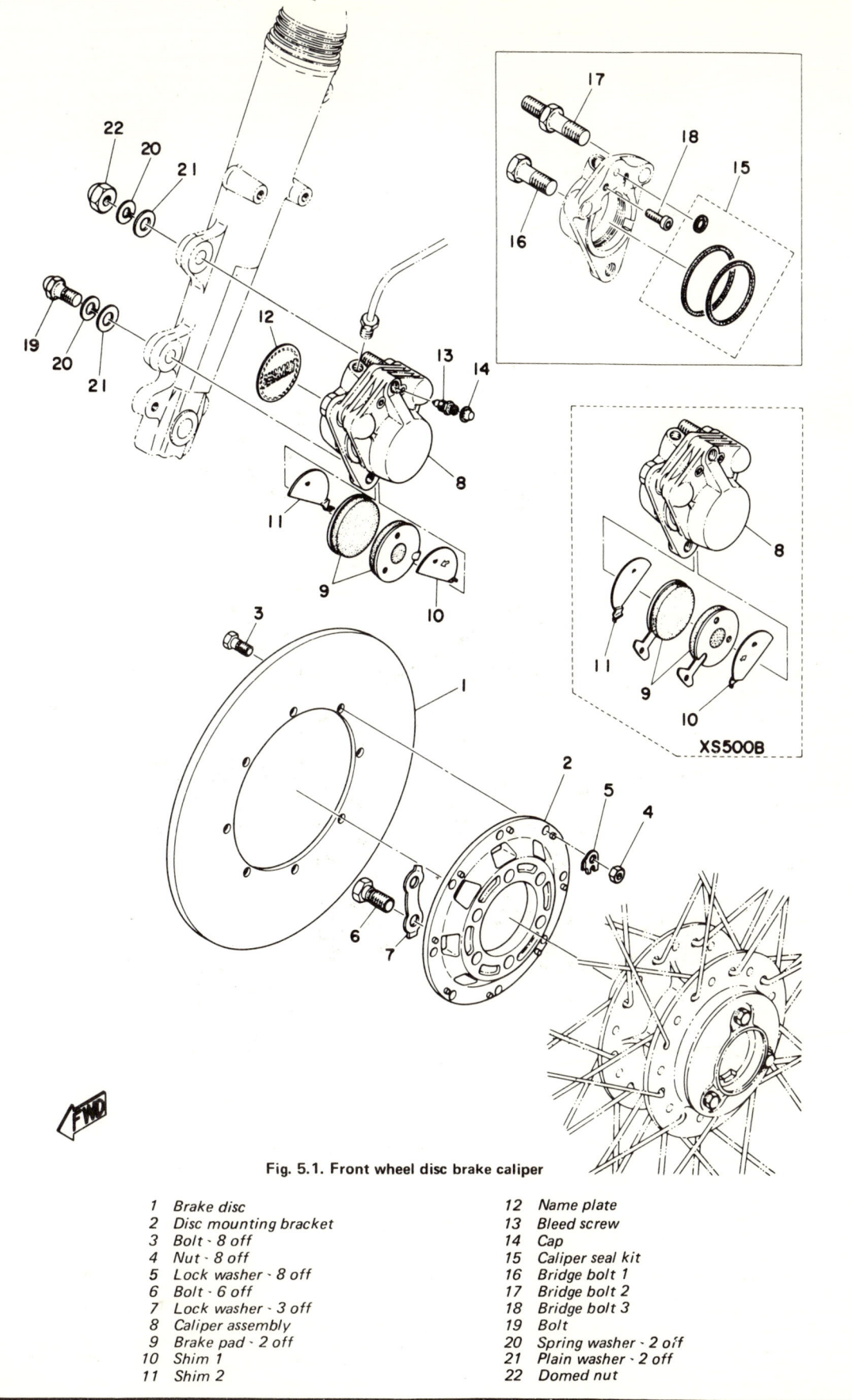

Fig. 5.1. Front wheel disc brake caliper

1 Brake disc
2 Disc mounting bracket
3 Bolt - 8 off
4 Nut - 8 off
5 Lock washer - 8 off
6 Bolt - 6 off
7 Lock washer - 3 off
8 Caliper assembly
9 Brake pad - 2 off
10 Shim 1
11 Shim 2
12 Name plate
13 Bleed screw
14 Cap
15 Caliper seal kit
16 Bridge bolt 1
17 Bridge bolt 2
18 Bridge bolt 3
19 Bolt
20 Spring washer - 2 off
21 Plain washer - 2 off
22 Domed nut

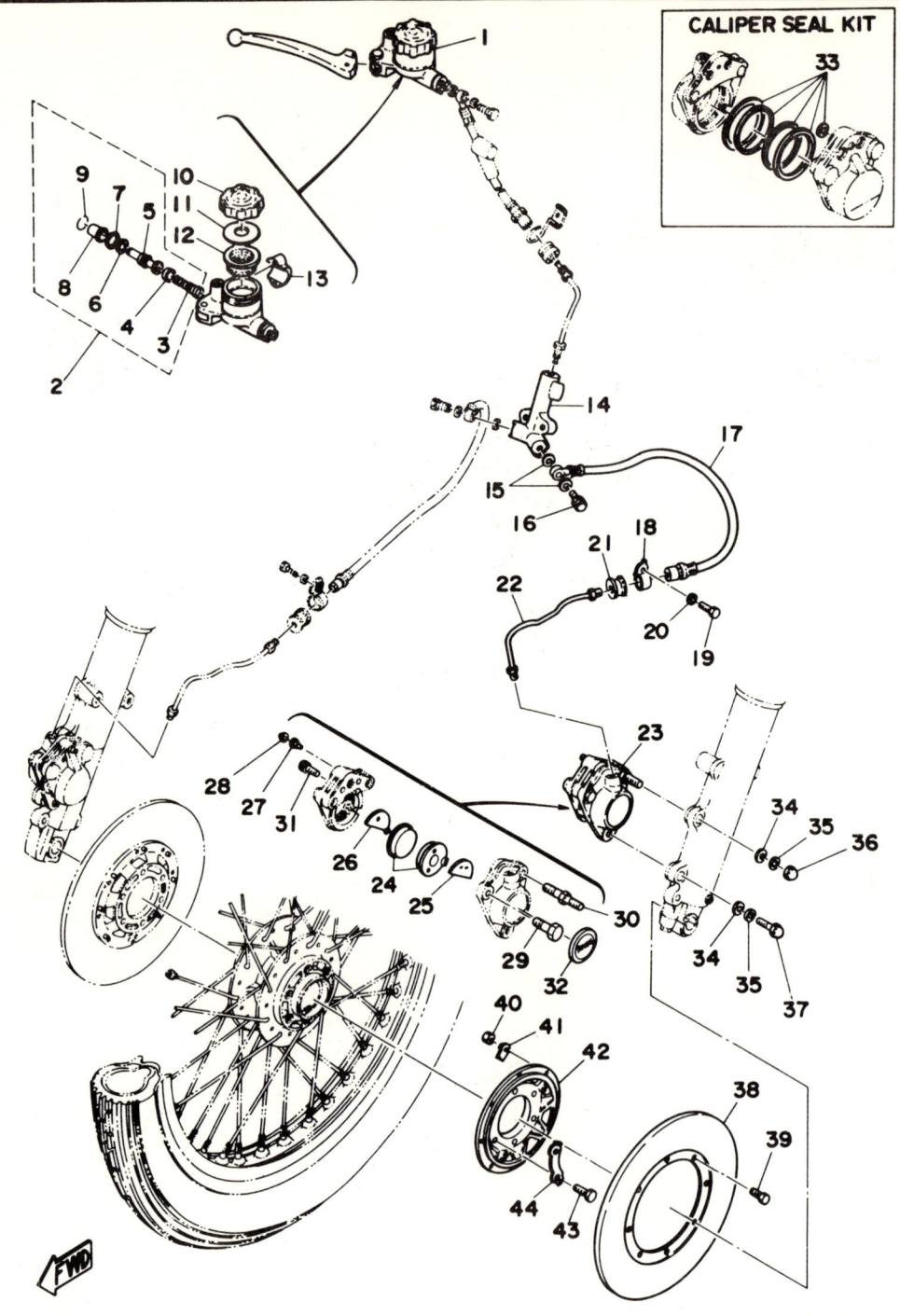

Fig. 5.2. Double front wheel disc brake (optional extra)

1 Master cylinder assembly
2 Master cylinder kit (items 3 - 9)
10 Reservoir cap
11 Diaphragm plate
12 Reservoir diaphragm
13 Master cylinder bracket
14 Joint
15 Washer - 2 off
16 Union bolt
17 Brake hose - lower - 2 off
18 Brake hose clamp - 2 off
19 Bolt - 2 off
20 Spring washer - 2 off
21 Brake hose protector - 2 off
22 Brake pipe - lower - 2 off
23 Caliper assembly - 2 off
24 Brake pad - 4 off
25 Shim 1 - 2 off
26 Shim 2 - 2 off
27 Bleed screw - 2 off
28 Cap - 2 off
29 Bridge bolt 1 - 2 off
30 Bridge bolt 2 - 2 off
31 Bridge bolt 3 - 2 off
32 Caliper emblem - 2 off
33 Caliper seal kit
34 Plain washer - 4 off
35 Spring washer - 4 off
36 Domed nut - 2 off
37 Bolt - 2 off
38 Brake disc - 2 off
39 Bolt - 16 off
40 Nut - 16 off
41 Lock washer - 16 off
42 Disc mounting bracket - 2 off
43 Bolt - 12 off
44 Lock washer - 6 off

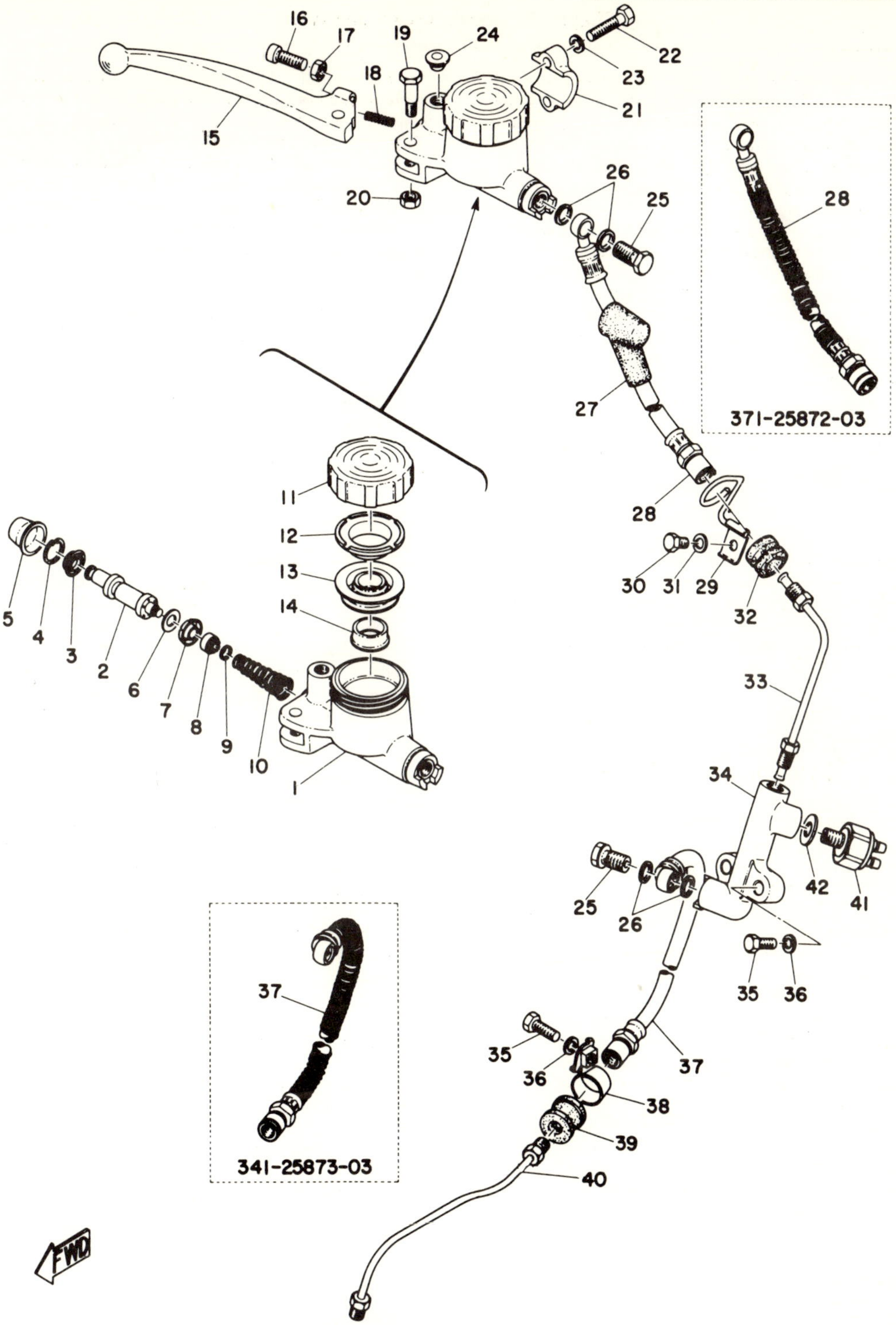

Fig. 5.3. Front brake master cylinder and hose

1 Master cylinder assembly	20 Nut	32 Brake hose protector
2 Master cylinder kit (items 2 - 10)	21 Master cylinder bracket	33 Brake pipe - upper
3 Master cylinder cup kit (items 3 - 7 and 9)	22 Bolt - 2 off	34 Joint
11 Reservoir cap	23 Spring washer - 2 off	35 Bolt - 3 off
12 Diaphragm bush	24 Plug	36 Spring washer - 3 off
13 Diaphragm	25 Union bolt	37 Brake hose - lower
14 Reservoir float	26 Sealing washer - 4 off	38 Brake hose clamp
15 Front brake lever	27 Master cylinder boot	39 Brake hose protector
16 Adjusting screw (for lever reach)	28 Brake hose - upper	40 Brake pipe - lower
17 Locknut	29 Brake hose clamp	41 Front brake stop lamp switch
18 Spring	30 Bolt	42 Washer
19 Bolt	31 Spring washer	

caused, necessitating renewal of the piston and probably the complete caliper unit. The pistons must be able to move quite freely within their housings, without evidence of any play, and must not be scored or have any form of surface damage that will encourage hydraulic fluid leakage. Whilst the caliper unit is separated, check the large 'O' ring seal that surrounds the piston housing, and renew it, if necessary.
7   When reassembling, each part must be scrupulously clean and the assembly itself must take place in ultra clean conditions. Use only hydraulic brake fluid to lubricate the moving parts, never petrol, paraffin or oil, which will attack the various seals and cause them to deteriorate. The caliper bolts must be tightened fully and if the brake pipe has been disconnected, the complete hydraulic system must be bled of air, after reconnection, by following the procedure described in Section 3, commencing at paragraph 4.
8   Do not omit to check the brake hose, pipe, and union connections. All must be in perfect condition for maximum efficiency.

5   Removing and replacing the brake disc

1   It is unlikely that the disc will require attention unless it is badly scored and braking efficiency is reduced. To remove the disc, first detach the front wheel from the forks as described in Chapter 4, Section 2.7. The disc is bolted to the left hand side of the wheel by eight bolts, the nuts of which are secured by tab washers. Bend back the tab washers and remove the nuts, to free the disc.
2   Replace the disc by reversing the dismantling procedure. Make sure that all eight nuts are tightened fully and that the tab washers are bent back into position.
3   Check the runout of the disc, when it is attached to the front wheel hub. It should not exceed 0.15 mm (0.006 in) at any point. If an excessive reading is obtained, check the wheel bearings before investigating further.

6   Master cylinder - examination and renovation (front brake)

1   The master cylinder is unlikely to give trouble unless the machine has been stored for a lengthy period or until a considerable mileage has been covered. The usual signs of trouble are leakage of hydraulic fluid and a gradual fall in the fluid reservoir content.
2   The satisfactory renovation of an hydraulic brake master cylinder is not a task to be taken lightly, since it is a somewhat skilled operation that must be carried out under clinically clean conditions. Remember that if the master cylinder is rendered inoperative in any way, a total brake failure will be the outcome.
3   To gain full access to the master cylinder, commence the dismantling operation by attaching a bleed tube to the caliper unit bleed nipple. Open the bleed nipple one complete turn, then operate the front brake lever until all fluid is pumped out of the reservoir. Close the bleed nipple, detach the tube and store the fluid in a closed container for subsequent re-use.
4   Detach the hose and remove the handlebar lever pivot bolt and the lever itself. Do not lose the spring that is released at the same time.
5   Access is now available to the piston and the cylinder and it is possible to remove the piston assembly, together with all the relevant seals. Take note of the way in which the seals are arranged because they must be replaced in the same order. Failure to observe this necessity will result in brake failure. Commence by removing the internal snap ring, which will release the piston. The spring will remain in the cylinder. Next, remove the conical spring, the 'E' clip and the retainer. This will free the cylinder cup.
6   Clean the master cylinder and piston with either hydraulic fluid or alcohol. On no account use either abrasives or other solvents such as petrol. If any signs of wear or damage are evident, renewal is necessary. It is not practicable to reclaim either the piston or the cylinder bore.
7   Soak the new seals in hydraulic fluid for about 15 minutes prior to fitting, then reassemble the parts IN EXACTLY THE SAME ORDER, using the reversal of the dismantling procedure. Lubricate with hydraulic fluid and make sure the feather edges of the various seals are not damaged.
8   Refit the assembled master cylinder unit to the handlebar, and reconnect the handlebar lever, hose etc. Refill the reservoir with hydraulic fluid and bleed the entire system by following the procedure detailed in Section 3.4 of this Chapter.
9   Check that the brake is working correctly before taking the machine on the road, to restore pressure and align the pads correctly. Use the brake gently for the first 50 miles or so to enable all the new parts to bed down correctly.
10 It should be emphasised that repairs to the master cylinder are best entrusted to a Yamaha agent, or alternatively, that the defective part should be replaced by a new unit.

7   Front wheel bearings - examination and replacement

1   Place the machine on the centre stand and remove the front wheel as described in Chapter 4, Section 2.7. Detach the speedometer drive gearbox, then remove the dust cover from the right-hand side and prise out the oil seal, which seats on a shouldered spacer. Working from the left-hand side, drive the right-hand wheel bearing outwards, using a drift of suitable size. Several sharp blows will be necessary. When the bearing has been displaced from its housing the bearing spacer can be withdrawn together with any flanged bearing seating that may be fitted. The left-hand bearing can then be displaced in similar fashion, using the same drift and driving it outwards from the right-hand side of the wheel. Note that both wheel bearings have one covered side, to impede entry of grit and other road debris.
2   Remove all the old grease from the hub and bearings, giving the latter a final wash in petrol. Check the bearings for play or any signs of roughness as they are rotated. If there is any doubt about their condition, renewal is essential.
3   Before driving the bearings back into position, pack the hub with high melting point grease, leaving room for any expansion that may occur. Pack the bearings with the same grease, and drive them back into position, not forgetting the spacer that separates them and any flanged bearing seatings that may be fitted. The closed faces of each bearing must face outwards. Make sure each bearing enters its housing square, otherwise there is risk of damage to the housing and the possibility of the bearing rotating in its housing, during use. Refit the shouldered spacer and oil seal to the right-hand side of the hub.

8   Front wheel: replacement

1   Replace the front wheel in the forks and reinsert the wheel spindle, making sure the speedometer drive gearbox is positioned so that the recess in its body aligns with the lower left-hand fork leg. This is important, as otherwise the speedometer drive gearbox can rotate with the wheel and will snap the speedometer drive cable.
2   Check that the lower left-hand fork leg clamp is tight and also the nut on the end of the wheel spindle. Do not omit to replace the split pin through the castellated nut, to prevent the nut from working loose whilst the machine is in use. Before taking the machine on the road, check that the wheel spins quite freely and that the front disc brake performs correctly.

7.1a Detach speedometer drive gearbox from hub

7.1b Prise out dust cover from right-hand side, followed by ...

7.1c ... oil seal

7.1d Working from left, drive out right-hand wheel bearing, followed by ...

7.1e ... bearing spacer

8.1 Position speedometer drive gearbox correctly, when replacing wheel

Chapter 5: Wheels, brakes and tyres

9 Rear wheel - examination, removal and renovation

1 Place the machine on the centre stand so that the rear wheel is raised clear of the ground. Check for rim alignment, damage to the rim and loose or broken spokes by following the procedure relating to the front wheel, as described in Section 2 of this Chapter. Note that it is also possible to have a matching alloy rear wheel.

2 To remove the rear wheel, use the procedure described in paragraphs 2 to 4 of Section 9, Chapter 4.

3 The rear wheel bearings have a similar arrangement to those of the front wheel and can be removed and replaced in a similar manner. In this instance there is less difficulty in gaining access because there is no speedometer drive gearbox to remove first. It will, however, be necessary to unscrew the threaded bearing retainer that screws into the left-hand side of the rear wheel hub, before the left-hand bearing can be drifted out. The exact arrangement varies, according to the model.

10 Rear brake assembly: examination, renovation and reassembly

Drum brake models

1 The rear brake is a single leading shoe of conventional design. The brake assembly is exposed when the brake plate is lifted off the wheel hub from the right hand side.

2 Examine the condition of the brake linings. If they are thin or uneven, the brake shoes should be renewed. The linings are bonded on and cannot be supplied separately.

3 To remove the brake shoes, turn the brake operating lever so that the brake is in the fully on position. Pull the brake shoes apart against their return spring pressure to free them from the operating cam after withdrawing the split pins and plates used to anchor their ends. The shoes can then be lifted away, complete with the return springs by reverting to a V formation. When they are clear of the brake plate, the return springs can be removed and the shoes separated.

4 Before replacing the brake shoes, check that the brake operating cam is working smoothly and not binding in the pivot bush. The cam is removed for greasing by detaching the operating arm from the splined shaft, after first marking its position in relation to the splines so that it is replaced in an identical position. Slacken the pinch bolt and draw the arm off the shaft. Grease the cam and spindle sparingly, or grease

8.2 Do not omit split pin through castellated wheel spindle nut

9.3a Rear wheel bearings do not have enclosed races

9.3b Drive bearings out in similar fashion

10.7 The rear brake pads (XS500C model)

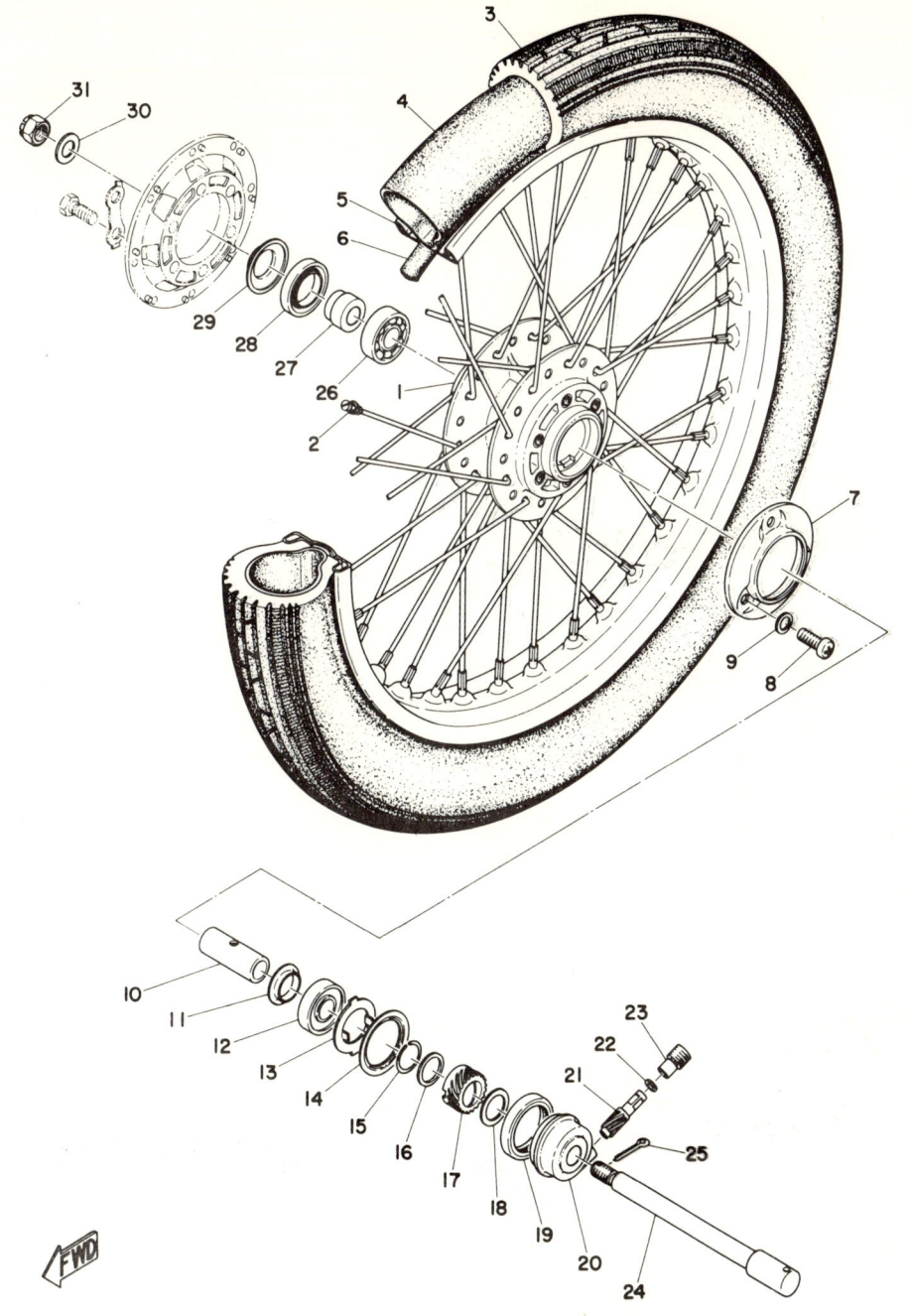

Fig. 5.4. Front wheel

1 Front hub
2 Spoke set
3 Front tyre
4 Inner tube
5 Wheel rim
6 Rim tape
7 Hub cover
8 Screw - 3 off
9 Spring washer - 3 - off
10 Bearing spacer
11 Spacer flange
12 Wheel bearing
13 Speedometer gearbox drive
14 Speedometer gearbox drive retainer
15 Circlip
16 Washer
17 Speedometer drive gear pinion (29 teeth)
18 Washer
19 Oil seal
20 Speedometer drive gearbox housing
21 Skew drive pinion (10 teeth)
22 Washer
23 Bush
24 Front wheel spindle
25 Split pin
26 Wheel bearing
27 Collar
28 Oil seal
29 Dust cover
30 Plain washer
31 Castellated wheel nut

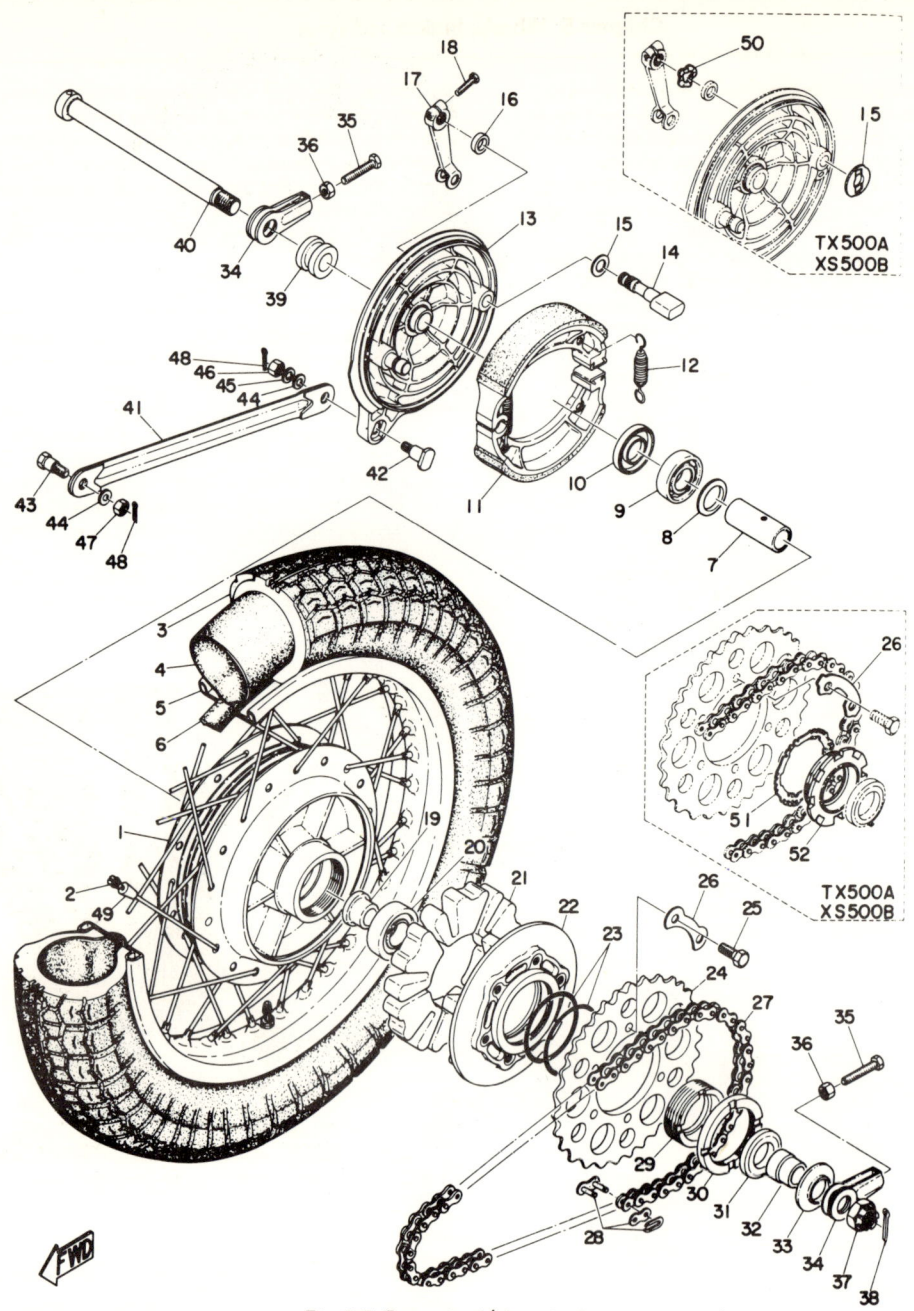

Fig. 5.5. Rear wheel (drum brake models only)

1	Rear hub	19	Collar	36	Locknut - 2 off
2	Spoke set	20	Wheel bearing	37	Castellated rear wheel spindle nut
3	Rear tyre	21	Cush drive rubber	38	Split pin
4	Inner tube	22	Sprocket carrier	39	Collar
5	Wheel rim	23	'O' ring - 2 off	40	Rear wheel spindle
6	Rim tape	24	Rear wheel sprocket - 42 teeth standard	41	Torque arm
7	Wheel bearing spacer	25	Bolt - 6 off	42	Bolt
8	Spacer flange	26	Lock washer - 3 off	43	Bolt
9	Wheel bearing	27	Final drive chain	44	Plain washer - 2 off
10	Oil seal	28	Chain joining link	45	Spring washer
11	Brake shoe - 2 off	29	Bearing retainer	46	Nut
12	Brake shoe return spring - 2 o	30	Locknut	47	Nut
13	Brake plate	31	Oil seal	48	Split pin
14	Brake operating cam	32	Collar	49	Balance weight
15	Shim	33	Dust cover	50	Wave washer
16	Seal	34	Chain tensioner - 2 off	51	Lock washer
17	Brake operating arm	35	Drawbolt - 2 off	52	Cush drive locking ring
18	Bolt				

Note: XS500C rear wheel is of somewhat similar construction, but is fitted with disc brake

Chapter 5: Wheels, brakes and tyres

may work onto the brake linings and impair their efficiency.
5   Check the inner surface of the brake drum. The surface on which the brake shoes operate should be smooth and free from score marks or indentations, otherwise reduced braking efficiency will be inevitable. Remove all traces of brake lining dust and wipe with a clean rag soaked in petrol to remove all traces of grease and oil.
6   To reassemble the brake shoes on the brake plate, fit the return springs and pull the shoes apart, holding them in V formation. If they are now located with the brake operating cam and pivots, they can be pushed back into position by pressing downward in order to snap them into position. Do not use excessive force, or there is risk of distorting the brake shoes permanently. Do not forget to replace the anchor plates and split pins which retain the shoes in position.

Disc brake model
7   The rear disc brake is virtually a copy of that fitted to the front wheel, with a rearrangement of the various components to suit the different layout of the brake. Access to the brake pads is obtained by removing the single crosshead screw that holds the fluted cover in position, and lifting the cover away.
8   Refer to Sections 3, 4, 5 and 6 of this Chapter when examining and renovating the rear disc brake components, as similar advice applies with only minor exceptions brought about by the different layout.

11 Adjusting the rear brake pedal

Drum brake models
1   If the adjustment of the rear brake is correct, the brake pedal will have a travel of from 20 to 30 mm (0.8 to 1.2 inch). Adjustment is made at the end of the brake operating rod, at the point where the rod passes through the trunnion in the brake operating arm. To decrease pedal movement, screw the adjusting nut inward, and outward for increase of travel.
2   Note that it may be necessary to re-adjust the height of the stop lamp switch if the range of pedal travel has been altered to any marked extent.

Disc brake models
3   The angle of the brake operating arm can be altered by adjusting the pedal stop on the underside. Ideally, the top of the pedal should be 5 mm (0.2 in) below the top of the footrest. The linkage with the rear brake master cylinder is also adjustable for length, so that the point at which the brake comes into operation can be adjusted to suit the rider's personal requirements. The rod should be set until it lightly touches the brake master cylinder, then turned outwards about ¾ turn. An ideal setting is that recommended in paragraph 1.
4   The connection to the stop lamp switch is made by means of a length of stout wire and an extension spring. As in the case of the drum brake models, the height of the stop lamp switch itself can be adjusted by moving the threaded body of the switch either upwards or downwards - the former to operate the lamp earlier and the latter to operate it later.

12 Cush drive assembly: examination and renovation

1   The cush drive assembly comprises a set of moulded synthetic rubber blocks arranged within a compartmentalised housing cast into the left-hand side of the rear wheel hub. Vanes cast in to the plate on which the final drive sprocket is mounted engage with these blocks and permit the sprocket to move in relation to the hub within certain limits. This action effectively cushions any surges or roughness in the transmission, which would otherwise convey the impression of harshness.
2   When the rear wheel is removed, it is advisable to examine the condition of the cush drive rubbers for signs of damage or general deterioration that may otherwise render them ineffective. The usual sign of a cush drive assembly requiring attention takes the form of excessive sprocket movement in relation to the wheel hub, or the presence of rubber dust.
3   When the rubbers are in good condition, it will prove quite difficult to prise the sprocket carrier plate from position. Before the sprocket and plate can be removed, the large diameter circlip and washer around the boss of the hub must be detached first.

13 Rear wheel sprocket: removal, examination and replacement

1   The rear wheel sprocket and its carrier plate can be removed from the rear wheel hub after the wheel itself is removed from the frame and the retaining circlip and washer withdrawn from the boss of the hub. If the cush drive rubbers are in good condition, it may prove quite difficult to prise the assembly clear from the hub without damaging the rubbers.
2   To separate the sprocket from the carrier plate, remove six bolts and three sets of paired tab washers which must be bent back first. The standard sprocket has 42 teeth, but it is possible to obtain a 43 tooth sprocket, as an alternative.

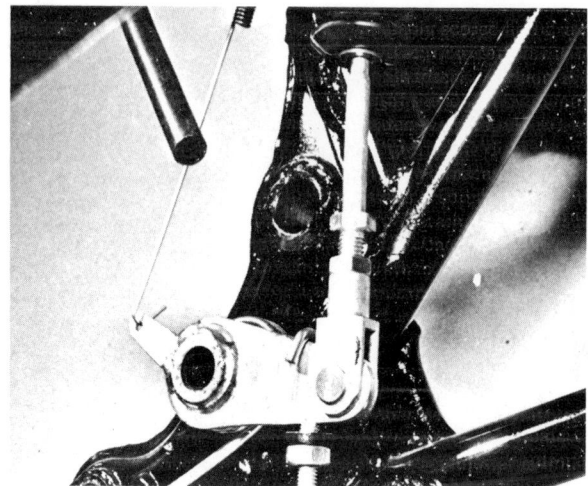
11.2 Linkage to rear brake master cylinder is adjustable in length

13.1 Large diameter external circlip retains sprocket on rear hub

120 Chapter 5 : Wheels, brakes and tyres

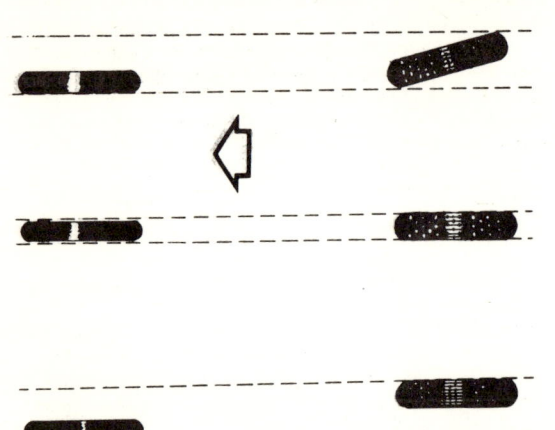

Fig. 5.6. Checking wheel alignment

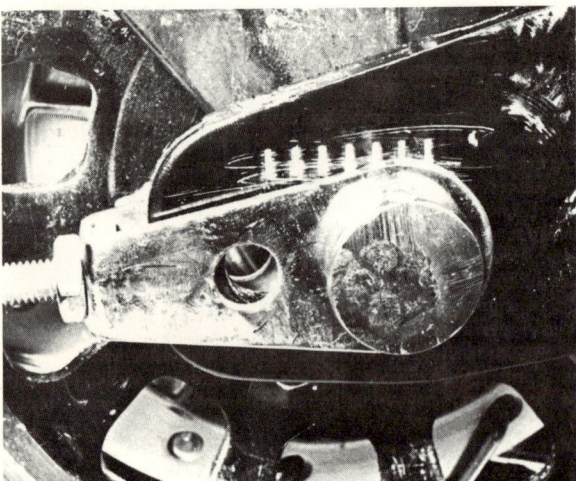

14.3 Fork ends are marked to aid rear wheel alignment

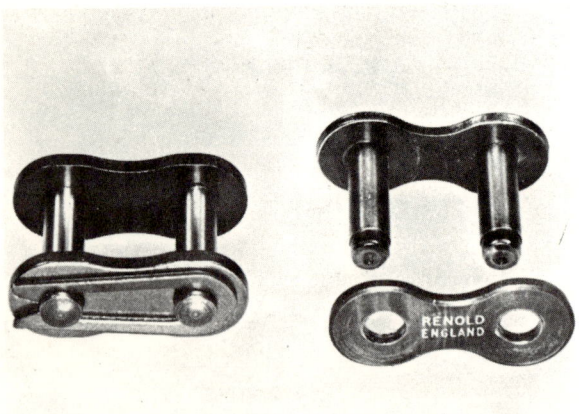

14.9 An equivalent British-made chain is available, of detachable type

No advantage is gained from varying the size outside these two choices, as the sizes have been selected by the manufacturer to give optimum performance, after extensive tests.
3 The sprocket will have to be renewed if the teeth are badly worn, chipped or broken. Wear is often evident by the sprocket teeth assuming a hooked formation. It is bad practice to renew one sprocket on its own and if possible, both final drive sprockets should be renewed as a pair, and a new chain fitted. If old and new parts are run together, more rapid wear will take place, necessitating even more frequent renewal of the parts concerned.

14 Final drive chain: removal, examination, lubrication and replacement

1 The final drive chain is fully exposed, apart from the protection given by the plastic chainguard above part of the upper run. Irrespective of the amount of protection provided, the chain tension will need adjustment at regular intervals, to compensate for wear. This is accomplished by slackening the rear wheel nut, after withdrawing the split pin, when the machine is on the centre stand. The draw bolt adjusters in each rear fork end are used to draw the wheel backward until the chain is again under correct tension. Note that it may be necessary to slacken the rear brake torque arm bolt during this operation.
2 Chain tension is correct if there is from 15 to 20 mm (0.6 to 0.8 inch) of slack in the middle of the lower run. Always check the chain at its tightest point; a chain rarely wears in an even manner during service.
3 Always adjust the draw bolts an even amount so that correct wheel alignment is preserved. The fork ends are marked with a series of vertical lines to provide a visual check. If desired, wheel alignment can be checked by rubbing a plank of wood parallel to the machine so that it touches both walls of the rear tyre. If wheel alignment is correct, it should be equidistant from either side of the front wheel tyre when tested on both sides of the rear wheel; it will not touch the front tyre because this tyre has a smaller cross section. See the accompanying diagram.
4 Do not run the chain overtight to compensate for uneven wear. A tight chain will place excessive stresses on the gearbox and rear wheel bearings leading to their early failure. It will also absorb a surprising amount of power.
5 After a period of running, the chain will require lubrication. Lack of oil will accelerate the rate of wear of both chain and sprockets and will lead to harsh transmission. The application of engine oil will act as a temporary expedient, but it is preferable to remove the chain, clean it by immersing it in a petrol/paraffin mix and then in a molten lubricant such as Linklyfe or Chainguard. These latter lubricants achieve better penetration of the chain links and rollers and are less likely to be thrown off when the chain is in motion. Alternatively, one of the spray-on lubricants recommended for chains can be applied from an aerosol can.
6 To check whether the chain is due for replacement, lay it lengthwise in a straight line and compress it endwise until all play is taken up. Anchor one end, then pull in the opposite direction to take up the play which develops. If the chain extends by more than ¼ inch per foot, it should be renewed in conjunction with the sprockets. Note that this check should ALWAYS be made after the chain has been washed out, but before any lubricant is applied, otherwise the lubricant may take up some of the play.
7 When fitting the chain on the machine, make sure the spring link is positioned correctly with the closed end facing the direction of travel.
8 Some models have an endless chain and it is not advisable to substitute a spring link if the chain has to be separated,

Chapter 5: Wheels, brakes and tyres

unless the chain and spring link are of the heavy duty type as used on the later models.

9 The chain fitted is of Japanese manufacture. When renewal is necessary, it should be noted that a Renold equivalent, of British manufacture, is available as an alternative for any of the Yamaha 500 four stroke twins. When obtaining a replacement, take along the old chain as a pattern or, if known, a note of the size and number of pitches (rollers). The XS 500C model has 106 pitches as standard.

15 Tyres - removal and replacement

1 At some time or other the need will arise to remove and replace the tyres, either as the result of a puncture or because a renewal is required to offset wear. To the inexperienced, tyre changing represents a formidable task yet if a few simple rules are observed and the technique learned, the whole operation is surprisingly simple.

2 To remove the tyre from either wheel, first detach the wheel from the machine by following the procedure in Chapters 4.2, paragraph 7 or 4.9, paragraphs 2 to 4, depending on whether the front or the rear wheel is involved. Deflate the tyre by removing the valve insert and when it is fully deflated, push the bead of the tyre away from the wheel rim on both sides so that the bead enters the centre well of the rim. Remove the locking cap and push the tyre valve into the tyre inself.

3 Insert a tyre lever close to the valve and lever the edge of the tyre over the outside of the wheel rim. Very little force should be necessary; if resistance is encountered it is probably due to the fact that the tyre beads have not entered the well of the wheel rim all the way round the tyre.

4 Once the tyre has been edged over the wheel rim, it is easy to work around the wheel rim so that the tyre is completely free on one side. At this stage, the inner tube can be removed.

5 Working from the other side of the wheel, ease the other edge of the tyre over the outside of the wheel rim which is furthest away. Continue to work around the rim until the tyre is free completely from the rim.

6 If a puncture has necessitated the removal of the tyre, re-inflate the inner tube and immerse it in a bowl of water to trace the source of the leak. Mark its position and deflate the tube. Dry the tube and clean the area around the puncture with a petrol soaked rag. When the surface has dried, apply the rubber solution and allow this to dry before removing the backing from the patch and applying the patch to the surface.

7 It is best to use a patch of the self-vulcanising type which will form a very permanent repair. Note that it may be necessary to remove a protective covering from the top surface of the patch, after it has sealed in position. Inner tubes made from synthetic rubber may require a special type of patch and adhesive if a satisfactory bond is to be achieved.

8 Before refitting the tyre, check the inside to make sure that the agent which caused the puncture is not trapped. Check the outside of the tyre, particularly the tread area, to make sure nothing is trapped that may cause a further puncture.

9 If the inner tube has been patched on a number of past occasions, or if there is a tear or large hole, it is preferable to discard it and fit a new one. Sudden deflation may cause an accident, particularly if it occurs with the front wheel.

10 To replace the tyre, inflate the inner tube sufficiently for it to assume a circular shape but only just. Then push it into the tyre so that it is enclosed completely. Lay the

Fig. 5.7a. Tyre removal

A *Deflate inner tube and insert lever in close proximity to tyre valve*
B *Use two levers to work bead over the edge of rim*
C *When first bead is clear, remove tyre as shown*

Fig.5.7b. Tyre fitting

D Inflate inner tube and insert in tyre
E Lay tyre on rim and feed valve through hole in rim
F Work first bead over rim, using lever in final section
G Use similar technique for second bead. Finish at tyre valve position
H Push valve and tube up into tyre when fitting final section, to avoid trapping

Chapter 5: Wheels, brakes and tyres

tyre on the wheel at an angle and insert the valve captive in its correct location.

11 Starting at the point furthest from the valve, push the tyre bead over the edge of the wheel rim until it is located in the central well. Continue to work around the tyre in this fashion until the whole of one side of the tyre is on the rim. It may be necessary to use a tyre-lever during the final stages.

12 Make sure that there is no pull on the tyre valve and again commencing with the area furthest from the valve, ease the other bead of the tyre over the edge of the rim. Finish with the area close to the valve, pushing the valve up into the tyre until the locking cap touches the rim. This will ensure the inner tube is not trapped when the last section of the bead is edged over the rim with a tyre lever.

13 Check that the inner tube is not trapped at any point. Re-inflate the inner tube and check that the tyre is seating correctly around the wheel rim. There should be a thin rib moulded around the wall of the tyre on both sides which should be equidistant from the wheel rim at all points. If the tyre is unevenly located on the rim, try bouncing the wheel when the tyre is at the recommended pressure. It is probable that one of the beads has not pulled clear of the centre well.

14 Always run the tyres at the recommended pressures and never under or over-inflate. The correct pressures for solo use are given in the Specifications Section of this Chapter. If a pillion passenger is carried, increase the rear tyre pressure only by approximately 4 psi.

15 Tyre replacement is aided by dusting the side walls, particularly in the vicinity of the beads, with a liberal coating of French chalk. Washing up liquid can also be used to good effect, but this has the disadvantage of causing the inner surfaces of the wheel rim to rust.

16 Never replace the inner tube and tyre without the rim tape in position. If this precaution is overlooked there is good chance of the ends of the spoke nipples chafing the inner tube and causing a crop of punctures.

17 Never fit a tyre which has a damaged tread or side walls. Apart from the legal aspects, there is a very great risk of a blow-out, which can have serious consequences on any two-wheel vehicle.

18 Tyre valves rarely give trouble, but it is always advisable to check whether the valve itself is leaking before removing the tyre. Do not forget to fit the dust cap, which forms an effective second seal. This is especially important on high performance machines where centrifugal force can cause the valve insert to retract and the tyre to deflate without warning.

16 Front wheel - balancing

1 It is customary on all high performance machines to balance the front wheel complete with tyre and tube. The out of balance forces which exist are eliminated and the handling of the machine is improved in consequence. A wheel which is badly out of balance produces through the steering a most unpleasant hammering effect at high speeds.

2 Some tyres have a balance mark on the sidewall, usually in the form of a coloured dot. This mark must be in line with the tyre valve, when the tyre is fitted to the inner tube. Even then, the wheel may require the addition of balance weights, to offset the weight of the tyre valve itself.

3 If the front wheel is raised clear of the ground and is spun, it will probably come to rest with the tyre valve or the heaviest part downward and will always come to rest in the same position. Balance weights must be added to a point diametrically opposite this 'heavy' spot until the wheel will come to rest in ANY position after it is spun. Balancing must be carried out with the dust cap fitted to the valve as its addition later will upset the balance.

4 Balance weights which clip around the wheel spokes are normally available in 5, 10 or 20 gramme sizes. If they are not available, wire solder, wrapped around the spokes close to the spoke nipples, form a good substitute.

5 There is no necessity to balance the rear wheel under normal road conditions, although it is advisable to replace the rear wheel tyre so that any balance mark is in line with the tyre valve.

17 Fault diagnosis

Symptom	Cause	Remedy
Handlebars oscillate at low speeds	Buckle or flat in wheel rim, most probably front wheel (spoked wheels only)	Check rim alignment by spinning wheel. Correct by retensioning spokes or rebuilding on new rim.
	Tyre not straight on rim	Check tyre alignment.
Machine lacks power and accelerates poorly	Rear brake binding (drum brake) Pads contacting disc (disc brakes)	Warm brake drum provides best evidence Re-adjust brake. Overhaul brake caliper unit(s).
Rear brake grabs when applied gently (drum brake only)	Ends of brake shoes not chamfered Elliptical brake drum	Chamfer with file. Lightly skim in lathe (specialist attention required).
Front or rear brake feels spongy	Air in hydraulic system	Bleed brake.
Brake pull-off sluggish	Brake cam binding in housing Wear brake shoe springs Sticking pistons in brake caliper (disc brakes)	Free and grease. Renew if springs have not become displaced. Overhaul caliper unit.
Harsh transmission	Worn or badly adjusted final drive chain Hooked or badly worn sprockets Worn or deteriorating cush drive rubbers	Adjust or renew as necessary Renew as a pair. Renew rubbers.

Chapter 6 Electrical system

Contents

General description ... 1	Headlamp: replacing bulbs and adjusting beam height ... 12
Alternator: checking the output ... 2	Stop and tail lamp: replacing bulbs ... 13
Battery: examination and maintenance ... 3	Flashing indicator lamps: replacing bulbs ... 14
Battery: charging procedure ... 4	Flashing indicator relay: location and replacement ... 15
Silicon rectifier: general description ... 5	Speedometer and tachometer heads: replacement of bulbs ... 16
Voltage regulator: location and characteristics ... 6	Indicator panel lamps: replacement of bulbs ... 17
Fuses: location and replacement ... 7	Horn: adjustment ... 18
Starter motor: removal, examination and replacement ... 8	Ignition switch: removal and replacement ... 19
Starter motor free running clutch: construction and renovation ... 9	Stop lamp switches: adjustment ... 20
Starter solenoid switch: function and location ... 10	Handlebar switches: general ... 21
Oil pressure warning switch: location and function ... 11	Fault diagnosis: electrical system ... 22

Specifications

Battery:
Make	GS or Yuasa
Type	12N14-3A or YB14-L
Voltage	12 volts
Capacity	14 amp hour
Earth	Negative

Alternator:
Make	Hitachi
Type	LD115-04
Output	14.5 volts, 13 amps

Regulator unit:
Make	Hitachi
Type	TR1Z-17 encapsulated solid state

Rectifier:
Make	Hitachi
Type	SB6B-15 full wave

Bulbs: *
Headlamp	50/40 watt or 45/40 watt
Tail lamp	8 watt (or, if combined, 8/21 watt)
Stop lamp	23 watt
Neutral indicator lamp	3 watt
Flasher indicator lamp	3 watt
High beam indicator lamp	3 watt
Speedometer lamp	3 watt (two)
Tachometer lamp	3 watt (two)
Flashing indicator lamps	27 watt (four) or 21 watt (four)

all rated at 12 volts

Fuses:
Ignition circuit	10 amp
Flashing indicators	10 amp
Lighting circuit	10 amp
Main fuse	20 amp
Spare fuses	10 amp and 20 amp (one each)

Chapter 6: Electrical system

1 General description

The Yamaha 500 cc four-stroke twin is fitted with a 12 volt electrical system. The system comprises a crankshaft mounted AC generator (alternator) of the brushless, three-phase type, the output of which is controlled by what is termed an IC voltage regulator - a regulator that provides a stable output voltage without relying upon mechanically-operated contact points. Because the output is alternating current (AC), a full wave rectifier is included in the charging circuit to convert the current to DC (direct current) for charging the battery.

Output is controlled by a Zener diode in the voltage regulator unit, whose voltage limiting characteristics change as the electrical demand increases, such as when the full lighting system is in use. Because the ancilliary components of the charging circuit (regulator, rectifier etc) are of the sealed type, if they should malfunction they will have to be renewed, as a repair is impracticable.

2 Alternator: checking the output

1 As explained in Chapter 3, Section 2, the output from the generator can be checked by a relatively simple test, using an electrical multi-meter of reasonable sensitivity. If the procedure described in this Section is followed, and a few simple checks carried out if the output is below par or non-exist, it must be stressed, however, that at their very best, these tests are only indicative and should not be relied upon to restore the system to full working order. If the existance of a fault is verified, the machine should be taken to a Yamaha repair agent or an auto-electrical expert for a more comprehensive test and the renewal of whatever components are found to be defective.

3 Battery: examination and maintenance

1 A GS 12N14-3A or a Yusa YB14-L battery, having a 14 amp hour capacity, is fitted as standard to the Yamaha 500 cc four-stroke twins. It is mounted in a compartment close to the air cleaner, underneath the dualseat, where it is retained by a rubber strap. A negative earth connection is used.
2 The transparent plastic case of the battery permits the upper and lower levels of the electrolyte to be observed without disturbing the battery by removing the left hand side cover. Maintenance is normally limited to keeping the electrolyte level between the prescribed upper and lower limits and making sure that the vent tube is not blocked. The lead plates and their sepatators are also visible through the transparent case, a further guide to the general condition of the battery.
3 Unless acid is spilt, as may occur if the machine falls over, the electrolyte should always be topped up with distilled water to restore the correct level. If the acid is spilt onto any part of the the machine, it should be neutralised with an alkali such as washing soda or baking powder and washed away with plenty of water, otherwise serious corrosion will occur. Top up with sulphuric acid of the correct specific gravity (1.260 to 1.280) only when spillage has occurred. Check that the vent pipe is well clear of the frame or any of the other cycle parts.
4 It is seldom practicable to repair a cracked battery case because the acid present in the joint will prevent the formation of an effective seal. It is always best to renew a cracked battery, especially in view of the corrosion which will be caused if the acid continues to leak.
5 If the machine is not used for a period, it is advisable to remove the battery and give it a 'refresher' charge every six weeks or so from a battery charger. If the battery is permitted to discharge completely, the plates will sulphate and render the battery useless.
6 Occasionally, check the condition of the battery terminals to ensure that corrosion is not taking place and that the electrical connections are tight. If corrosion has occured, it should be cleaned away by scraping with a knife and then using emery cloth to remove the final traces. Remake the electrical connections whilst the joint is still clean, then smear the assembly with petroleum jelly (NOT grease) to prevent recurrence of the corrosion. Badly corroded connections have a high electrical resistance and may give the impression of a complete battery failure.

4 Battery: charging procedure

1 Since the ignition system is dependent on the battery for its operation, if the battery discharges completely it must be removed and recharged before the machine can be used. A battery charger is necessary for this purpose.
2 The normal charge rate is 4 amps for about 4 hours for a 14 amp hour battery. A more rapid charge at a higher rate can be given in an emergency, but this should be avoided if at all possible because it will shorten the useful working life of the battery. Always ensure the battery is topped up before charging.
3 When the battery is replaced on the machine, make sure that it is protected by the rubber pads in the battery compartment, which help damp out the undesirable effects of vibration. Do not reverse connect the battery, or the silicon rectifier may be damaged by the reverse flow of current.

5 Silicon rectifier: general description

1 The function of the silicon rectifier is to convert to AC current produced by the alternator into DC so that it can be used to charge the battery.
2 The rectifier is located beneath the battery, beneath the dualseat, a location where it is afforded reasonable protection. The question of access is of relatively little importance because the rectifier is unlikely to give trouble during normal service. Should it malfunction, a repair is not practicable. It must be renewed.
3 Damage to the rectifier will occur if the machine is run without a battery for any period of time, or with one that no longer holds its charge. A high voltage will develop in the absence of any load across the coils of the alternator which will cause a reverse flow of current and subsequent damage to the rectifier

5.2 Silicon rectifier is found under battery. Is recognisable by finned cover

cells. Reverse connection of the battery will have a similar undesirable effect.

4 There is no simple means of checking whether the rectifier is functioning correctly without the appropriate test equipment. A Yamaha agent or an auto-electrician are best qualified to advise, particularly if the battery is in low state of charge.

6 Voltage regulator: location and characteristics

1 The voltage regulator unit is located to the rear of the battery, in the electrical compartment underneath the dualseat. Being of the electronic type, it is quite compact and is easily recognised on account of its ribbed cover.
2 The voltage regulator unit comprises an assembly of transistors and zenor diodes which maintain the voltage of the charging current by either accepting or interrupting the current to the field coil of the alternator. This function is determined by the electrical characteristics of the components in the control circuit, which cannot be adjusted in the normally accepted manner. In consequence, if the unit malfunctions and tests show the fault is within the unit itself, renewal will be necessary.
3 Electrical testing by anyone other than a skilled electrician is not recommended. If the flow of current during testing is reversed inadvertently, the transistors will be damaged.
4 The usual symptoms of a defective voltage regulator are inability to keep the battery fully charged, or over-charging, which will cause the battery electrolyte to discharge via the pipe, necessitating frequent topping up.

7 Fuses: location and replacement

1 A 20 amp fuse is included in the positive lead of the battery, and there is a spare 20 amp fuse mounted close by, in a small container. The fuse provides the weak link in the chain, to protect the electrical system from any sudden overload or short circuit. Other fuses are in the ignition circuit (10 amp), flashing indicator circuit (10 amp) and headlamp wiring (10 amp). There is an additional spare 10 amp fuse as a replacement for any of these.
2 If a fuse, blows, it should not be renewed until a check has shown whether a short circuit has occurred; there is usually a reason other than old age. This will involve checking the electrical circuit to identify and correct the fault. If this precaution is not observed, the replacement fuse which may be the only spare, may blow immediately on connection.
3 When a fuse blows whilst the machine is running and no spare is available a 'get you home' remedy is to remove the blown fuse and wrap it in silver paper before replacing it in the fuse holder. The silver paper will restore electrical continuity by bridging the broken wire within the fuse. This expedient should never be used if there is evidence of a short circuit or other major electrical fault, otherwise more serious damage will be caused. Renew the 'doctored' fuse at the earliest possible opportunity to restore full circuit protection. The fuses are located under the dualseat, behind the battery.

8 Starter motor: removal, examination and replacement

1 An electrical starter motor, operated from a small push-button on the right hand side of the handlebars, provides an alternative and more convenient method of starting the engine, without having to use the kickstarter. The starter motor is mounted within a compartment at the rear of the cylinder block. Current is supplied from the battery via a heavy duty solenoid switch and a cable capable of carrying the very high current demanded by the starter motor on the initial start-up.
2 The starter motor drives a free running clutch immediately behind the generator rotor. The clutch ensures the starter motor drive is disconnected from the primary transmission immediately the engine starts. It operates on the centrifugal principle; spring loaded rollers take up the drive until the centrifugal force of the rotating engine overcomes their resistance and the drive is automatically disconnected.
3 To remove the starter motor from the engine unit, first disconnect the positive lead from the battery, then the starter motor cable from the solenoid switch. It is not possible to detach the starter cable from the starter motor itself; in consequence the cable must be threaded through the frame so that it is free when the starter motor is lifted away. Detach the two allen screws in the finned cover over the starter motor housing and lift the cover away, complete with gasket. The starter motor is secured to the crankcase by two allen screws which pass through a clamp securing the right-hand end of the motor and two bolts that pass into the left-hand side of the casting. When these allen screws and bolts are withdrawn, the motor can be prised out of position and lifted out of its compartment, with the heavy duty cable still attached. If necessary, detach the lead and grommet from the oil pressure switch, which may get in the way.
4 The parts of the starter motor most likely to require attention are the brushes. The end cover is retained by the two long screws which pass through the lugs cast on both end pieces. If the screws are withdrawn, the end cover can be lifted away and the brush gear exposed
5 Lift up the spring clips which bear on the end of each brush and remove the brushes from their holders. Each brush should have a length of 12 - 13 mm (0.472 - 0.512 in). The serviceable limit is 5.5 mm (0.217 in), which denotes when the brushes must be renewed.
6 Before the brushes are replaced, make sure the commutator is clean, on which they bear. Clean with a strip of fine emery cloth pressed against the commutator whilst the latter is revolved by hand. Wipe with a rag soaked in petrol to ensure a bright, grease-free surface is obtained. At the same time, check that the mica insulator between the copper segments of the armature is undercut. If the difference in height is less than 0.012 in (0.3 mm) it must be re-cut - a task for a Yamaha dealer or an auto-electrical expert.
7 Replace the brushes in their holders and check that they slide quite freely. Make sure the brushes are replaced in their original positions because they will have worn to the profile of the commutator. Replace and tighten the end cover, then replace the starter motor and cable in the housing, tighten down and re-make the electrical connection to the solenoid switch. Check that the starter motor functions correctly before replacing the compartment cover and sealing gasket.

9 Starter motor free running clutch: construction and renovation

1 Although a mechanical and not an electrical component, it is appropriate to include the free running clutch in this Chapter because it is an essential part of the electric starter system.
2 As mentioned in Chapter 1, the free running clutch is built into the alternator rotor assembly and will be found in the back of the rotor when the latter is removed from the left-hand end of the crankshaft. The only parts likely to require attention are the rollers and their springs, or the driven sprocket. Access to the rollers is gained by removing the three countersunk crosshead screws which retain the clutch body to the rear of the alternator rotor. Signs of wear or damage will be obvious and will necessitate renewal of the worn or damaged parts.
3 The driven sprocket behind the clutch will need renewal only after very extensive service.
4 To check whether the clutch is operating correctly, turn the driven sprocket anticlockwise. This should force the spring loaded rollers against the crankshaft and cause it to tighten on the crankshaft as the drive is taken up.
5 If the starter clutch has been dismantled, make sure the three crosshead screws are staked over after reassembly, to prevent them working loose.

Chapter 6: Electrical system

6.1 Voltage regulator is mounted to rear of battery. Cannot be repaired

7.1 The fuse box of the XS500C model is mounted above battery

10.3 Starter solenoid switch is below flasher unit. Has stout cable attached

10 Starter solenoid switch: function and location

1 The starter motor switch is designed to work on the electromagnetic principle. When the starter motor button is depressed, current from the battery passes through windings in the switch solenoid and generates an electro-magnetic force which causes a set of contact points to close. Immediately the points close, the starter motor is energised and a very heavy current is drawn from the battery.

2 This arrangement is used for at least two reasons. Firstly, the starter motor current is drawn only when the button is depressed and is cut off again when pressure on the button is released. This ensures minimum drainage on the battery. Secondly, if the battery is in a low state of charge, there will not be sufficient current to cause the solenoid contacts to close. In consequence, it is not possible to place an excessive drain on the battery which, in some circumstances, can cause the plates to overheat and shed their coatings. If the starter will not operate, first suspect a discharged battery. This can be checked by trying the horn or switching on the lights. If this check shows the battery to be in good shape, suspect the starter switch which should come into action with a pronounced click. It is located under the dualseat, close to the battery, and can be identified by the heavy duty starter cable connected to it. It is not possible to effect a satisfactory repair if the switch malfunctions; it must be renewed.

3 The starter motor solenoid switch is mounted close to the battery, on the right-hand side of the machine. It is readily identified by the heavy duty cable attached to it.

11 Oil pressure warning switch: location and function

1 A circular oil pressure warning switch screws into the top of the upper crankcase, immediately behind the cylinder block. It has a taper thread, so that it can be tightened fully to preclude the possibility of oil seepage.

2 The operating range of the switch cannot be adjusted and if it malfunctions, renewal is essential. When the engine is stationary, there is no oil pressure and the warning light in the instrument console between the speedometer and tachometer should glow when the ignition is switched on. Immediately the engine starts, the light should go out, showing that the lubrication system is performing correctly and that there is full oil pressure. Always check that the warning light is operating when starting the engine. If the bulb should fail, renew it with one of similar wattage at the earliest possible opportunity.

3 If the warning light glows at any time whilst the engine is running, stop the engine immediately and investigate the cause. If the engine is run with reduced pressure, serious damage will be caused, especially as the main and big-end bearings are of the shell type. Note that if the electrical lead from the switch to the warning lamp is earthed at any point along its run, this will cause the lamp to glow at all times.

12 Headlamp: replacing bulbs and adjusting beam height

1 In order to gain access to the headlamp bulbs it is necessary first to remove the rim, complete with the reflector and headlamp glass . The rim is retained by two crosshead screws through the headlamp shell. Remove the screws completely and draw the rim from the headlamp shell.

2 Early models have a main headlamp bulb which is a push fit into the central bulb holder of the reflector. The bulb holder can be replaced in one position only to ensure the bulb is always correctly focussed. It is retained by a spring under tension. A bulb of the twin filament type is fitted which has a 50/40W rating (machines imported to the UK). The pilot lamp bulb is bayonet fitting and fits within a bulb holder which has the same form of attachment as the headlamp reflector. This bulb has a 6W rating.

12.3 UK imported models have separate headlamp bulbs

12.4a Slot permits headlamp to be tilted upwards or downwards

12.4b Turn this screw to move headlamp beam to right or left

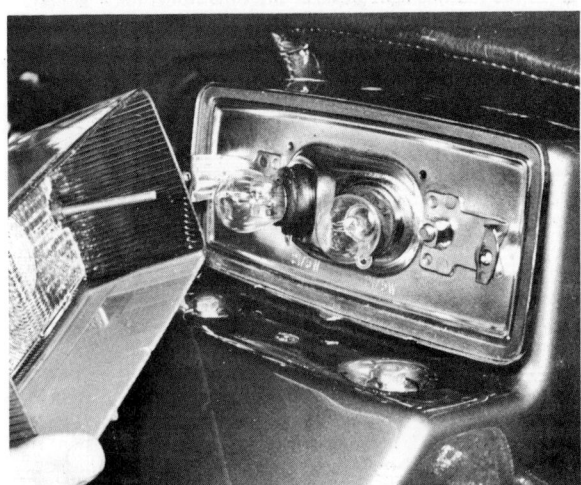

13.1a Twin bulb stop lamp fits behind dualseat on XS500C models

3 Later models have a sealed beam headlamp unit, rated at 50/40W with no provision for a pilot lamp except those imported into the UK and countries where this is a statutory requirement. If one filament blows, the complete unit must be renewed. To release the lamp unit, remove the horizontal adjusting screw, and the other two screws from the collar which clamps the light unit to the headlamp rim. Make a note of the setting of the adjusting screw, otherwise it will be necessary to re-adjust the beam height after installing the new light unit by reversing the dismantling procedure.

4 Beam height is adjusted by turning the adjusting screw fitted at the bottom of the headlamp shell. Loosen the screw and move the shell either upwards or downwards, as required, before re-tightening. Horizontal adjustment is made by turning the small crosshead screw in the righ-hand side of the rim, viewed from the front of the machine. If the screw is turned inwards, the beam will be moved towards the left.

5 UK lighting regulations stipulate that the lighting system must be arranged so that the light will not dazzle a person standing at a distance greater than 25 feet from the lamp, whose eye level is not less than 3 feet 6 inches above the plane. It is easy to approximate this setting by placing the machine 25 feet away from a wall, on a level road, and setting the height so that it is concentrated at the same height as the distance of the centre of the headlamp from the ground. The rider must be seated normally during this operation and also the pillion passenger, if one is carried regularly.

13 Stop and tail lamp: replacing bulbs

1 The stop lamp has two bulbs of 27W rating, to indicate when the rear brake is applied. On some models the stop lamp also also operates in conjunction with the front brake; the stop lamp switch is incorporated in the front brake assembly to meet the statutory requirements of the country or state to which the machine is exported.

2 The rear number plate has a separate lamp above it, rated at 8W, which also illuminates the index numbers.

3 To gain access to the stop and tail lamp bulbs unscrew the two crosshead screws which retain the plastic lens covers in position.

4 Earlier models have one lamp which performs both functions and is fitted with an 8/27W bulb with offset pins. This prevents the tail lamp filament operating with the stop lamp switch and vice-versa.

Chapter 6: Electrical system

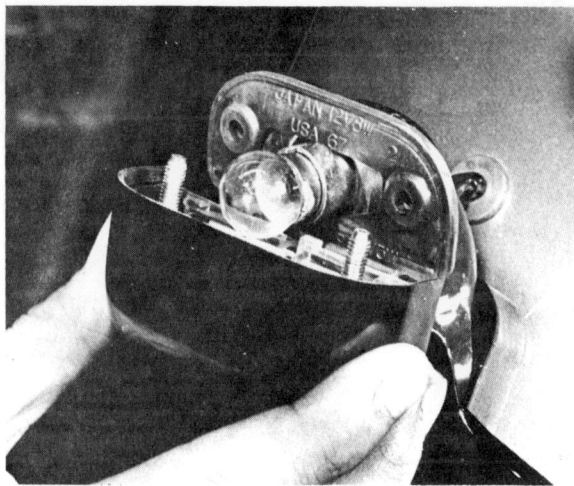

13.1b XS500C model has separate rear lamp above number plate

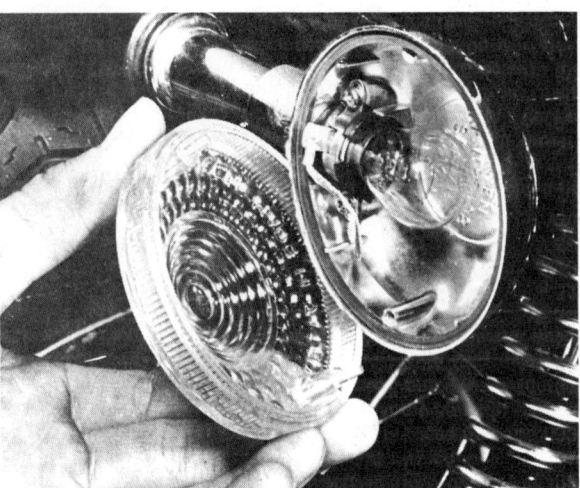

14.2 Plastic lens covers are retained by two crosshead screws

16.2 Instrument head will lift up to expose bulb and holder

14 Flashing indicator lamps: replacing bulbs

1 Flashing indicator lamps are fitted to the front and rear of the machine. They are mounted on short 'stalks' through which the electrical leads pass. One set of indicators is attached to either side of the fork lug to which the headlamp is attached. The other set are attached to the rear mudguard, immediately beneath the end of the dualseat.

2 Each flasher unit has a bayonet fitting 27W bulb. To replace a bulb remove the plastics end cover which is retained by two crosshead screws. US models have twin filament bulbs which provide clearance lights when the headlamp is switched on.

15 Flashing indicator relay: location and replacement

1 The flashing indicator relay fitted in conjunction with the flashing indicator lamps is located with the other electrical components in the compartment under the dualseat. It is rubber mounted to isolate it from the harmful effects of vibration.

2 When the relay malfunctions it must be renewed; a repair is impracticable. When the unit is in working order, audible clicks will be heard which keep pace with the flash of the indicator lamps. If the lamps malfunction, check firstly that a bulb failure is not responsible, or the handlebar switch faulty. The usual symptom of a fault is one initial flash before the unit goes dead.

3 Take great care when handling a flashing indicator relay. It is easily damaged, if dropped.

16 Speedometer and tachometer heads: replacement of bulbs

1 Apart from the bulbs use to illuminate the dial of each instrument during the hours of darkness, the speedometer head and the tachometer head fitted to the earlier models contain the warning lamps which indicate when neutral is selected (green), when oil pressure is below the pre-set limit, when the flashing indicators are operating (amber) and when the headlamp is on main beam (red). All bulbs fitted to either of the instrument heads have identical bulb holders, which are a push fit into the vase of the instrument case. Access is gained by slackening the chromium plated clamp around both instruments and lifting each upward so that the two screws can be removed from the underplate and the bulb holders exposed. It may be possible to remove the undercovers without need to raise the instruments, if the mounting angle permits good access to the crosshead screws.

2 On XS 500C models, the instrument head is released from its holder when the domed nut and washer on the underside are removed.

17 Indicator panel lamps: replacement of bulbs

An indicator panel is clamped to the handlebar centre which contains the four warning lamps which were previously included in the tachometer and speedometer heads. The bulb holders are similar to those fitted in the tachometer and speedometer heads and can be detached from the base of the indicator panel by pulling them away. The panel cover is retained by four small crosshead screws.

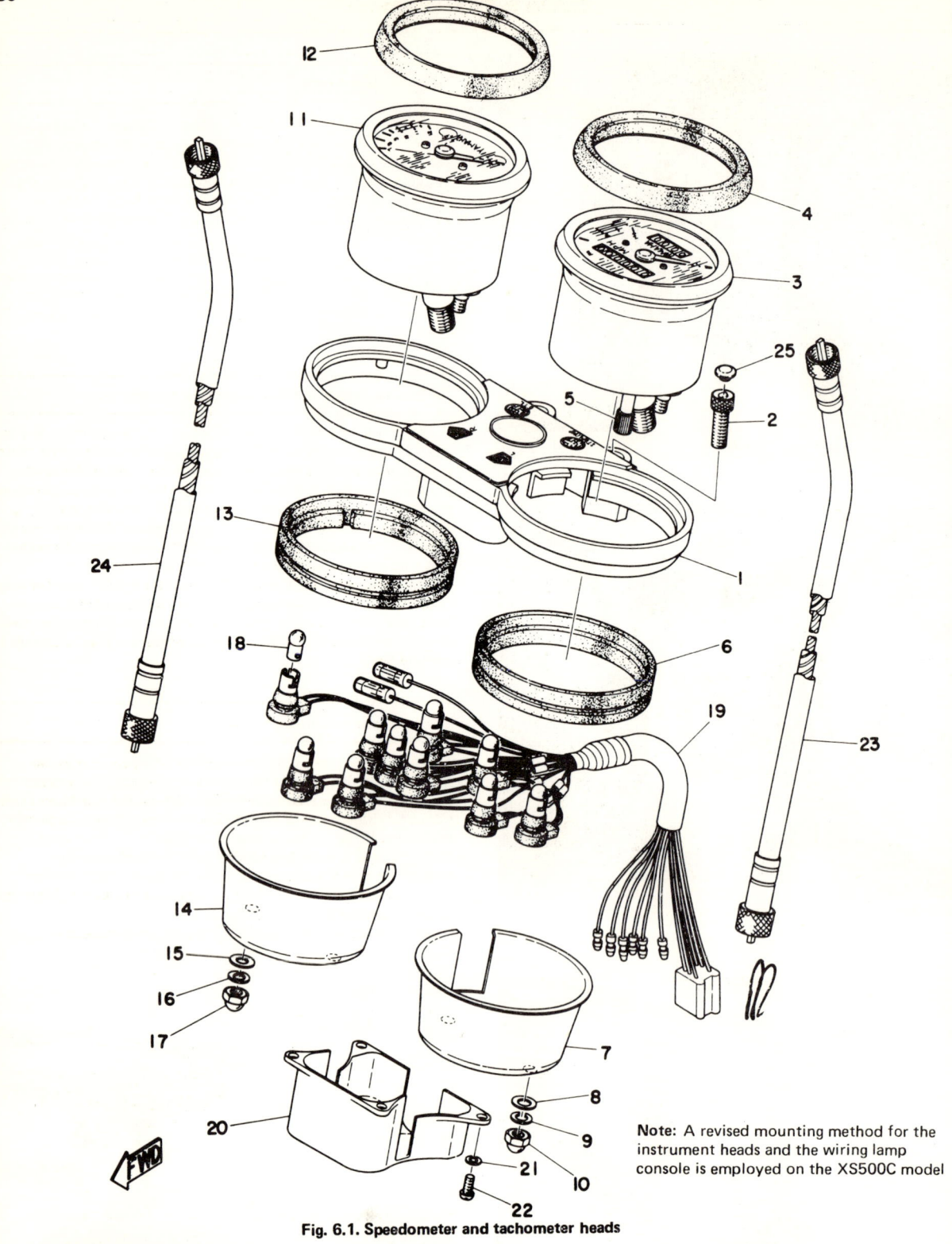

Fig. 6.1. Speedometer and tachometer heads

Note: A revised mounting method for the instrument heads and the wiring lamp console is employed on the XS500C model

1 Instrument mounting bracket
2 Bolt - 2 off
3 Speedometer head
4 Damping rubber
5 Speedometer reset knob
6 Damping rubber - lower
7 Speedometer cover
8 Plain washer - 2 off
9 Spring washer - 2 off
10 Domed nut - 2 off
11 Tachometer head
12 Damping rubber
13 Damping rubber - lower
14 Tachometer cover
15 Plain washer - 2 off
16 Spring washer - 2 off
17 Domed nut - 2 off
18 Bulb - 10 off
19 Bulbholder and lead wire assembly
20 Lamp console cover
21 Spring washer - 4 off
22 Screw - 4 off
23 Speedometer drive cable assembly
24 Tachometer drive cable assembly
25 Cap bolt - 2 off

Chapter 6: Electrical system

17.1a XS500C panel is retained by four small crosshead screws

17.1b Bulbs (and ignition switch mounting) are exposed when cover is removed

18 Horn: adjustment

1 The horn is provided with an adjusting screw in the back of the horn body so that the sound volume can be varied, if necessary. To adjust the horn note, turn the screw not more than one half turn in either direction and test. If the note is weaker, or lost altogether, turn in the opposite direction. Continue adjusting by one half turn at a time until the desired volume and note is obtained.
2 The horn button is located on the left hand side of the handlebars. If the horn does not operate and an electrical meter shows no current is passing through the horn when the horn button is depressed, check the continuity of the light green coloured wire within the headlamp shell.

19 Ignition switch: removal and replacement

1 The main switch which controls both the ignition system and the lighting is attached to the warning light console in the centre of the handlebars, between the speedometer and tachometer.
2 If the switch proves defective, it can be removed by unscrewing the two bolts which secure the bracket to the frame and separating the terminal connector at the end of the short wiring harness. To release the switch unit itself, unscrew the threaded ring around the outside of the lock.
3 Fit the new switch through the bracket, tighten the threaded ring, then bolt the switch bracket to the warning light console. Reconnect the wires at the terminal connector. Remember that when a new switch is fitted, it will be necessary also to change the ignition key.

20 Stop lamp switches: adjustment

1 All models have a stop lamp switch fitted to operate in conjunction with the rear brake pedal. The switch is located immediately to the rear of the crankcase, on the right-hand side of the machine. It has a threaded body, permitting a range of adjustment.
2 If the stop lamp is late in operating, then slacken the locknuts and turn the body of the lamp in an anticlockwise direction so that the adjustment seems near correct; tighten the locknuts and test.
3 If the lamp operates too early, the locknuts should be

20.1a Rear brake stop lamp switch is adjustable

20.1b Front brake stop lamp switch cannot be adjusted

slackened and the switch body turned clockwise so that it is lowered in relation to the mounting bracket.
4 As a guide, the light should operate after the brake pedal has been depressed by about 20mm (0.75 in).
5 A stop lamp switch is also incorporated in the front brake, to give warning when the front brake is applied. This is not yet a statutory requirement in the UK, although it applies in many other countries and states.
6 The front brake stop lamp switch is built into the hydraulic system and contains no provision for adjustment. If the switch malfunctions, it must be renewed.
7 If the stop lamp bulb fails, special circuitry in the electrical system causes a warning lamp to flash in the warning light console, to draw attention to this fault.

21 Handlebar switches: general

1 Generally speaking, the switches give little trouble, but if necessary they can be dismantled by separating the halves which form a split clamp around the handlbars. Note that the machine cannot be started until the ignition cut-off on the right-hand end of the handlebars is turned to the central 'ON' position.
2 If a switch malfuctions, it will have to be renewed. Repairs are virtually impracticable, on account of the minute dimensions of the internal.

22 Fault diagnosis

Fault	Cause	Remedy
Electrical failure	Blown fuse in inoperative circuit	Check wiring and electrical components for short circuit before fitting new fuse.
Complete electrical failure	Isolated battery	Check battery connections, also whether connections show signs of corrosion.
Dim lights, horn and starter inoperative	Discharged battery	Remove battery and charge with battery charger. Check generator output and voltage regulator output.
Constantly blowing bulbs	Vibration or poor earth connection	Check security of bulb holders. Check earth return connections.
Starter motor sluggish	Worn brushes	Remove starter motor and renew brushes.
Parking lights dim rapidly	Battery will not hold charge	Renew battery at earliest opportunity.
Flashing indicators do not operate	Blown bulb Damaged flasher unit	Renew bulb. Renew flasher unit.

Wiring diagram overleaf

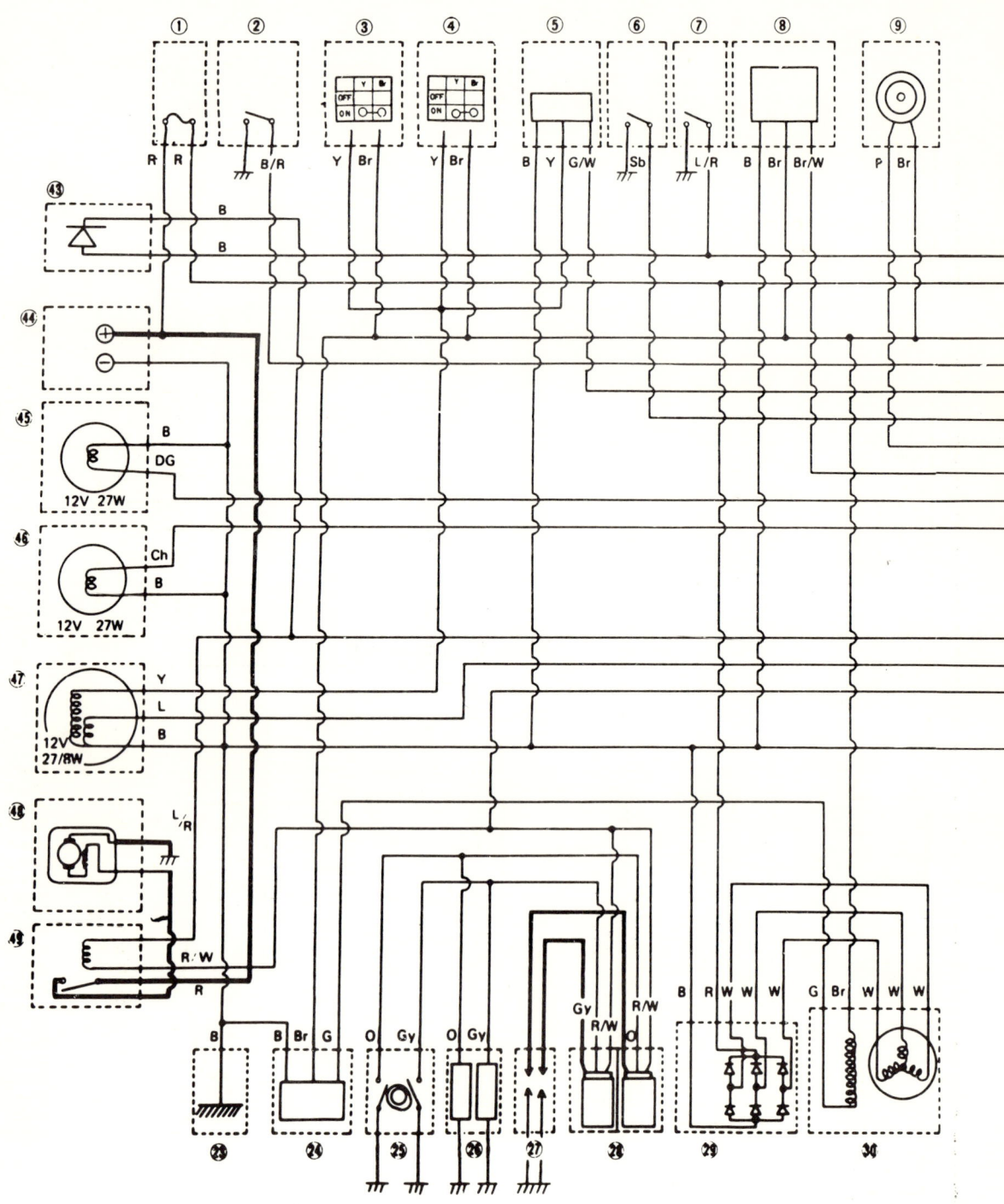

Fig. 6.2. Yamaha XS500 twin wiring diagram

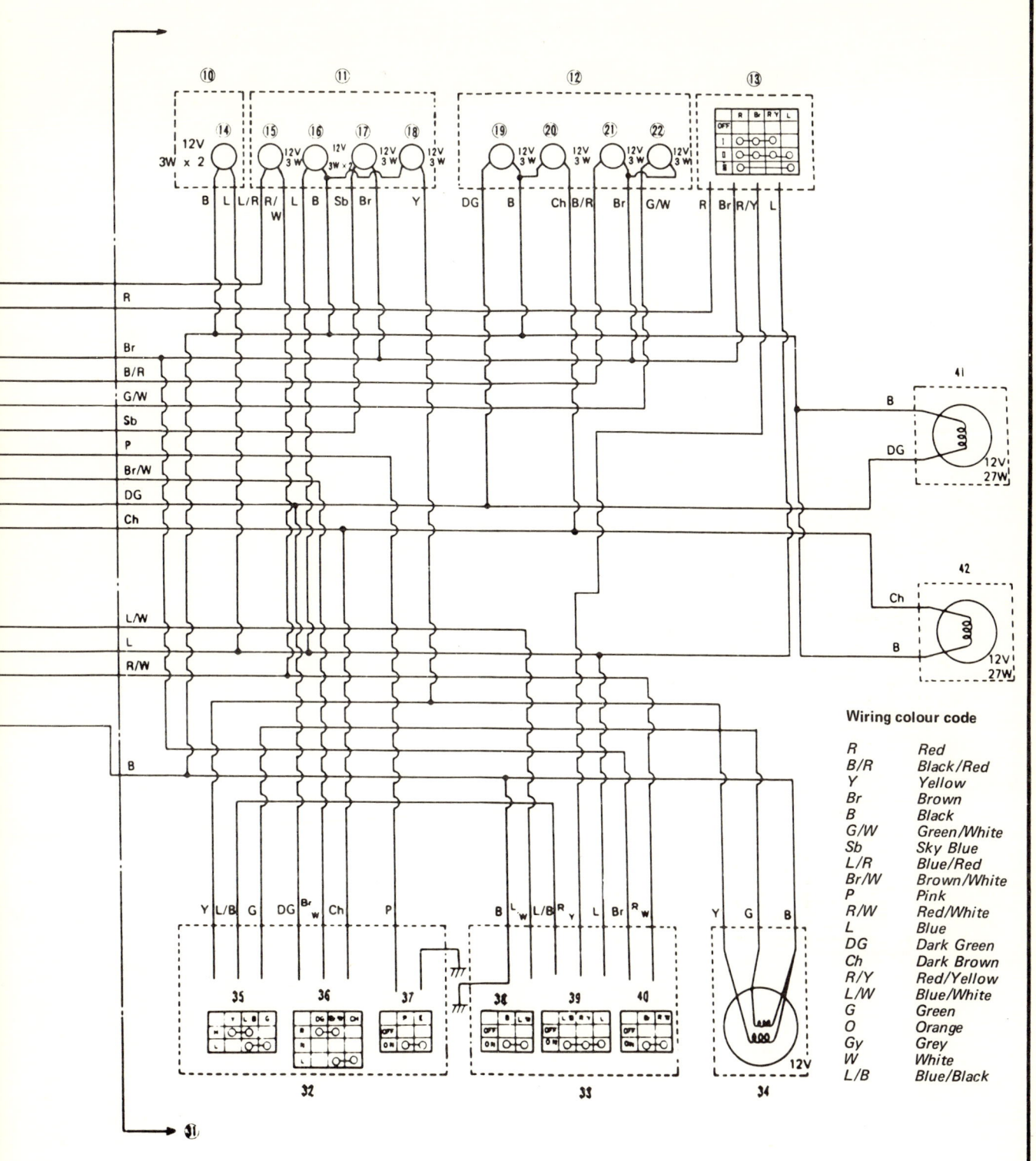

Metric conversion tables

Inches	Decimals	Millimetres	Millimetres to Inches mm	Inches	Inches to Millimetres Inches	mm
1/64	0.015625	0.3969	0.01	0.00039	0.001	0.0254
1/32	0.03125	0.7937	0.02	0.00079	0.002	0.0508
3/64	0.046875	1.1906	0.03	0.00118	0.003	0.0762
1/16	0.0625	1.5875	0.04	0.00157	0.004	0.1016
5/64	0.078125	1.9844	0.05	0.00197	0.005	0.1270
3/32	0.09375	2.3812	0.06	0.00236	0.006	0.1524
7/64	0.109375	2.7781	0.07	0.00276	0.007	0.1778
1/8	0.125	3.1750	0.08	0.00315	0.008	0.2032
9/64	0.140625	3.5719	0.09	0.00354	0.009	0.2286
5/32	0.15625	3.9687	0.1	0.00394	0.01	0.254
11/64	0.171875	4.3656	0.2	0.00787	0.02	0.508
3/16	0.1875	4.7625	0.3	0.01181	0.03	0.762
13/64	0.203125	5.1594	0.4	0.01575	0.04	1.016
7/32	0.21875	5.5562	0.5	0.01969	0.05	1.270
15/64	0.234375	5.9531	0.6	0.02362	0.06	1.524
1/4	0.25	6.3500	0.7	0.02756	0.07	1.778
17/64	0.265625	6.7469	0.8	0.03150	0.08	2.032
9/32	0.28125	7.1437	0.9	0.03543	0.09	2.286
19/64	0.296875	7.5406	1	0.03937	0.1	2.54
5/16	0.3125	7.9375	2	0.07874	0.2	5.08
21/64	0.328125	8.3344	3	0.11811	0.3	7.62
11/32	0.34375	8.7312	4	0.15748	0.4	10.16
23/64	0.359375	9.1281	5	0.19685	0.5	12.70
3/8	0.375	9.5250	6	0.23622	0.6	15.24
25/64	0.390625	9.9219	7	0.27559	0.7	17.78
13/32	0.40625	10.3187	8	0.31496	0.8	20.32
27/64	0.421875	10.7156	9	0.35433	0.9	22.86
7/16	0.4375	11.1125	10	0.39370	1	25.4
29/64	0.453125	11.5094	11	0.43307	2	50.8
15/32	0.46875	11.9062	12	0.47244	3	76.2
31/64	0.484375	12.3031	13	0.51181	4	101.6
1/2	0.5	12.7000	14	0.55118	5	127.0
33/64	0.515625	13.0969	15	0.59055	6	152.4
17/32	0.53125	13.4937	16	0.62992	7	177.8
35/64	0.546875	13.8906	17	0.66929	8	203.2
9/16	0.5625	14.2875	18	0.70866	9	228.6
37/64	0.578125	14.6844	19	0.74803	10	254.0
19/32	0.59375	15.0812	20	0.78740	11	279.4
39/64	0.609375	15.4781	21	0.82677	12	304.8
5/8	0.625	15.8750	22	0.86614	13	330.2
41/64	0.640625	16.2719	23	0.90551	14	355.6
21/32	0.65625	16.6687	24	0.94488	15	381.0
43/64	0.671875	17.0656	25	0.98425	16	406.4
11/16	0.6875	17.4625	26	1.02362	17	431.8
45/64	0.703125	17.8594	27	1.06299	18	457.2
23/32	0.71875	18.2562	28	1.10236	19	482.6
47/64	0.734375	18.6531	29	1.14173	20	508.0
3/4	0.75	19.0500	30	1.18110	21	533.4
49/64	0.765625	19.4469	31	1.22047	22	558.8
25/32	0.78125	19.8437	32	1.25984	23	584.2
51/64	0.796875	20.2406	33	1.29921	24	609.6
13/16	0.8125	20.6375	34	1.33858	25	635.0
53/64	0.828125	21.0344	35	1.37795	26	660.4
27/32	0.84375	21.4312	36	1.41732	27	685.8
55/64	0.859375	21.8281	37	1.4567	28	711.2
7/8	0.875	22.2250	38	1.4961	29	736.6
57/64	0.890625	22.6219	39	1.5354	30	762.0
29/32	0.90625	23.0187	40	1.5748	31	787.4
59/64	0.921875	23.4156	41	1.6142	32	812.8
15/16	0.9375	23.8125	42	1.6535	33	838.2
61/64	0.953125	24.2094	43	1.6929	34	863.6
31/32	0.96875	24.6062	44	1.7323	35	889.0
63/64	0.984375	25.0031	45	1.7717	36	914.4

Metric Conversion Tables

1 Imperial gallon = 8 Imp pints = 1.16 US gallons = 277.42 cu in = 4.5459 litres

1 US gallon = 4 US quarts = 0.862 Imp gallon = 231 cu in = 3.785 litres

1 Litre = 0.2199 Imp gallon = 0.2642 US gallon = 61.0253 cu in = 1000 cc

Miles to Kilometres		Kilometres to Miles	
1	1.61	1	0.62
2	3.22	2	1.24
3	4.83	3	1.86
4	6.44	4	2.49
5	8.05	5	3.11
6	9.66	6	3.73
7	11.27	7	4.35
8	12.88	8	4.97
9	14.48	9	5.59
10	16.09	10	6.21
20	32.19	20	12.43
30	48.28	30	18.64
40	64.37	40	24.85
50	80.47	50	31.07
60	96.56	60	37.28
70	112.65	70	43.50
80	128.75	80	49.71
90	144.84	90	55.92
100	160.93	100	62.14

lb f ft to Kg f m		Kg f m to lb f ft		lb f/in^2 : Kg f/cm^2		Kg f/cm^2 : lb f/in^2	
1	0.138	1	7.233	1	0.07	1	14.22
2	0.276	2	14.466	2	0.14	2	28.50
3	0.414	3	21.699	3	0.21	3	42.67
4	0.553	4	28.932	4	0.28	4	56.89
5	0.691	5	36.165	5	0.35	5	71.12
6	0.829	6	43.398	6	0.42	6	85.34
7	0.967	7	50.631	7	0.49	7	99.56
8	1.106	8	57.864	8	0.56	8	113.79
9	1.244	9	65.097	9	0.63	9	128.00
10	1.382	10	72.330	10	0.70	10	142.23
20	2.765	20	144.660	20	1.41	20	284.47
30	4.147	30	216.990	30	2.11	30	426.70

Index

A

Adjustments
    brake pedal - 119
    carburettor(s) - 80, 82
    contact breakers - 88
    headlamp beam - 127
    horn - 131
    ignition timing - 90
    valve clearances - 43
Air filter - 82
Alternator - 25, 87, 125
Automatic advance unit - 91

B

Battery - 124, 125
Big-end bearings - 39
Brakes - 109, 110, 114, 116
Brake adjustment - 119
Brake bleeding - 110
Brake hydraulic cylinders - 114
Brake pads - 110
Brake pedal - 106
Bulbs, ratings - 124
Bulbs, replacement - 127, 128, 129

C

Camshaft - 44
Camshaft chain - 28, 45, 58
Camshaft chain tensioner - 45
Camshaft drive sprocket - 25
Carburettor(s) - 77, 79, 80, 82
Centre stand - 106
Chains
    camshaft - 28, 45, 58
    final drive - 120
Cleaning the machine - 107
Clutch - 28, 45, 58
Condenser - 90
Connecting-rods - 40
Contact breakers - 28, 88
Crankcases - 33
Crankcase side covers - 20
Crankshaft - 33, 40, 47
Crankshaft balancer - 25, 37, 47, 54, 63
Cush drive - 119
Cylinder block - 25, 40, 68
Cylinder head - 20, 40, 70

D

Direction indicator relay - 129
Direction indicator - 129
Dualseat - 107

E

Engine
    dismantling - 20
    examination and renovation - 39
    reassembly - 47

Index

refitting - 72
removal - 15
Exhaust system - 82

F

Fault diagnosis
    brakes - 123
    clutch - 75
    electrical system - 132
    engine - 74
    frame and forks - 108
    fuel system - 86
    gearbox - 75
    ignition system - 93
    lubrication system - 86
    tyres - 123
    wheels - 123
Flashing indicator relay - 129
Flashing indicator - 129
Footrests - 106
Forks, front - 94, 96, 99
Frame - 101
Fuel tank - 77
Fuel taps - 77
Fuses - 124, 126

G

Gearbox
    bearings - 47
    dismantling - 33
    examination and renovation - 45
    reassembly - 47
    refitting - 72
    removal - 15
Gearchange mechanism - 33, 54
Gear cluster - 33
Gear selector mechanism - 35

H

Handlebar switches - 132
Headlamp - 127
Horn - 131

I

Ignition advance unit - 91
Ignition coil - 90
Ignition switch - 90, 131
Ignition timing - 90
Indicator panel - 129
Instrument drive cables - 107
Instrument heads - 107, 129

K

Kickstart - 28, 54

L

Lubrication system - 82

M

Main bearings - 39
Maintenance, routine - 7
Master cylinder - 114
Metric conversion tables - 136, 137
Modifications - 5

O

Oil filter - 25, 84
Oil pressure release valve - 33, 84
Oil pressure switch - 127
Oil pump - 35, 37, 84
Oil seals - 40
Oil strainer - 33, 52
Ordering spare parts - 5

P

Petrol tank - 77
Petrol taps - 77
Pinions:
    camshaft drive - 45
    primary drive - 28, 45
Piston rings - 40
Pistons - 25, 40
Primary drive - 58
Primary drive pinion - 28
Prop stand - 106

R

Rectifier - 87, 125
Regulator - 87, 126
Relay, flashing indicators - 129
Rev-counter - 37, 107, 129
Rocker gear - 44
Routine maintenance - 7
Running-in - 74

S

Seat - 107
Silicon rectifier - 125
Spare parts, ordering - 5
Spark plugs - 87, 93
Specifications:
    brakes - 109
    clutch - 14
    electrical system - 132
    engine - 13
    frame and forks - 94
    fuel system - 76
    gearbox - 14
    ignition system - 87
    lubrication system - 76
    tyres - 109
Speedometer drive - 107
Speedometer head - 107, 129
Sprockets:
    camshaft - 28, 45
    final drive - 25, 119
Starter motor - 25, 126
Starter solenoid switch - 127
Steering head bearings - 99
Steering head lock - 99
Stop lamp - 128
Stop lamp switches - 131
Sump - 33, 52, 84
Suspension units - 106
Swinging arm - 101
Switches - 90, 127, 131, 132

T

Tachometer drive - 37, 107
Tachometer head - 107, 129
Tail lamp - 128
Tools - 6
Tyres - 109, 121
Tyre pressures - 109

V

Valves (engine) - 70
Valve clearances - adjustment - 43
Voltage regulator - 126

W

Wheel balancing - 123
Wheel bearings - 114
Wheel, front - 109, 114, 123
Wheel, rear - 109, 116
Wiring diagram - 134, 135
Working conditions - 6

Printed by
J. H. HAYNES & Co. Ltd
Sparkford Yeovil Somerset
ENGLAND